FORTIFICATIONS
AND
SIEGECRAFT

FORTIFICATIONS AND SIEGECRAFT

Defense and Attack through the Ages

Jeremy Black

ROWMAN & LITTLEFIELD
Lanham • Boulder • New York • London

Published by Rowman & Littlefield
An imprint of The Rowman & Littlefield Publishing Group, Inc.
4501 Forbes Boulevard, Suite 200, Lanham, Maryland 20706
https://rowman.com

Unit A, Whitacre Mews, 26-34 Stannary Street, London SE11 4AB,
United Kingdom

British Library Cataloguing in Publication Information Available

Library of Congress Cataloging-in-Publication Data
Names: Black, Jeremy, 1955– author.
Title: Fortifications and siegecraft : defense and attack through the ages /
    Jeremy Black.
Description: Lanham, MD : Rowman & Littlefield, [2018] | Includes biblio-
    graphical references and index.
Identifiers: LCCN 2017058552 (print) | LCCN 2017060288 (ebook) | ISBN
    9781538109694 (ebook) | ISBN 9781538109687 (hardcover : alk. paper)
Subjects: LCSH: Fortification—History. | Siege warfare—History.
Classification: LCC UG401 (ebook) | LCC UG401 .B565 2018 (print) | DDC
    355.4/409—dc23
LC record available at https://lccn.loc.gov/2017058552

Printed in the United States of America

For David Miller

CONTENTS

ABBREVIATIONS

Add	Department of Manuscripts, Additional Manuscripts
AE	Paris, Ministère de Relations Extérieures
BB	Oxford, Bodleian Library, Bland Burges Papers
BCE	Before Common Era, same dates as BC, before Christ
Beinecke	New Haven, Beinecke Library
BL	London, British Library
CE	Common Era, same dates as AD, *anno Domini*
Cobbett	William Cobbett, ed., *Parliamentary History of England from . . . 1066 to . . . 1803* (36 vols., London, 1806–20)
CP	*Correspondance Politique*
CRO	County Record Office
JMH	*Journal of Military History*
IO	India Office Library
NA	London, National Archives
SP	State Papers
WO	War Office

PREFACE

As centers for defense and bases for attack, fortifications are a crucial aspect of military history. In practice, with all its ramifications, the history of fortification is, in one respect, a history of mankind, indeed a global history. Moreover, the remains of fortifications offer a still potent, and often dramatic, testimony to the past, notably with the strength of the sites, the power of the works, and the resources expended. This book provides a history of fortifications, but fortifications have scant meaning without an understanding of the real and potential threat to them posed by their counterpoint, siegecraft, and that is also considered.

This is not a technical history of the fort, nor of the techniques of siegecraft, but instead is a study of how attack and defense have interacted across time. Examinations of forts and their defensive abilities (and therefore the methods of defeating them) can tend toward the specific, with emphases on particular conflicts or architectural styles. In contrast, placing them within the wider development of government, society, and culture correctly fits them into human history. Moreover, the examination of the future of these installations, as well as of potential methods of destroying them, only reaffirms their omnipresence in history. Fortifications are not relics of the past but rather elements fundamental to military and social interaction across the world. Fortification and siegecraft used skills that were not combat skills, notably masonry and carpentry. In part, they are ways to use money to replace manpower, ensuring a degree of attrition by wealth rather than blood.

Ambitious, problem-solving, and complex engineering tasks and tech-nological change interacted to create a major civilizational force—the urge to fortify.

As emerges repeatedly in this book, there is no clear definition of fortification. Visiting Japanese castles from the sixteenth century or the coastal defenses on Guernsey built by the Germans in 1940–45 during their occupation of the island in World War II, this comment might appear absurd. Each is a dramatic type of fortification. However, there are, in practice, many issues of definition. To take just those examples, is a castle less of a fortification if its prime function was residential or to act as a jail? Fortifications were ownership markers or bases as much as serving any defensive function. Are the World War II German subma-rine pens on the west coast of France, ones that, as at Saint-Nazaire, remain impressive to this day, any less fortifications because they were designed to protect the submarines against air attack? These are all examples of fixed fortifications.

So also with the most emblematic fortification over the last century, the Berlin Wall. Constructed in 1961 and presented as a defensive structure, the "Anti-Fascist Protection Wall" was, in fact, created to stop the exodus of East Germany's population. The wall was supported by underground corridors, which allowed border guards to move rapid-ly. It was lined by watchtowers and minefields, and many were shot dead as they sought to flee across the wall. The breaching of the wall on November 9, 1989, was totemic of a new German, indeed world, order and a key event in the collapse of European Communism.

What also to make of digital fortifications, notably against electronic enemies? Given reliance on the Internet, such fortification may well entail operating without any external supply of information for a pro-longed period of time.

Moreover, fortifications can be readily improvised. Thus, in the aftermath of the fall of the Roman Empire, all sorts of structures that were not designed as fortifications found themselves admirably suited to the role, at times with little modification. This was true in Rome of the Colosseum, Domitian's Circus, and even Hadrian's Tomb. Similar-ly, during World War II, the Soviets turned industrial plants and planned cities into fortifications.

Terminology is also an issue. Thus, in Russian the only real word for fortress is *krepost'*, and that was around from at least the sixteenth century. Under Peter the Great (r. 1689–1725), Western terms, including *fortaleza* and *fortaletsiia*, were imported, but they were soon discarded as barbarisms. *Fortifikatsiia* had a longer life and is still used.

An agreed definition of fortifications would also have to work across time and across cultures. Fixed means to control space is one possibility, but it does not include field fortifications, unless fixed is understood as possibly temporary. Many, often most, fixed fortifications are in practice temporary. This was certainly the case with those erected before and during World War II. One definition that has been used—defensive means to control space—must be adapted to refer to static methods, as otherwise forms of mobile defense come into the subject and its equations of capability. There is a need not to place too much emphasis purely on defense. Fortifications were often used offensively. It is necessary to distinguish between the tactical defensive value of a fortified position, for example, a Roman legionary *castrum*, and the use of the tactical defense within a larger offensive strategy.

In *The Wealth of Nations* (1776), Adam Smith began book 5, "On the Revenue of the Sovereign or Commonwealth," by arguing that

> the first duty of the sovereign, that of protecting the society from the violence and invasion of other independent societies, can be performed only by means of a military force. But the expense both of preparing this military force in time of peace, and of employing it in time of war, is very different in the different states of society, in the different periods of improvement.
>
> Among nations of hunters, the lowest and rudest state of society, such as we find it among the native tribes of North America . . . an army of hunters can seldom exceed two or three hundred men. . . . An army of shepherds on the contrary, may sometimes amount to two or three hundred thousand.[1]

Smith linked complexity to the socioeconomic developments that permitted the establishment of professionalized regular armies able to sustain themselves and presented this establishment as an inevitable consequence of these developments. He referred to the "opulent and civilized" in contrast to the "poor and barbarous."[2] Fortification was an important part of this equation, as notably with Edward Gibbon's consideration, in his *History of the Decline and Fall of the Roman Empire*, soon after, of the role of Russian fortifications in preventing the movement forward of another "barbarian" invasion. This use of fortification was not only descriptive but also culturally encoded. Fortification was identified with progress. Siegecraft also reflected technological, economic, and social development.

However, there was also an enduring identification of fortification with oppression, as with the Saxon opposition to Emperor Henry IV in 1070. The fortress building of the latter was presented as a way to reduce the Saxon people to slavery, a slavery to be enforced by royal garrison forces. This helped ensure that the capture, and therefore defense, of these fortresses played a key role in campaigning.[3] This theme was to be long-standing and to play a major role in the Western political imagination. Thus, for the Romantic intellectuals of the nineteenth century, fortresses represented tyranny, imprisonment, and murderous dark deeds. This was seen in fiction, in art, and in opera, as with Beethoven's opera *Fidelio* (1805) and Puccini's *Tosca* (1900).

The range of belief and symbolism in fortification and sieges, as well as in their discussion, extended to the location and design of fortresses and to the role of prophecies in sieges, as with Alexander the Great in the sieges of Tyre and Gaza.[4] So also with the conduct of operations in Julius Caesar's successful siege of Munda in Spain, which was held by Pompey's sons:

> Shields and javelins taken from among the enemy's weapons were placed to serve as a palisade, dead bodies as a rampart; on top, impaled on sword points, several human heads were ranged in a row all facing the town, the object being not merely to enclose the enemy by a palisade, but to afford him an awe-inspiring spectacle by displaying before him the evidence of valour.[5]

The focus on garrisons, a key adjunct to fortifications, by both the opposition to Emperor Henry IV and the Romantic intellectuals, was appropriate. Garrisons had multiple political, social, economic, and cultural meanings and consequences,[6] and continue to do so, although the garrison is now far less significant as an experience of life, both for the military and for civilians. Indeed, as a result, there is far less need for bases than in the last century. At the same time, military bases overseas can still be major irritants, as with the Americans in Okinawa.[7]

Leaving to one side the ideological dimension, there was a civilizational component, in that major state forms, for long, established fortifications, both to protect particular locations and as part of a broader pattern of defense. The form this takes has changed greatly over the last eighty years, and fortifications have become less important. This means that the subject can be historicized in a misleading fashion as if it is not still relevant, but that is not the case.

Turning more narrowly to particular types of fortification, the developmental model has to be used with caution. In particular, "cutting edge" fortifications were not always those that were pursued. They were the most costly and, for that and other reasons, not necessarily the most appropriate. Lower-specification fortifications were frequently effective, and, notably, cost effective, especially for private individuals. As a separate complication of the notion of development, there was often continuity in the sites defended and in the forms adopted, such as ditch-surrounded palisaded earthwork fortifications, for example the *palankas* of the Ottoman Balkans.[8] The issue of specifications, and indeed of the interaction of offensive and defensive techniques, needs to be located in terms of a general overview of the place of fortification and siege in the patterns of war as a political undertaking and, separately, with reference to the logistical exigencies and possibilities of particular environments. Politics and logistics both tended to influence technological adoption.

Even if a definition of fortification and its purpose could be agreed, and one that works across cultures past and present, there are the problems posed by the changing "data set" that requires analysis and, linked to that, the question of emphases and priorities within this "data set." For most of human history, the prime form of investigation has been that by means of archaeology. This remains significant to the present, and not least as the archaeology of sites from over the last half millennium has attracted more attention, as opposed to the earlier, classic, period of archaeology. Archaeological work is greatly affected by the extent, nature, understanding, and accessibility of the available remains. In addition, there are the issues raised by the possibility and availability of archaeological research, factors that are greatly affected by politics, both international and domestic, and by resources. As a result, changes such as the collapse of Soviet Communism or developments in the attitudes of the Chinese government toward China's past can be highly significant, and so also with those in states that are somewhat more obscure.

Recent and current research alters the fortifications that can, and should, be discussed, and sometimes greatly so. For example, there have been important recent advances in the archaeology of the Ottoman (Turkish) Empire which offer much, notably in areas for which written sources are limited. Some major fortifications in the Ottoman Empire have only been considered or excavated relatively recently.[9] The same is the case elsewhere. The 195-kilometer-long "Great Wall of Gorgan," or "the Red Snake," the longest and most elaborate Persian (Iranian) defensive work, on which there has been recent work from 1995, reached from the east of the Caspian Sea into the Elburz Mountains and appears to be a work of the Sasanian rulers that was designed to stop invasions by the White Huns who were based to the north. Constructed and maintained in the fifth to seventh centuries CE (AD), this wall was matched by the Wall of Derbent to the west of the Caspian Sea. The extent to which these and other Sasanian works deserve recognition alongside the Chinese and Roman counterparts that receive so much attention is noteworthy.[10]

So, even more, is the question of what else remains undiscovered, or not yet brought into the archaeological and historical mainstreams. These (and other) mainstreams are clearly selective in their chronological and geographical coverage, a point repeatedly made by world historians, not that they do not create their own patterns. For example, Madagascar, no small island, is commonly ignored in military history, and it can be highly instructive to ask military historians about its history.

But what of fortifications that were not fixed and were never intended to be fixed? They were fortifications and designed for protection. Here we really are in conceptual, methodological, and historiographical difficulties. If the emphasis is on protection, then, at the level of individuals, armor, or any form of protective clothing, is their fortification. Secondly, if we move to the use of temporary or, very differently, enhanced positions, then the trench or earthen breastworks hastily dug or the farm complex with bolted windows and doors becomes a fortress.[11] So also with urban warfare as a whole, including irregular war in the urban jungle.[12] That approach may appear flawed, but given the emphasis in recent literature on both insurgencies and counterinsurgency warfare, it seems particularly mistaken to omit the relevant defenses from any discussion of fortifications. So also with the responses to irregular warfare and, indeed, with changing patterns of symmetrical conflict.

There is less confusion if policing or law and order are considered, because a major purpose of fortifications was indeed to provide internal security. This purpose could be directed as much against lawlessness as against rebellion, with the two of these sometimes scarcely separable. In this case, as others, fortification ensures or enhances the capacity for defense. Given that many modern states, notably, but not only, in South America and Western Europe, do not fear invasion or, even more, plan attacks on other states, it is these protections against internal disorder that are most relevant. This dimension has been enhanced by the recent emphasis on terrorist threats, but also by broader questions about governability in the face of populist action.

The ambiguous nature of warfare extends to the dubious use of the language of warfare to discuss very different activities. This can be seen, for example, in the use of the terminology of war, including fortification and siegecraft, defenses and attack, to describe cancer and other diseases, or the impact of the weather, or indeed politics, as in "political siege warfare."[13] There is also use of such language in investment policies and practices. The American investor Warren Buffett argued that a "wide economic moat" separates successful firms from their rivals and is therefore a major aspect of strong long-term stocks.

The uncertainty about definitions affects the presentation of past fortifications. "*Chateau en ruines sur un rivage* [shore]" is the label attached to a painting by the fine French painter of ruins Hubert Robert (1733–1808), which is displayed by the Fondation Bemberg in Toulouse, one of the many excellent provincial art galleries and museums in France. But look at the painting. The castle is old, rather than in ruins, and the painting includes a sentry post and a soldier on guard holding a gun. Clearly the position was still adequate to supervise the river traffic that is shown. Far from being in ruins, it was fit for a then-current purpose. This, indeed, is true of most fortifications, both public and private.

The issue of capacity for defense can be taken further into fresh fields for conceptual uncertainty by thinking, first, of the fortified nature of weapons and of platforms designed for, or at least used for, defensive purposes, for example armored trains, as in the Russian Civil War (1918–21).[14] Second comes the fortified nature of those used for attacking purposes, as with armor and secondary defensive weaponry on warships, aircraft, and tanks, for example the antiaircraft guns added to warships in World War II, and notably by the Americans in response to Japanese kamikaze attacks in 1944–45. The notion of a bomber as a "Flying Fortress," to give the name widely applied to the B-17, a key American bomber from World War II, captures only part of its function (that of protecting itself from attack), and certainly not that which might be more accurately conveyed by an interceptor fighter designed to block such bombers. To add to the complexity, escort fighters in the air, for example the American P-51D Mustangs (and the equivalent warships), had defensive tasks as part of the process of fortifying (i.e., protecting) the strike force. One recent work refers to tank destroyers as moving pillboxes.[15] This description captures their role as a part of the defenses of the German West Wall (Siegfried Line) when attacked by the Allies in 1945. But it also poses major questions as to how best to treat field fortifications that were mobile. In this context, fortification becomes any form of enhanced defense, which is a definition too far.

To offer a clear definition of fortification and one of logical weight across place, time, and context is not credible. That, moreover, leaves out the question of comparative insights from the fortifications produced by other species, such as moles, bees, or ants (a far from complete list), although the relationships between site, structure, and protective behavior seen in these cases are more generally instructive.

In this book, a number of criteria are offered. There is no discussion of the situation as far as war at sea or war in the air are concerned, although coastal defenses require mention. The last, however, are handled at greater length in my recent book on combined operations.[16] Here it is necessary to note that, as more generally with mobile defense and with a wider defense strategy, warships able to sink attacking ships were a key element in coastal defense, as was the capacity and willingness to attack the naval bases of opponents. Moreover, building coastal defenses was significant as an aspect of a wider defense system. It served to force the enemy to send a large army with artillery and other bulky equipment, thereby increasing the chances of successful interception at sea. Separate to such purposes, there was also reliance on coastal defenses against a naval power that could not be readily opposed at sea because it was much stronger or because, notably to do with the weather but also a result of the range of commitments for the defending navy, there was no guarantee of interception at sea. This was the case with coastal defenses in England, from the Roman forts of the Saxon Shore to nineteenth- and twentieth-century works, such as American coastal fortifications and those of many other states.

There is full consideration here of nonfixed, alongside fixed, fortifications; although this nonfixed character does not extend to vehicles, whether horses, chariots, tanks, or tank destroyers. Although body armor will be mentioned and offers fruitful comparisons, notably in terms of the relationships between utility and show, the emphasis here is very much not on the protection and "fortification" of individuals, which also means that shields are not considered. However, the enhancement of their protection by means of positional defenses, whether permanent (or, rather, intended thus) or not, is the subject.

Correspondingly, the means employed to attack these defenses will also be considered, although siegecraft, as conventionally understood, focuses far more on fixed defenses. Fortifications provide an opportunity to assess the significant, but changing, balance between defense and offense: how one comes to dominate the other. This is a classic topic in the study and practice of strategy.

Ultimately, the intention is to encourage readers to think widely about the subject. Reflecting on its complexities, not least in definitional terms, is a central part of this process of thought. In particular, it is necessary to appreciate that the variety of forms taken by fortifications reflected a range of utilitarian considerations in a multiplicity of social, economic, technological, political, cultural, and military contexts, contexts that, while also far from internally consistent or fixed, did not compose a fixed matrix. The military dimension was very important but was not outside this matrix. Instead, it was affected by the other contexts. So, in particular, with the key relationships between domestic fortification, in other words that against internal challenges, and its international counterpart. Alongside overlaps, there were important contrasts between these elements, but these differences can be overstated to define the subject.

I have benefited from opportunities to visit fortifications around the world, from Japan to the United States, from New Zealand to Panama, and to lecture at a number of fortified sites, including the Tower of London and the positions at Yorktown. I can also recall the little boy who made a papier-mâché motte-and-bailey castle and put his little soldiers in it. While working on this book, I particularly profited from being asked to lecture on a tour to Peninsula War (1808–13) sites and at Gibraltar. I am most grateful to Pete Brown, Stan Carpenter, James Cowan, Kelly DeVries, John France, Bob Higham, Luigi Loreto, Tim May, Stephen Morillo, Steven Nicklas, Albert Nofi, Kaushik Roy, Frédéric Saffroy, Anthony Saunders, Mark Stevens, Ulf Sundberg, Heiko Whenning, and three anonymous reviewers for their advice on all or part of an earlier draft. I have also benefited from discussing the subject with Gabor Agoston, Alejandro Amendolara, Gunnar Åselius, Jacek Burdowicz-Nowicki, Richard Butterwick, Mike Cailes, Borislav Chernev, Stephen Church, Tony Cross, Mike Dobson, Theo Farrell, Steven Fischer, Maurice Fitzgerald, David Fursdon, Richard Hitchcock, Faisal Husain, Tony King, Mark Lawrence, Malyn Newitt, David Parrott, Alexander Querengässer, Levi Roach, Gareth Stansfield, Michael Talbot, Harold Tanner, Peter Waldron, Alan Warren, Ireneusz Wojewódzki, and Adam Zeman, and from the help of Ryan Patterson in tracking down relevant items. It is a great pleasure to dedicate this book to David Miller, a good friend and a man who joins *bon* to *viveur*.

I

ORIGINS

At the most basic of levels, humans protected themselves from the outset against animals with their claws and teeth. In this context, many "fortifications" were natural features that provided shelter and/or enhanced strength, a situation that has lasted to the present. Caves and ridges were key examples, but so were thickets of vegetation or marshlands, in both of which men on foot could protect themselves from more mobile opponents. These three sentences can readily be written, and read, but they account for most of human history. Caves, which provided shelter and protected their residents against outflanking, were particularly important for humans as for other animals. Thornbushes long provided the palisades in Africa. They also provided shelter. This was not only necessary against predators but also against the elements (weather), as with caves in Gibraltar for Neanderthals and early *Homo sapiens*.

In part, these two goals of protection and shelter were on a continuum, and the extent to which the search for protection was the key element underlines the variety of goals this might entail, let alone the methods. Bears, however, do not use caves to store food as humans do. Gorillas build daily "sleep" nests, but this is for comfort, not for protection. The human need for protection could lead to a kind of "permanent" rest or "shelter." While the sheltering need and building capacity can be widespread, the nature and expression of the idea are more complex. The nature of the environment was, and is, an important variable: arid environments were more dangerous than jungles, and both humans and animals are more exposed in flatlands. In the latter, fortifications were a form of self-made caves for protection.

Natural fortifications were eventually enhanced in a process that may appear obvious but in which, as throughout the history of fortifications, perception, understanding, implementation, and diffusion all played a role. This form of protection, which generally entailed barricades of stones and earth, as well as the use of fire, which deterred animals and provided light for fighting, became palisades of wood when domestic animals also had to be protected, as well as to restrain and control these animals. In the absence of wood, which was easier to carry and to interweave with other natural and manufactured materials, stone could be used, and so also could earth.

Thus, the domestication of animals is a key element in the history of fortification, and notably so on flatlands. This domestication occurred in very different environments, at varied times, and in the context of a range of threats. Alongside animals—notably, but not only, wolves, bears, tigers, and lions—other humans were opponents, not least in seizing livestock, a goal they shared with animal predators. It is much easier to impound livestock in a small shelter or fortress in order to protect them against humans and predators than it is to protect large fields of crops. The value of the protected food is also much higher with the protected livestock, while the granary or silo, the product of the fields, is a kind of fortress for the products of agriculture. It provides protection against pests and weather and a site to defend against raiders. Predators and the elements were closely linked, with the latter fostering the former.

The principle of fortification is more fundamental than the means employed, a point that is repeatedly clear across history and that helps explain the wide definition used in this book. Moreover, this approach captures the value of comparative approaches.[1] Such approaches can clarify, but also supersede, the differences that emerged from particular environments. So also with definitions. Indeed, the focus for most of the history of fortification on sociobiological, evolutionary-biological, and anthropological modeling linked to archaeological assessments has encouraged broad-ranging definitions, for example: "Fortifications, which are the physical means by which humans defensively occupy a location . . . defines fortifications solely as habitations or occupations that incorporate defense into their location or construction."[2]

Alongside issues with definitions, there are also those with causes. For example, to take a famous site in England, Offa, king from 757 to 796 CE of Mercia, the kingdom in Midland England, in about 784–96 created a frontier line—the ditched earth rampart known as Offa's Dyke—running from the Severn estuary to the Dee, that may well have been a defensive work. The structure was 103 kilometers long and the rampart eight meters high and ten wide. The construction probably absorbed over seven million man-hours. It was built after the Welsh attack on Mercia in 784. It has also been argued that the dyke was essentially a boundary between Mercia and the Welsh principalities to the west, not a defensive line, and that it may have arisen from an agreed frontier. It certainly was to mark the definition of a border. At least some sections of the dyke, however, probably had a defensive function, being intended to deter raiding by creating an effective barrier and providing the best views. Nevertheless, the building of the dyke was not the end of Mercian expansion. In 822, Offa's successor, Cenwulf, invaded northern Wales, destroyed the fortress of Deganwy on the River Conwy, and annexed the principality of Powys. Fortification? Boundary? Base for further offensives? All in practice, as is most probable, but in what ratio? The last is more generally true as an issue in analysis, and fortifications as a subject are no different.

So also, for example, with the contemporary Danish earthwork in south Jutland,[3] or, for the Romans, with Hadrian's Wall, which was constructed in northern England between 122 and 128 CE. After the unsuccessful forays into Scotland and the withdrawal from the Antonine Wall farther north, Hadrian's Wall marked a limit of expansion and a northern boundary. It was a defensive work and one that made the most effective use of available troops, but it also served to limit southward migration and to control any trade. Questions as to purpose and usage are far harder to address satisfactorily for structures for which the historical context cannot be recreated so readily and for which the evidence is only archaeological, such as ditches and dykes in fifth- and sixth-century England, which may have been the work of Romano-Britons resisting Angle advances.[4]

THE ANCIENT WORLD

Fortifications of a more sophisticated type than palisades followed the development of states, not least because human attackers could achieve far more than animal counterparts, notably in the scale, duration, sophistication, and range of attack. The need for protection,[5] a determination to establish control, and clashing interests between states encouraged the walling of settlements[6] and also large-scale conflict.

At the same time, it is necessary to be wary of any teleology. It is, in addition, important not to erode the distinctions between society and state, and also between conflict and large-scale conflict. In particular, state forms, and therefore conflict on a large scale, developed in a patchy fashion. Much of the world remained with hunter-gatherer or pastoral socioeconomic systems, and without the concentrations of population or state developments seen with intensive agriculture. These social and state developments led to a process of resource accumulation and allocation and to a specialization of function that made large-scale fortification possible. Possible does not mean inevitable.[7] Nevertheless, a society that had a working agrarian system with regular harvests would have a larger population and one with leisure time during the growth period of the grain. This provided greater opportunities for fortification and conflict. Moreover, granaries and stables required protection and could be defended.

More generally, there is room for considerable skepticism over how far there was any clear understanding by ancient fort builders of what a fortress was, a situation that prefigures that today. As a consequence, some scholars use the word in inverted commas and argue, for example, that "most 'fortresses' were simply fortified settlements," not purpose-built specifically as military positions, in this particular case a reference to about sixty enclosed structures in the Negev highlands that were constructed in the eleventh–tenth centuries BCE, the period of the kings of Judah and Israel. The sites were probably linked to the protection of trade routes, but also to the enforced resettlement of nomads, a purpose that was related but different. If the sites were fortresses, they were intended as bases for soldiers and administrators, not to resist siege,[8] and their role as bases provided continuity in usage.

In many areas, fortified settlements were a norm, with the fortification being an aspect of enhanced protection. This "foundational" fortification was associated with population and settlement rather than with political complexity and centralization. Where possible, much of the protection continued to be provided by terrain features, such as height and slope, a situation still valid today. In the *Alexandrian War*, a work ostensibly by Julius Caesar but in practice of uncertain authorship, there is mention, with reference to 47 BCE, of Zela, a town in modern Turkey, with "adequate natural defences, considering its position in a plain: for its battlements are reared upon a hillock . . . whose summit is loftier than all the terrain surrounding it."[9] In the event, the struggle with Pharnaces of Bithynia was decided by a battle fought in the open country between the defenses and Caesar's camp.

Aside from height, the steepness of the slope was a key feature in hindering attackers, as was the presence or absence of covering vegetation and the nature of the rock, in particular the ease of gaining a foothold, let alone a secure foothold. The nature and stories surrounding the sites of Athens, Rome, and many other cities focused on these factors. There is a distinction, as well as a possible continuum, between naturally defensible and enhanced defenses. Defenders of any kind of fortification enjoyed advantages in an age when decisive fighting had to take place at close quarters. Anyone attacking a wall could go over, under, or through, but each posed considerable difficulties. Missile weapons had only limited impact on walls. Bow fire was dependent on individual skill or mass fire. Siege warfare could be bloody. Attackers had to be prepared to suffer heavy casualties.

In China, the spread of agriculture led to, or was related to, fortification. In the Neolithic period (c. 4500–2000 BCE), defended sites appeared in both the Yellow and the Yangzi River regions. Compressed-earth techniques, achieved by stamping down the earth, were to the fore, as they also were for Chinese city walls. Banpo village near Xian, which dated to about 4500 BCE, was heavily fortified with a fifteen-foot-deep ditch divided by cross walls. In contrast, in the Chifeng area of the Inner Mongolian region of modern northeastern China, as revealed in recent work on a dam, settlements were ringed in the early second millennium BCE with double stone walls. Semicircular towers were also built there, as were fortified gates. Fortified sites were generally located on steep slopes. Semicircular towers reduced the space in which attackers could not be seen and fired upon.[10]

The history of armor may seem to be very much part of another story, but it overlaps with that of field fortifications, capturing especially the extent to which the latter might be movable, in particular during the course of a conflict or part of a siege. Providing cover for troops from fire was an aspect of armor and of the more conventional understandings of fortification, whether fixed or field. So, also, with protecting troops from shock action. As with other types of protection, armor could have symbolic as well as utilitarian purposes. So also with shields. The evolution of both reflected an adaptation of natural materials, such as hide and wood. Wooden shields were depicted in prehistoric cave paintings. As the range of worked material increased, flexibility was enhanced.

The role of spiritual protection further complicates the issue of fortification, and in a dual sense. Religious rites and buildings were an aspect of the protection of communities but also required protection. Indeed, protected temple complexes were a prominent feature in early cities, as with Nippur in Mesopotamia (Iraq), which, from c. 2100 BCE, had a series of temple walls. Moreover, such complexes went on being significant and have remained so to the present. In part, this is a matter of symbolism, and historic fortification features can be seen, as with temples built in Japan over the last four centuries as well as earlier.

However, attacks on religious sites, notably terrorist attacks, ensure that their protection remains important, especially in the Middle East where Shia and other shrines were attacked in Iraq in the early twenty-first century. Religious sites have also been attacked in Afghanistan and Pakistan. The continued threat means an emphasis on gates and walls, notably the former, and on the guards necessary to man them. As so often, the human dimension of fortification, that of the human protectors, is a key element.

City-states developed in the fertile valleys of the Euphrates and, later, Tigris in modern Iraq from the fourth millennium BCE, Ur being the most prominent early one. The wall of another city, Uruk, was about 9.5 kilometers long. By about 3300 BCE, walled towns had begun to be built along the Nile in Egypt, Nekhen (Hieraconpolis) and Naqada being the earliest.

Walled towns were subsequently found across China, in areas with an appreciable density of population, as with Chengziya in about 2500 BCE. Built in about 1550 BCE, the walls of the Shang city Zhengzhou were about ten meters high and nearly seven kilometers in circumference and would have required millions of working days to construct. Such works indicate the level of political control, social cohesion, and organizational ability prevalent at the time. The development of walled towns and cities in China was widespread, beginning at an early stage and achieving a "cultural" dimension, in the sense that every self-respecting city had to have a wall. The scale of Chinese walled cities dwarfed those elsewhere. The construction of Chinese walls, using rammed earth and a plentiful supply of labor, produced extremely thick walls that were impervious to siege engines. This resulted in additional defensive features focusing on gates, which became the main point of attack. The gates protruded from the walls and usually had a number of additional internal gates and courtyards that served as "killing zones" for archers on the walls above.

Walled towns also became more common in other areas. Thus, in Turkmenistan in Central Asia, on the trade route between China and the West, the first city in the Merv oasis, the walled Erk Fala, was founded in the sixth century BCE.

More generally, fixed defenses were significant for controlling communications. This was particularly so for river crossings and for transshipment points linked to sea, lake, and river travel. Fortresses were also important for road links. For example, the Bronze Age fortress of Mycenae, between c. 1550 BCE and 1100, dominated the main road between Argos and Corinth, the two great ports of the Peloponnese.[11] The same emphasis on the control of communications can be found in every age. The ability to provide protection for, and thus to encourage, direct, and tax, passing trade at choke points, whether natural or artificial, often funded the construction of fortresses. In the history of fortification, this is more generally an indicator of the presence of concepts and practices across time and space, in this case of fortresses as controllers and protectors of trade.

Most sites that required protection were not at the scale of cities, but that did not mean that protection was any less necessary. Instead, it was seen at a variety of levels of social development and form and continued to be introduced even while larger-scale works were constructed elsewhere. For example, the Agaric Bronze Age of southeastern Spain, which flourished in about 2200–1550 BCE, was characterized by hilltop, stone-built settlements and an expansion of control to cover eventually all of southeastern Spain. Archaeological research has provided evidence of fortifications, for example at the site of La Bastida where, in 2012–13, masonry walls were discovered, which in part flanked an entrance passage, and five solid square protruding towers resting on carefully prepared foundations to prevent sliding down the steep hill, a considerable feat. The close-backed towers provided an opportunity to throw objects, while the main entrance was protected by special defensive design measures that would have exposed attackers.

There was also a water cistern. While that was necessary for settlements, whether fortified or not, the presence of cisterns made it easier for defenders to sustain a blockade and thus could encourage attackers to mount an assault.

Earlier fortified precincts in Iberia survive from c. 3000 BCE, in the Copper Age, usually with concentric walls to protect successive walled precincts, and an emphasis on defensive archery ensuring loopholes in the walls. In contrast, in La Bastida, a center of power, the location was in a mountain environment, and the settlement was probably more clearly military in purpose, with the emphasis apparently on close combat. It is unclear how far this different style of fortification, notably the solid square towers, reflects diffusion from the Eastern Mediterranean where there are earlier examples.[12]

Fortifications located in mountainous areas or on hills or tells were widespread and seen, for example, with the Hittites in Anatolia. Tells were defensive settlements built up above the surrounding plain by piling up and compacting earth. These fortifications proved important in conflict between states and in resistance to the expansion of imperial control. However, there was also a pattern by which the consolidation of states led to the abandonment of such fortifications distant from the frontiers. For example, some Hittite tells were abandoned in about 2300 BCE.[13] Instead, fortifications were concentrated in frontier zones, as by the Egyptians to their south, in Nubia.

More generally, rural homesteads across much of the world were built with defense in mind. The ground floor often had no windows and served as a barn. The stairway from the ground floor to the upper floor was very steep, narrow, and eminently defensible. Such farmsteads can still be seen in many rural areas, including, in Europe, in Greece, Italy, and Spain, as well as in other continents.

Fortifications in the Ancient world were also found within states, notably in the towns in populated valleys which acted as centers of government and control. Some fortifications were on a considerable scale, as with the Hittite capital of Hattushash. The citadel, built in the seventeenth century BCE and containing the palace, was the core of a city whose walls, extended by about 1400 BCE to encompass the Upper City, were supported by projecting towers and twin-towered gateways. The standard fortification materials in the Near East were stone and mud bricks.[14] More generally, a series of devices could make fortifications stronger. These included recessed gates, towers overtopping walls, towered gates, concentricity, and, in particular, layered defenses.

Returning to southeastern Spain, there are still many stone-built settlements in the hills, notably the so-called white villages. The defensive character of these sites is readily apparent, not least in terms of visibility over valley routes into the hills, thus also providing warning against raiders, as well as in having only one entrance. This pattern continued with walled medieval Spanish villages such as Pedraza de la Sierra, north of Madrid, where the castle dates to the thirteenth century. Issues of visibility, surveillance, and sight lines are all significant in terms of fortification, this being the case at every level and for all types. These issues help to explain both the location of particular fortifications and the response to the possibilities and problems of the site. With reference to Julius Caesar's campaigns against Pompey's sons in Spain in 45 BCE, a Roman writer noted

> the hilly type of country by no means unsuitable for the fortification of camps. In fact, practically the whole region of Further Spain, fertile as it is and correspondingly well watered, makes a siege a fruitless and difficult task. Here too, in view of the constant sallies of the natives, all places which are remote from towns are firmly held by towers and fortifications, as in Africa, roofed over with rough-cast, not tiles. Moreover, they have watch-towers in them. . . . A large proportion of the towns are established in naturally elevated positions, with the result that the approach to them, involving as it does a simultaneous climb, proves a difficult task.[15]

Hilltop watchtowers were also built in coastal positions such as Castell de Ferro on Spain's Mediterranean coast, a tower that may have Phoenician origins alongside its Arab features.

The need for attackers to come to close quarters with an enemy in order to seize a position, and thus suppress the defenders, gave fortifications their significance as well as strength. This was a strength that was only to be eclipsed (and then only partially) by dependable and powerful missile weapons. Such weapons altered the parameters of attack and defense, as well as the requirements from defenses. The viability of fortifications, moreover, was enhanced by limitations in siegecraft. However, fortifications, and the capability and drive to build them, were always in a dynamic relationship with the means to overcome them.

Indeed, improvements in the latter, for example by the aggressive and expansionist Iraqi-based Assyrian empire in the ninth–seventh centuries BCE, ensured that Assyrian advances, whether or not they led to battle, could not be resisted by remaining behind walls, as was often the case in warfare, both between and within states. The dramatic stone reliefs from the palace of Nineveh, the Assyrian capital, depict the sieges of walled cities in the mid-seventh century. The Assyrians used battering rams. The carvings that show them have men fighting from the tops of the towers that protect the rams: they are siege towers with battering rams or vice versa. As so often, the evidence on the course of development in the nature and use of weapons is limited. The Assyrians also used mining operations and siege ladders. Their conquests included Babylon (689) and the Elamite cities (648–647).[16]

Siege towers are a form of fortified gantry. Indeed, the technology to build a wall was often the same as that to take it down. This situation continued until the age of explosives, as explosives had no use in construction.

Aside from devices that came into direct contact with the walls, notably battering rams and siege towers, there were siege engines, including those that fired projectiles, especially catapults, although their range, accuracy, and aiming required fire from close proximity. As with other weapons, catapults served a variety of purposes and could be fired from a number of platforms. Large catapults could throw heavy stones designed to inflict damage to the structure, while medium-size catapults launched bolts, and lighter, handheld ones fired arrows and small stones designed to clear away defenders from their positions. Such anti-personnel weaponry provided an opportunity for gaining tactical dominance and thereby for the use of siege engines close up against the walls. Thus, they were an aspect of the degree to which sieges involved stages in order to suppress the defenses, just as defenses involved stages with which to resist attack. In turn, these stages required different facets for the defense. This included firepower mounted on the walls and notably in the towers, which were their strongest features. The use of primitive "firebombs" was particularly effective against wood, especially in a dry country.

A threat-response sequence in fortifications can be seen in the Greek world. The Greeks for long relied chiefly on terrain features, with fortifications running along slopes and no multistory towers. Prior to the sixth century BCE, Greek fortifications were less sophisticated than those in the Near East, while the Persian Empire contained a network of forts and the Persians proved adept at siegecraft. After Cyrus the Great of Persia defeated Croesus, king of the Lydians in 547 BCE, his general, Harpagus, captured the wealthy Greek cities on the Ionian coast of Anatolia, a major part of the Greek world. Having surrounded their target with a rampart, the Persians weakened it before capturing it by storming. In response, in the fifth century BCE, the Greeks strengthened their defenses, building higher towers and using carefully hewn masonry.

Greek warfare is famous for the sieges of Troy and Syracuse, although they took place about 800 years apart, and saw the development of defensive architecture, not least with the Theban general and statesman Epaminondas (c. 418–362 BCE) building new city walls.[17] The extensive discussion of the siege of Troy by Homer in the *Iliad*, and of that by the Athenians of Syracuse in 415–413 BCE by Thucydides in his *The Peloponnesian War*, ensures that these are the sieges first described at great length and ones frequently held up for the lessons they offer. Syracuse had to be innovative due to the challenge from Carthage but, as Thucydides made clear, the mismanagement of the campaign by the Athenians was a key element. Syracuse was also helped by the lack of Athenian security, such that they knew that the expedition was coming.[18]

In general, Greek warfare appears to have focused on operations that brought more rapid results, notably the destruction of crops. The remorselessness seen with Roman operations did not generally characterize those of the Greeks. There was therefore on the Greek part a preference for taking cities by storm, as when the Argives unsuccessfully tried to take Epidaurus by the use of scaling ladders. The Roman Republic was a far larger and stronger state than any one Greek city-state.

In Sicily, part of the Greek world, Dionysius of Syracuse in 398 attacked the Carthaginian city of Motya, a city off western Sicily situated on an island in the lagoon and surrounded by a wall with at least twenty watchtowers. Having built a mole, Dionysius used siege towers and battering rams. The Carthaginians responded with burning pitch, but the Greeks doused the flames. The Greeks broke holes in the walls and also used gangways to advance troops from the siege towers into the city, which they captured.

Alexander the Great of Macedon successfully besieged the well-fortified port city of Tyre in 332 BCE during his conquest of the Persian Empire. This was the major siege in his long campaigns. In it, the catapults were able (alongside more rapid-firing archers) to provide covering fire for battering rams employed to breach the walls, and also for boarding bridges from which troops moved into breaches from ships. Alexander's success in this operation reflected the multipurpose effectiveness of Macedonian armies. At the same time, it is instructive that far more attention is devoted to Alexander's victories in battle, notably Issus (333) and Gaugamela (331). Cannon were later to provide the breaching force of the battering rams without needing their close contact, although they long displayed similar characteristics to catapults in requiring direct sight and close range.

Alexander had earlier besieged the Persian naval base of Halicarnassus on the southeastern coast of the Aegean in 334 BCE. This siege had been less successful because sortieing forces had burned the siege towers that Alexander used in addition to filling in the castle ditch and undermining the walls. There, as at Miletus that year, storming was part of Alexander's siege methods.[19]

The Hellenistic powers that succeeded Alexander's empire and dominated Southwest Asia and the Eastern Mediterranean until the first century BCE built fortresses such as the citadel of Gyaur Kala, founded by the Seleucid ruler Antiochus I (281–261 BCE) at Merv, and also developed siegecraft. They produced more formidable siege weapons, for example battering rams sheathed with iron and mounted on rollers, early versions of armored vehicles. At the siege of Rhodes in 305–304 BCE by Demetrius "Poliorcetes" ("the Besieger"; 336–283

BCE), the son of Alexander's general Antigonus I, there were also iron-tipped borers (made effective by a windlass, pulleys, and rollers) that were designed to make holes in the walls, as well as a massive iron-plated mobile tower carrying catapults. The siege, which was part of the attempt by Antigonus to maintain his sphere of control, failed. However, siegecraft as a whole became more successful in this period.[20] Rhodes, with an excellent natural harbor on the route between the Levant and the Ionian Sea, continued to be an important and contested fortified position into the sixteenth century.

Siege towers became larger and heavier and thus able to project more power. They were also better defended, for example with iron plates and goatskins to resist the fire missiles and catapults launched from the positions they were attacking. Fire was a key weapon for both attackers and defenders and therefore had to be protected against. Flexibility in usage was crucial, as these siege towers could be assembled and disassembled or, alternatively, made on-site if timber was available. Indeed, for these and other purposes, such as palisades, siege operations frequently entailed a denuding of woodland that had a long-term impact on the vegetation. This was seen for example with Roman operations in Spain, France, and Israel in the first centuries BCE and CE[21] and is also apparent on a shorter timescale, as with the effect of the American Civil War (1861–65). This denuding continued into the twentieth century. Thus, neutral Spain supplied part of the wood required by the Western Allies for their trench system in France during World War I, but part of the country was denuded as a consequence.

Siegecraft became more successful because of heavier and better-armed siege towers, accumulated knowledge preserved in manuals, and the extent to which stronger states with more resources, material, and intelligence could both conduct sieges more successfully and build effective fortifications. The Hellenistic period saw publications on warfare. In the mid-third century BCE, Philon wrote the *Poliorketika*, the sole surviving Hellenistic manual on fortification. It provided information on how to construct, defend, and attack city walls.

The Romans developed the tactical formation of the testudo, by which troops grouped together and advanced under the cover of their shields, which provided cover against arrows, javelins, and stones. This method, which required a very high degree of training and discipline to be effective, first used at the siege of Aquilonia in 293 BCE, and more particularly at that of New Carthage (in Spain) in 209 BCE by Scipio Africanus, provided a way to approach walls sheltered from most defensive fire and thus to be better prepared for an assault. The Romans also used heavy siege engines, as at Lilybaeum in 250 BCE and Ategua in 45 BCE. In his account of the campaigning in Sicily in the First Punic War, Polybius made frequent references to the Roman use of siege engines, as at Camarina in 258 BCE, where they made a breach in the walls, and Panormus in 254 BCE, a key position:

> They threw up works in two places and after making the other necessary preparations brought up their battering rams. The tower on the sea shore was easily knocked down, and the soldiers pressing in through this breach, the so-called New Town was stormed, and the part known as the Old Town being now in imminent danger, its inhabitants soon surrendered.[22]

Moreover, they employed battering rams, as against Macedonian-held Oreus in 200 BCE.

Sieges continued to be important over the following century. Scipio Aemilianus Africanus, the Roman commander in the Third Punic War, besieged and captured Carthage in 146 BCE after a siege that became a house-to-house struggle. In 134–133 BCE, his siege of Numantia, another difficult struggle, followed again by the destruction of the city, brought to an end a harsh war in northern Spain. These provided impressive instances of the application of superior resources by a state with administrative and policy continuity.

At Alesia in Gaul (France), in 52 BCE the Gauls under Vercingétorix made their last stand on a hilltop town, only to be surrounded by Julius Caesar with a ditch and earthworks. After breakout attempts to avoid being starved out were defeated, as well as those by a relief force to break through the fortified line of contravallation established facing against relief forces in order to protect the besiegers, Vercingétorix surrendered. Such lines were part of Roman lines of fortification.[23] The attempted relief of fortified positions was a key element in the fighting of the period. Earlier in the year, Vercingétorix was unable to relieve Avaricum (Bourges) when Caesar besieged it, but his scorched-earth tactics helped lead to the supply problems that contributed to the failure of Caesar's siege of Gergovia, a formidable position.

In the subsequent civil war, Caesar's success in siegecraft was shown at the expense of Massilia [Marseilles], which supported one of his opponents, Lucius Domitius Ahenobarbus, who was proconsul of Gaul. Caesar, refused access to the city on his march through Gaul to Spain, laid siege to it. The port was blockaded, and then in order to help compress the soil for a mighty ramp, "all the woods were felled." Two towers on rollers were placed on the ramp, and from them fire was directed at the defenders. The catapults of the attackers bombarded the towers, while in turn the attackers' testudos were pummeled by stones dropped from the walls. The Romans also used battering rams, only for these to be hit by stones and inflammables dropped from above. The towers were eventually burned down in a sally, but inexorable effort won Caesar success after a siege that took from April to September 49 BCE.[24]

The Roman general Gnaeus Domitius Corbulo (d. 67 CE), who fought in Germany and conquered Armenia, observed that the pick was the weapon with which to beat the enemy,[25] an observation that was to be valid for many generals. Indeed, the Romans built a massive earthen ramp at Masada as a key element in their successful siege in 72–74 CE of this fortress where Jewish resistance came to focus after the successful siege of Jerusalem in 69–70 by Titus, the elder son and successor of Emperor Vespanian. Such ramps overcame the advantages of terrain and walls enjoyed by defenders. At Masada, the Romans located their siege engines on a stone platform constructed on the ramp.[26]

Adept in capturing fortresses, the Romans established permanent garrisons on, or close to, their frontiers and fortified these garrison bases. In addition, both China and the Romans built series of walls, including the Long Walls of Wei, Zhao, and Yan (c. 350–290 BCE) in China and the Roman *limes* notably between the upper Rhine and the upper Danube. These walls were supported by fortresses, leading to an interplay of defensive positions that was also seen at the scale of individual fortresses. Both the Chinese and the Romans constructed formidable systems, and archaeological research has recently provided plentiful evidence of both.[27] The patterns of attack and defense of a single strongpoint are different from those of campaigns shaped by strategic-level, long-wall fortification of frontiers. These wall systems, as also with those of the Byzantines and Persians, provided a limited physical barrier, but also an excellent observation and early-warning structure when

combined with regularly spaced lookout posts. They were able to com-
municate rapidly, using flag or light signals, with centrally placed reserve forces, which were held back and could then respond rapidly to
the main incursions once they had been identified. It meant that an
economy of force was achieved, without tying down large numbers of
troops. Walls served not only to control "barbarians," but also as an
economic influence zone, a source of intelligence catchment, a means
to impose order on local citizens, and a way to regulate trade.

In China, lengthy and continuous border walls were constructed
during the Warring States period (403–221 BCE) and were intended
for defense against other Chinese states, rather than against invading
northern "barbarians." In turn, once China had been unified by the
Qin, the emperor, in 215 BCE, ordered the construction of a long wall
fortifying the northern frontier against "barbarians." Subsequently, the
Western and Eastern Han dynasties (206 BCE–220 CE) repaired the
Qin wall and built new walls to the north and south of it, in part in order
to support territorial expansion. Military garrisons were established in
Ferghana (an important valley on the Silk Road), Korea, and Champa
(Vietnam).[28] The Chinese also used mountain fortresses in order to
protect against "barbarians" and to maintain order during periods of
social instability, as in the last years of the Han dynasty when the central
government was weak. So also in Korea.

The formidable fortresses along Rome's frontiers were designed to
provide both sites for defense and bases for attack.[29] Roman defenses
made use of ditches to protect positions, both permanent and temporary. These were sloped or pointed V-sectioned ditches that were difficult for attackers to cross, not least because of their steep slopes and
pointed bottoms. Trajan's Column shows Roman soldiers digging. The
Romans used baffled (offset) gates as part of the system. Such gates
obliged attackers to open their flanks and rear to defending fire.

The Romans had frontiers (a much-debated concept and practice[30])
with "barbarians" and those with more developed governmental systems such as the Parthian and then Sasanian empires of Persia (Iran).
Usually the Romans had to build from new, not least because they did
not tend to use Iron Age fortifications and, as a related point, did not
tend to build on hilltops. However, in the Near East, they could develop existing, mostly Hellenistic, defenses, as with the major antisiege
glacis and rampart added to Dura-Europos. This Macedonian military

colony on the Syrian Euphrates, a long-standing area of fortification, became a Roman fortress before falling to Sasanian siege in about 256 CE, with the attackers constructing a massive siege ramp. Sapping, tunneling, and countermining were major elements in this siege. Antioch had fallen to the Sasanians three years earlier.

Evidence from the disposition of bodies and artifacts has suggested that at Dura-Europos the Sasanians used bitumen and sulfur to gas their opponents underground, a variant on the Hellenistic, Roman, and Chinese use of smoke in siege mines. More generally, this episode indicated the degree to which, in fortification and siegecraft, past practices were adopted and then improved incrementally. The Romans did so with Hellenistic practices, while the Parthians and Sasanids drew on the same, namely Seleucid skills, as seen with the ability of the Parthian city of Hatra to deploy powerful artillery in repelling Roman sieges. As a result of this derivation, both sides used similar siege techniques, and this provided another way to transmit ideas.[31] Within their empire, the Romans also built forts against pirates, for example in Asia Minor in the first century BCE.

Roman forces were trained and adept at building marching camps every time they stopped. These generally occurred at 15-mile intervals, the average daily rate of march expected of a legion. The camps followed a standardized pattern and, in what would today be referred to as a standing operation procedure, each element of the marching group understood its role in the construction process. They provided security and good communications on their line of advance.

As Rome came under "barbarian" pressure, more fortifications were built and more widely. In Gaul in the late third and fourth centuries CE, about one hundred urban centers were fortified by the Romans with impressive stone walls, while there were also many lesser fortifications.[32] Rome had a new multitowered wall in the 270s, built by the orders of Emperor Aurelian, and it held off Alaric and the Goths until they starved the city into submission in 410. In Germany, Constance was fortified with new walls in the fourth century. Major Roman cities including Cologne and Trier were fortified.

In China, siege warfare developed with the use of siege towers and stone-throwing catapults (both also employed by the Romans) against cities protected by thick earth walls behind deep, wide ditches. Due to their large armies, a product of strong states and plentiful population, the Chinese and Indians were able to surround fortified positions in order to establish blockades. The Chinese made extensive use of siege artillery from an early period, and this included fire weapons. These could be explosive or flammable and were launched by a variety of means, including bows, catapults, and rockets. However, their primary function was to clear battlements of enemy defenders and artillery rather than to weaken or breach a wall, and necessarily so due to the thickness of the walls.

The origins of the most powerful engine in terms of the projectile that could be fired, the trebuchet, are controversial. It is claimed that it was invented in China in the fifth to third century BCE and was certainly not then known in western Europe. The trebuchet was a traction piece that contained a rotating beam placed on a fulcrum. A sling was hung from the beam, and the projectile was placed in it. On the shorter side of the beam, ropes were hung, and when they were pulled (by humans), the projectile was thrown forward. Experiments have shown that if the slings of traction trebuchets were hung onto, as is depicted in the illustrations, the arc is flattened and the ballistic force is increased, which is the way it would usually have been used. The trebuchet was essentially antipersonnel until the thirteenth century CE. From its origin in China, the trebuchet spread westward.

South Asia saw the development in the third millennium BCE of agricultural settlements that were walled, such as Mundigak (near Kandahar), which eventually had massive walls. Archaeological remains extend to fortifications of a formidable scale. This is notably so for the Indus Valley–based Harappan culture of 2800–1600 BCE, as with the citadels at Harappa, Kalibangan, and Mohenjo-daro. In addition, the lower towns were protected with thick walls. These were of mud bricks or baked bricks. The Vedic Aryans in the early second millennium BCE identified themselves as the "destroyers of forts." In turn, in the early first millennium BCE, fortified settlements reappeared in the Punjab. Moreover, major cities across southern India were fortified in the context of intense competition. So also in the mid-Ganges valley with the Magadhan capital, Rājagrha, and the city of Pātaliputra, which was fortified against the Vajji confederation in the sixth century BCE. On what was later the North-West Frontier of British India (and now of Pakistan), the tribes who unsuccessfully opposed Alexander the Great in

327 BCE relied on walled towns, such as Arigaion, and rock fortresses, such as Aornos.

Alongside the emphasis in this chapter on, as it were, "state" fortifications, it is also appropriate to note those that could be seen as "private," although this is generally more a case of continuum than of contrast.

BRITAIN

In the case of England, a useful example of early developments, the remains of forts are readily apparent from the Bronze Age on, although there are issues with assessing how many there were. Archaeology and aerial reconnaissance have provided more information in recent decades. Aerial reconnaissance has focused on cropmarks in order to throw much light on the location of forts. Hilltop sites date back to the Neolithic era. Hill forts became more common with the Iron Age from c. 700 BCE. They were probably places of refuge during conflict rather than inhabited sites. In particular, this was because, depending on the surface geology and soil cover, hilltops and promontories could face major issues with water availability, although this also meant that they were not vulnerable to flash floods. More positively, hilltops were often within visual contact of each other and were thus able to send and receive messages. As defended places for storing foodstuffs, hill forts had permanent value. Archaeology also suggests that a number of forts had permanent communities, including Danebury, Maiden Castle, and South Cadbury.

The role of conflict in Wales, where the Iron Age began in about 600 BCE, is indicated by surviving weapons and by approximately six hundred hill forts from the period, some bank-and-ditch, others stone-walled. The latter were probably a testimony to territorialization in the shape of the control of particular territories and the existence of distinct tribes. The existence of numerous hill forts, for example over fifty in the Welsh county of Caernarfonshire alone, does not mean that they were occupied simultaneously. The Iron Age there lasted to c. 100 CE. Economic prosperity was a key element. The largest surviving known hill forts in the region of Wales were to the east of central Wales, in what is now good farmland in the neighboring English counties of Herefordshire and Shropshire. Some were larger than twenty acres, and that at Llanymynech, between Oswestry and Welshpool, was 140 acres.[33]

Most English sites were relatively modest, for example Woodbury and Cadbury Castles in Devon. Although *castle* appears in the names, these hill forts were never castellated and date from a period before that of castles. Yet again, the imprecision of the relevant vocabulary emerges clearly. Maiden Castle outside modern Dorchester survives as a striking manifestation of the task the invading Romans faced. The serried banks (closely spaced ramparts) of the hill fort, which belonged to the tribe of the Durotriges, were calculated to break up an attacking charge. The innermost bank would have carried a palisade. These hill forts, however, were to be vulnerable to Roman siegecraft after a large-scale invasion was launched in 43 CE. Maiden Castle was among the over twenty stormed by the II Augusta Legion under the future Emperor Vespasian, with the Romans benefiting in the attack on Maiden Castle from covering firepower. It was not refortified and thus remained as a historical site. The Roman practice was not to refortify Iron Age forts, but, in addition, most British hill forts appear to have fallen out of regular use before the end of the first millennium BCE.[34] Vespasian was later to besiege Jerusalem in 69.

In turn, the Romans were major fort builders in Britain, not least with their substantial legionary bases, particularly Deva (Chester), Eboracum (York), and Isca Augusta (Caerleon), as well as with shorter-lived legionary bases, such as Exeter (Isca Dumnoniorum) and Wroxeter. In addition, the Romans built supporting forts, such as Housesteads, as part of Hadrian's Wall, a seventy-mile-long fortified stone wall constructed from about 122 across Britain at its narrowest point from the River Tyne to the Solway Firth (estuary). Wallsend on the Tyne remains as a place-name at the eastern end of the onetime wall. This wall took advantage of features in the terrain, notably a sill of hard volcanic rock that gave added height. The Emperor Hadrian was a consolidator of empire who also built defensive works in Germany.

The Romans later built the Antonine Wall farther north in Britain. A turf rampart set upon a stone base, defended by forts, this wall was not retained for as long. Also in the reign of Antonius Pius (138–61), the frontier was advanced in Germany, with a palisade defended by stone watchtowers and forts. Rather than being intended to resist attacks, the walls and their forts were bases for operations, as well as being a control

Figure 1.1.   Maiden Castle

on transit into the area of Roman rule. Vindolanda Fort on Hadrian's Wall is a good example of a large fort used as a legionary operating base.

The style of Roman defenses altered. From the mid-first century CE, gate towers projecting in front of the defensive wall appear, and there was a trend toward an auxiliary gateway, the entrances of which could be enfiladed from the ramparts. This style developed into projecting semicircular towers that were able to provide enfilading fire against attackers, for example at Jerusalem.[35]

The ten forts of the Saxon Shore were built in England by the Romans from the 270s onward, from Brancaster, Norfolk, to Portchester, Hampshire, in order to limit attacks on the east and south coasts by seaborne raiders from Germany. With their thick and high walls, these forts, most of which had protruding towers, were designed to protect harbors and estuaries. The construction and improvement of town defenses in Roman Britain from the third century also indicated an attitude of growing defensiveness in the face of outside attack. This was seen in London and, more generally, in Roman town defenses.[36] The Saxon Shore forts worked and could be adapted in the late third and fourth centuries, but they finally failed through a lack of manpower.

There were also forts on the Continental side of the Channel, from the mouth of the river Seine as far north as the river Rhine, notably at Boulogne.[37]

THE "DARK AGES": EUROPE

This pattern of town walls remained significant under the "barbarian" conquerors of the Roman Empire, for example the Anglo-Saxon conquerors of England, once they had established states of their own. Thus, Roman city fortifications and traditions were significant under the Visigoths in Spain and southern France, as at Carcassonne and Toulouse, and under the Franks in France, and, indeed, Roman fortifications were maintained or revived if in a defensible condition for centuries, for example Doncaster in tenth-century England.[38] There was also a reoccupation of some pre-Roman fortifications, both in the late Roman period and in the post-Roman one, as with Cadbury Castle in Somerset. Innovations were seen. As a defense against Viking advances along rivers, fortified bridges were used under the Franks in the ninth century, certainly at Pont-de-l'Arche on the Seine from 862 and probably at Les Ponts-de-Cé on the Loire in 873.[39] Fortifications, moreover, had a place in protecting the role of rivers in the transport of supplies. The Vikings, in turn, fortified their bases, as with their winter camp at Repton in England in 873–74.[40] They also had siege engines, at least as indicated by their siege of Paris in 885–86.

Fortifications fulfilled many functions, such that when towns were founded, they were often accompanied by a castle, for example Bonifacio on the Corsican coast by Bonifacio of Tuscany in 828. Fortifications were a symbol of power but also a tool of rule as well as a place of refuge and a protection for food. These varied purposes encouraged a spread of fortresses into areas where they had been uncommon before, in part because the areas were beyond the Roman Empire, notably east of the Rhine. There, fortresses were associated with Frankish expansion from the second half of the seventh century and were used to locate, anchor, and express both lay and religious authority. There could be considerable density in fortifications. During Henry I's wars against the Slavs in 924–26 in what is now central Germany, a roughly triangular area of about seven thousand square miles between the Saale and Elbe

Rivers had about fifty timber-and-earthen fortifications, roughly one for every 140 square miles.

There was also considerable continuity from the Carolingian rulers of the seventh to ninth centuries to the Ottonian rulers of the tenth and eleventh, not least in the use of particular sites. There was also a process of further expansion, as with the Ottonians building fortifications against Slavs, Magyars, and Danes, for example Meissen in 928.

Yet there were also significant political changes. For example, throughout southern Germany, fortress construction continued with the ruler as the main builder until the ninth century. In contrast, in the tenth century, fortified centers of lordship became more common, being linked to two-part fortresses: a main stronghold and a fortified bailey. There was also a change in building technology. In place of an earlier emphasis on drywall construction (an English term meaning the placing of rocks on top of each other without being mortared together) or "heaped up" walls, mortared walls, which could be seen in the region of Hesse possibly from the end of the seventh century, became widespread by the tenth century, bringing added strength. This was an aspect of a political crisis focused on the need for protection against Magyar (Hungarian) expansion and the fissiparous weakness of the political order. Monasteries, such as St. Gall, and episcopal seats, such as Würzburg and Eichstätt, were fortified, as were towns, such as Regensburg, an episcopal seat and center of lay government, in about 920. In the tenth century, following the Edict of Pîtres (864), which loosened and delegated the royal right to build fortifications, aristocratic fortresses became more common. They were intended to secure lordship and to assert interests, as with the Counts of Schweinfurt in northern Bavaria. Their fortresses, however, were destroyed by Emperor Henry II in 1003 following the overthrow of the family. On the general pattern of fortifications, one that reflected not only cost but the value of particular sites, most of their fortresses were not new but rather improved older strongholds.[41] More mundanely, the castle at Burg Hayn in Germany was built in 1077 in order to protect hunting rights.

The standard emphasis on feudal cavalry in popular views of medieval European warfare (an emphasis similar to the tank-based view of the German army in World War II) has been qualified in scholarship by a stress on the extent to which large numbers of infantry were both involved and important. In part, this importance relates to the significance of sieges and the need for infantry this entailed, both in order to mount sieges and so as to resist them.[42] Linked to this came a need for specialists in siege warfare, notably those able to construct and operate siege engines and catapults, as in the campaign of Otto III and Henry II in the 990s–1010s.[43] This need was closely related to the sphere of operations and the defensive sites there.[44] A resource drain, cavalry was not useful in the "attack" phase of a siege, although important in thwarting relief attempts.

In southern England, Alfred, king of Wessex, encouraged the creation of thirty *burhs* (fortified towns or proto-towns) in the late ninth century connected by roads and beacons as a key part of a comprehensive defensive system drawing on wide-ranging militia obligations to provide military service designed to resist renewed Viking attacks.[45] The fortifications were earth and timber. There had been ditch-and-rampart defenses for towns before the Viking attacks, for example at Hereford and Tamworth in Mercia,[46] as well as palisades and defensible gates to protect Wessex's palaces. Some of the *burhs*, such as Bath, Chichester, Exeter, and Winchester, were former Roman towns and made use of refurbished Roman town defenses. Others, such as Bridport, were new.[47] On the whole, the *burhs* were less impressive than Roman town defenses, though at their best, for example Lydford overlooking a river gorge, they could be quite impenetrable. The *burhs* existed within interlocking communications and logistical support systems.

So also with Viking settlements. Some were refurbished Roman fortifications, as at York, where the walls of the legionary fortress (although not of Roman York as a whole) were rebuilt and extended. Others were newly fortified, notably in the East Midlands, as with Nottingham and Derby.

The *burh* system was continued by Alfred's successors, as they established the Old English state in the tenth century, notably conquering the Viking-held East Midlands. Chester was fortified in 907; Hertford in 911; Tamworth in 913; Buckingham and Warwick in 914; Cambridge, Colchester, Derby, and Huntingdon in 917; Nottingham and Stamford in 918; and Manchester in 919. Fortification and siegecraft were important to warfare. In the 990s, 1000s, and 1010s, in response to new Viking attacks, existing defenses were strengthened, emergency *burhs* were constructed, and Iron Age hill forts were reoccupied. In addition, private defended residences, the basis of castles, existed in England in the late Saxon period, some built by Norman and French protégés of Edward the Confessor (r. 1042–66), notably in Herefordshire on the troubled frontier with Wales.

BYZANTIUM

In terms of fortification, the Dark Ages is a term that is out of place. It may have been appropriate in western Europe, but not in the Byzantine Empire, the Middle East, or East Asia.

The Eastern Roman (Byzantine) Empire, which suffered repeated invasions, maintained formidable defenses, for example to protect the city of Salonika. Existing fortifications were improved as with the massive city wall at Antioch (near modern Aleppo) in the sixth century, which had about sixty towers divided into two groups: large polygonal master towers and smaller square towers dependent on them. Strongly defended Constantinople (modern Istanbul), the Byzantine capital, saw off Arab attacks in 674–78 and 717–18, in part by the use of Greek fire, an incendiary device. However, its strong walls were more significant. The Theodosian Wall built in the 440s to protect Constantinople had two bastioned curtains fronted by a ditch and containing sophisticated well-defended gateways. It was not broken through until 1453, when artillery could be used, as in 1204 the Crusader attack came on the sea walls. The defenses of Constantinople were an anomaly, but fortification was important to Byzantine strategy, both in the Balkans and in Asia. In the latter, between the rise of the Islamic caliphate in the seventh century and its fragmentation around 900, it could launch nearly annual attacks on Byzantium that the Byzantines could not meet head on. The essential Byzantine strategy involved letting Arab armies across the border, having the whole population and their livestock retreat into fortified settlements to deny easy plunder to the raiders, and shadowing the larger Arab armies with field forces. Thus the fortified points served as refuges with a mobile defense force, the refuges providing crucial logistical support.

There was also the discussion of fortification and siegecraft in Byzantine military treatises. For example, the tenth-century *Parangelmata Poliorcetica* by "Heron of Byzantium" focuses on how to conduct sieges, dealing with various types of siege writings. Illustrating the continuity of the subject, much of the text is a rewriting of a second-century text by Apollodorus of Damascus, while other Classical sources are also widely used. As the work contains only two contemporary allusions, it was probably not written by anyone with direct experience of siegecraft. A sister work that covered surveying techniques needed for sieges draws heavily on Hero of Alexandria's *Dioptra*.[48]

CHINA

In China, the pressure from northern "barbarians" encouraged the need for wall building or wall repairing under a series of dynasties: the Western Jin (265–316 CE), Northern Wei (386–534), Eastern Wei (534–50), Northern Qi (550–77), Northern Zhou (577–81), and Sui (581–618). Reflecting the pressure of attack, these walls were far further south than the Qin and Han walls. In turn, as a reminder of the significance of tasking, the early Tang dynasty (618–907) was interested in territorial expansion, notably into Xinjiang, and not in new walls. As a result, new fortified settlements were more to the fore under the early Tang. With the "Four Garrisons," the Tang kept order among the oasis kingdoms of the Tarim Basin in the mid-seventh century. In the Tibet borderlands, from Xinjiang to Gansu and Sichuan, the Tang established a major system of fortresses with large garrisons and military colonies, a system that increased in size in the mid-eighth century. Walls could be part of a larger strategy in which tribute payment played a role. In short, as with Byzantium, although different due to the availability in China of more troops, fortifications were part of a larger strategic system.[49]

Aside from walls, there were also a large number of walled cities in China, for example Guangzhou, in some of which were garrisons including cavalry, the cities and their garrisons providing defense in depth. The roads and rivers linking these fortresses were a key element of the defensive system as they not only provided supply routes for the defenders but also denied them to attackers. Logistics were made even more significant by the size of armies, as their supply needs were greater. As a result, advancing forces were unwilling to bypass major fortified places. However, made of rammed earth and frequently supported by deep moats, city walls themselves were strong.[50] Sieges could be lengthy and costly, while attacking means, such as mining, could be countered.[51]

As elsewhere, battles could determine the fate of fortresses. For example, the Tang defeat by the An Lushan rebels at Tongguan in 756 greatly weakened Tang capability and led to the fall of the capital, Chang'an. At the same time, fortresses, if held, could limit the effects of battle and provide opportunities for rallying support. In 756, the emperor's heir apparent, the future Suzong, fell back to Lingwu, a major fortress, from which he successfully organized resistance.

The Chinese largely faced "barbarians" who lacked much skill in siegecraft, but some of their opponents were more able. In 819, the Tibetans besieged Yanzhou, using Chinese-style siege engines, but the refortification of the fortress, combined with a firm defense, held it. In 829, Chengdu's citadel survived attack by Nanzhao. The Chinese also strengthened their frontiers with roads and post stations that helped them move troops and messages. Within China, city walls were also important when Chinese factions fought each other.

Under the Northern Song (960–1127), who lacked effective cavalry, the problems of using infantry to defend against cavalry attackers encouraged linear defenses, including a network of hydraulic defenses such as deep irrigation channels and marshes to protect the vulnerable province of Hebei. They also developed new fertile land, which helped to sustain the garrisons and new towns. The Song also put an emphasis on fortified cities, which provided another powerful defense against the cavalry of the Liao dynasty of the Kitans (907–1125). These cities dissuaded the Liao from invading in the 980s. In 1004–05, the Liao launched a major attack on the city of Ying, with massed archery to cover scaling attempts that were repelled.

The Song constructed new city walls of brick rather than of earth and stone. Long portions of the Song border coincided with the remains of earlier walls. This provided a continuity, seen also with the later Ming era, that reflected both a practical understanding of the topography and its possibilities and, on the other hand, beliefs about the structure of the universe and concerning a border between China and the "barbarians."[52] Such beliefs have been studied for China, but not for most societies.

NEW WORLD

In the New World, there was also a range of defensive works, including major sites such as the fortified hilltop cities of Central America, including, in modern Mexico, Cacaxtla and Xochicalco, both of which were developed from about 650, being abandoned in c. 8500 and c. 900, respectively. Village locations and designs also reflected the extent of warfare. Thus, in about 900, in northeast North America, there was a move from sites that were generally small and located along major waterways to larger and more compact villages, usually on defendable terrain such as hilltops and away from major river valleys. However, here, as elsewhere, archaeological research, both by excavations and by GIS-based analyses, may well throw up much new material.[53] The archaeological coverage so far is far patchier for much of Latin America than for North America, and this is particularly the case for forested regions, notably Amazonia and Caribbean coastal regions.

CONCLUSIONS

Most of human history has been covered in this chapter, and therefore most of the history of fortification and sieges. Dating the age of fortification is not easy given multiple issues of definition and application. Nevertheless, even if prehistoric protection against animals is omitted and the conventional focus beginning on Jericho in 8000–6000 BCE, with its ditch, massive rock wall, and later circular tower, is taken, then most of history is covered in this chapter (although these features of Jericho are not universally accepted as military in nature). Moreover, this approach is one that contests accounts of prehistoric human life as inherently peaceful. The disproportionately slim nature of the coverage compared to the remainder of the book is lessened if weighting is introduced for the size of the world's population, which was then relatively small, but, nonetheless, it remains an issue. So, even more, does that of methodology. This period is one in which the evidence is archaeological, with little or no literary material to help with intentionality or usage. There are clashes over basic points such as whether ancient Egypt had walled towns: it did.[54]

Processes of development are difficult to assess, not least the extent to which (semi-) automatic processes of cause and effect, notably of challenge and response, are the most appropriate. They are certainly the simplest to employ. However, comparisons between societies in apparently similar circumstances are made more difficult by a lack of understanding of how threats were perceived, an issue that extends to the question of how the potential for change was understood. Thus, in his *Strategema*, Sextus Julius Frontinus (c. 30–104 CE), who was a Roman consul three times between 73 and 100, saw no possible improvement in siege artillery: "works and engines of war, the invention of which has long since reached its limit, and for the improvement of which I see no further hope in the applied arts." As a result, he focused on other means and tactics, for example, surprise attacks, inducing treachery, diverting streams, contaminating water supplies, terrorizing the besieged, attacking from an unexpected quarter, and setting troops to draw out the besieged.[55] The last was frequently attempted but often did not work, as at Panormus in 258 BCE when the Carthaginians refused to come out to fight the Romans, leaving the latter to withdraw.[56]

It is generally argued that fortifications reflected concentrations of power that indicated the need to control as well as to protect both fertile plains and trade routes, as in the southern Caucasus in the Bronze and Iron Ages. Such a pattern becomes more apparent if research focuses on settlements and the landscape, rather than on the fortified sites themselves, and then locates and understands the sites with reference to the criteria reflected in the distribution of settlements.[57]

Separately, there is also the danger of simplifying the military system of particular ages or specific societies as part of a process of locating and explaining fortification. In practice, complexity is frequently more appropriate. Thus, Sasanid Persia should be known for its fortifications, as well as for the heavy cavalry that tends to attract attention.

Moreover, alongside the tendency to focus on societies' external protection against other societies, it is necessary to note the continual process by which they protected themselves internally against lawlessness and disorder. The wall, the gate, and the fence, ubiquitous forms, were central to the definition of space and to its protection. So, even more, was the idea of a threatening outside. This is an aspect of focusing on

settlements and the perceived landscape and then considering the fortifications accordingly.

The standard developmental model for warfare does not adequately
capture the need for fortification. This is not only the case for lawlessness and disorder within settled societies. In addition, nomadic, semi-
nomadic, and other peoples who did not develop large-scale governmental structures often relied on raiding their opponents and lacked
the specialization in fortifications and siegecraft seen with powerful
states. However, due to the frequently endemic violence between villages, clans, and tribes, many, if not most, settlements were fortified.
The impact of "little war" on fortification awaits systematic study.

So also with the role of "natural fortresses." Prime contenders included passes through mountains, such as Thermopylae in Greece,
where a small number of Greeks, most prominently Spartans, delayed
the attacking Persians in 480 BCE, and Hulao in China where a road
wound through high loess escarpments. The Tang were blocked there
in 621 CE until the defenders came out to fight. The defeat of the
defenders led to the surrender of the besieged city of Luoyang, now
without hope of relief.[58]

The points made about the period covered in this chapter as a whole
can also be advanced more specifically for the "Dark Ages," which in
western Europe took up over half a millennium, from c. 400 to c. 1000.
It is again difficult for this period to establish patterns of causation. The
general narratives relate to responses to "barbarian" invasions and to
weaknesses in political/military consolidation. However, as before, the
nature of response mechanisms was far from clear.

The utility of the fortifications of this period, and indeed of earlier
centuries, could be long-lasting. Some of China's many walls proved
useful against the Japanese in the twentieth century. Trajan's Wall in
Moldavia had some use into the nineteenth century, while Aurelian's
Wall was still the primary defense of Rome then. Chester's Walls are
essentially those the Romans built, Constantinople/Istanbul's Theodosian Walls were the key defense in 1453, and the Danevirke was still
useful in the Schleswig-Holstein Wars of the mid-nineteenth century
and was employed by the Germans in 1945 as an antitank feature.

What is readily apparent is the extent to which fortification conveyed
security, and thus affirmed power and legitimacy. This was captured by
Bai Juyi (772–846), a Chinese scholar and court official who in c. 808

wrote "Walling Yanzhou," a poem for the emperor. Not the most gripping of works, it described the construction in 792 of a fortress on a main road into China from Tibet. Lines included the following:

Ten years have now passed since Yanzhou's walls were built,
And the barbarians dressed in furs and felts have not since crossed our border.
. . . they keep far from the new fortress.

There was also reference back in the poem to Zhang Renyuan (d. 714) who, in 711, had built three fortresses, each controlling one of the trade and invasion routes into Guangzhong:

His three forts towered firm as the legs of a tripod.
. . . the soldiers never heard the sound of barbarians' horses.[59]

2

THE MEDIEVAL CASTLE

Castles and fortified cities were a potent display of power and an impressive force multiplier, and much warfare focused on the capture and defense of these positions.[1] Surviving examples of castles, whether in Europe, the Near East, or the Far East, provide ample illustration of how they literally towered over, and thus physically and symbolically commanded, the surrounding countryside. Stone was not vulnerable to fire, as wood very much was. Moreover, the strength of the defenses posed tactical and organizational problems for attackers, especially the difficulty of providing supplies for besieging forces. Western European states tended to put more emphasis on stone than their counterparts in China, India, and Southeast and East Asia, where the emphasis instead was generally on the use of earth, timber, or brick.

At the same time, so-called stone castles had plenty of wooden components as an integral part of their infrastructure, and the mining of their defenses by means of a fire-filled tunnel under a wall threatened the collapse of the wall. The collapse of the burning wooden support props brought the heavy masonry walls or towers above them crashing down, creating a breach. The very weight of the stone edifice could add to the vulnerability of the structure to attack by means of mining.

In terms of power and display, there was also the issue of scale, and notably the size of fortified cities, such as Milan, Antioch, Constantinople, Baghdad, or Xian, when contrasted with the often relatively modest numbers in attacking forces. This situation helped lead to a pattern of focusing the attack on the gates, rather than trying to attack along the walls. However, as earlier, such a concentrated focus left besieging armies vulnerable to sallies by the defenders. When combined with the operation of relief forces, as with the eventually successful siege of Antioch during the First Crusade, this vulnerability ensured that sieges were, or at least could be, an aspect of field operations as a whole. Linked to or separate from this, they could also be lengthy, as with the eventually successful Crusader siege of Acre (in modern Israel) during the Third Crusade in 1189–91. In this siege, the Crusaders had to battle both the determined defenders, who were being resupplied by sea, and relief attempts.[2] Partly as a result of their cost in time and resources, some leaders did not seek sieges, and they certainly sought to avoid lengthy ones, although the capture of fortified positions was desirable, and much medieval strategy revolved around this goal.

EAST AND SOUTH ASIA

Fortified cities, rather than stand-alone fortresses, were the key defensive means and target in many parts of the world, including East and South Asia. These cities were capable of putting up strong resistance, as in 1126 when the Jurchen Jin attacked Kaifeng, the capital of Song China, situated in central China (Henan) just south of the Yellow River, only to face strong walls, a deep moat, and fortifications that included bastions, all supported by gunpowder weaponry. However, in 1127 the Jurchen Jin succeeded in part because they used gunpowder bombs fired from catapults. The Mongol invasion of the Tangut kingdom of Xi Xia in 1209 saw the storming or blockade of fortified cities. The key siege was that of Zhongxing, the western capital of the Xi Xia in Sichuan, but the Mongols found that their battering rams were ineffective and they lacked more sophisticated weapons. As a result, Chinggis Khan (Genghis Khan), using the winter rains in 1209–10, had a dyke built to redirect the Huanghe River, which began to flood the city and undermine its walls. In consequence, the Tangut made peace in 1210.

In 1212, the apparently inexorable Mongols pressed on to invade the Jin empire of northern China with two armies, each equipped with a train of camels carrying Chinese siege weapons that could be assembled on-site. The Mongols, however, did not want lengthy sieges, and this ensured that, in the 1214 campaign, Chinggis did not initially attack

Zhongdu (Beijing), the Jin capital, preferring instead to blockade it, a key choice for attackers. However, a resumed offensive led to a focus on the city, one supported by siege weapons and engineers. With relief efforts beaten off, the city surrendered in 1215.[3]

Invading the Khwarazmian empire in Central Asia in 1219, the Mongols also took the major cities, notably Bukhara and Samarqand. The local people were driven into the fort cities, flooding them with refugees and spreading terror. As at the successful siege of Kaifeng, the new Jin capital, in China in 1232, local people were also used in sieges in order to fill moats with debris and man the siege weapons. Once captured, the walls of cities were destroyed by the 'Mongols in order to leave them vulnerable. Cutting cities off from supplies could also be important, as when Karakorum/Qarqorum, the Mongol capital, located in what is today Mongolia, was captured by Khubilai in a Mongol civil war in 1262.[4]

There were also stand-alone fortresses, such as the mountain fortresses in Armenia and Georgia that slowed, but did not stop, Mongol invasion in 1238. These fortresses took on much of their significance from their position, as the tactical significance of their mountainous position was given operational importance by their role in guarding the passes through which advances were funneled. In 1256, the Mongols under Hülegü, a grandson of Chinggis, captured the castles of the Assassins. These were located in the mountainous northwest of Iran and were built on high crags in commanding positions. The Seljuks had failed to capture one of the principal castles, Lambsar, after a siege lasting eight years. However, the ferocious reputation of the Mongols persuaded the Assassins to surrender.

Technology also played a role. In the twelfth century, the ropes on a trebuchet, which had been pulled down by men, were replaced with a counterweight, although not everywhere or always. This development began probably in the Middle East, although it is not certain who was responsible. Possessing Persian technology from the 1220s, the Mongols took up the innovation, using these trebuchets to pound Baghdad, the capital of the Abbasid caliphate, into surrender in a week in 1258, bringing that long-lasting caliphate to an end in a key episode in Islamic history. The counterweight trebuchets are clearly depicted in illustrated Persian accounts of the siege. At Aleppo (which the Crusaders had not captured) in 1260, the Mongols focused all their trebuchets on one point, the gate facing Iraq, and broke through there.[5]

From the Middle East, the innovation spread. For example, the Mongol ruler in Persia, the Il-Khan Abaqa, sent two engineers to his uncle, Khubilai, to help the latter in his conquest of Song (southern) China. The engineers built seven counterweight trebuchets, previously unknown in China, each able to hurl stones weighing hundreds of pounds. The effectiveness of these stones depended on the thickness and structural integrity of the walls. The cities of Xiangyang and Fancheng fell in 1273. Shayang followed in 1274 and Changzhou in 1275, with gunpowder bombs fired by trebuchets adding to the destructiveness.

Technology was not the sole element. To move from raiding and victory in battle to seizing territory required an ability to capture fortified positions. Largely by using Chinese expertise, the Mongols acquired skill in siege warfare during the numerous campaigns required to conquer the Jurchen Jin empire of northern China and the Song empire of southern China, campaigns that represented the most impressive use of force in the thirteenth century. The lengthy nature of the sieges was possible only because of Mongol organization and persistence, while the ability to elicit and coerce support was also important.[6]

At the same time, the Koreans and Southern Song had considerable success in delaying the Mongols by means of mountain fortresses and (in the case of the Koreans) island positions. New mountain fortresses, to which local governmental bodies were relocated, were constructed in the early 1240s by the Southern Song in Sichuan, and a multipoint defense network was established accordingly, providing defense in depth and weakening enemy forces. The mountains chosen were generally close to rivers or at the confluence of two. Thus, Diaoyucheng, a fortress in Hezhou, had walls that extended to the Jialing River. It survived a major Mongol attack in 1259, only falling in 1279.[7]

Less happily, in 1343–45, during the siege of the well-fortified Genoese-ruled trading city of Kaffa (modern Theodosia) in Crimea, the Mongols used trebuchets to fire corpses into the city, spreading the bubonic plague. Fleeing Genoese brought the disease back to Europe. Such biological warfare, firing human or animal corpses, was not uncommon and had been used since Antiquity. The poisoning of water supplies was also a significant ploy for both attackers and defenders.

Although both sides were willing to take heavy casualties, the Mongols proved less adroit with siegecraft at the expense of the Mamluks in Syria, not least because the Mongols did not use gunpowder weaponry. Neither the Mongol army under Hülegü nor the Ilkhanid army of his son appear to have had any superior knowledge in the field of siege warfare, which is a demonstration of the importance to the Mongols of captured knowledge in the form of recruitment from captives.[8] Nevertheless, Hülegü captured Damascus in 1260. A later inner-Asian invader, the wide-ranging Timur the Lame, captured Delhi (1398), Damascus (1401), and Baghdad (1401), among much else.

In Japan, clans and daimyo (autonomous princes) built castle seats, as with Tsuroka in northern Honshu, the castle seat of the Sakai clan. Broad moats were a major feature, as at Hagi. Stone castles were built from the fifteenth century, notably Nakagusuku (c. 1450) on Okinawa, the castle of a feudal lord. There was also a process of expansion. Himejī Castle, built in 1333, on a strategic hilltop overlooking the coastal route along the Inland Sea west of Kobe, was strengthened in 1467 with the addition of two baileys.

INDIA

The spread of innovations can be difficult to chart and therefore explain, but it is apparent. For example, in 1468–69 the sultan of Bahmani in India incorporated state-of-the-art military engineering from the contemporary Middle East, including projecting bastions equipped with counterweight trebuchets and gunports in curtain walls for cannon, and the use of cannon for sieges followed in the early 1470s.[9] It is possible that this use of cannon was introduced from Mamluk Egypt.

Prior to the spread of cannon, Indian fortification focused on cities, where it was a question of walls and citadels, or fortresses in the countryside, usually on hilltops. Particular effort was devoted to citadels at capitals. This was especially so at Delhi, the key center of power in northern India. The citadel there was a residence, political center, military stronghold, and protector of both mosque and mausoleum. Particular rulers founded their own citadels or adapted those of their predecessors. Thus in Delhi, Ghiyās ud-din Tughluq, the sultan in 1320–25, speedily built a citadel. So also did Firūz Shāh, sultan from 1354 to

1388. The Lodis moved the capital to Agra in 1505 and built there accordingly, but Sher Shāh, who returned the capital to Delhi in 1540 when he captured it from the Mughals, built a citadel prior to his death in 1545. Regaining Delhi in 1555, the Mughals used his citadel as a quarry for cut stone.[10] Separately across India, the town dwellings and rural centers of prominent families were fortified, with walled and gated compounds being a significant feature in towns.

THE CRUSADES

Proclaimed in 1095, what became the First Crusade was mounted to recapture the Holy Land for Christendom. The Crusades exposed the Western military system to particular challenges.[11] Establishing states in the Middle East from the end of the eleventh century in the face of militarily sophisticated opponents with large armies obliged the Crusaders to create a series of strongholds to protect their positions, although there are conceptual issues over the relationship between castles and frontiers.[12] There were a variety of types of fortification including cities with citadels, towns with castles, castles in mountainous areas and on coastal plains, towers, and fortified caves. For each type, archaeological work has been patchy.[13] As a result, the phases of construction of some, notably minor, works is unclear, as therefore is the analysis of the process of development. The combination of terrain features and shooting fronts was a key element in most castles as each was crucial to the defense.[14]

Major, stand-alone castles have attracted the most archaeological and scholarly attention and are found across a range of countries, including Japan as well as the Crusader kingdoms and European states. With the development of the concentric plan from the late 1160s (Belvoir 1168–70 is an early example of a concentric castle, but it is difficult to date many of the Crusader castles), castle design in the Crusader lands was possibly more advanced than in Europe because of the major challenges the Crusaders had to face from larger Muslim armies (most of the soldiers were Turks or Kurds) and their effective siege techniques. Possibly, there was also a better-skilled local workforce. Castles, however, were affected by the danger of denuding them of troops in order to create a field army and by the psychological effects of the defeat of such an army, as when Saladin's defeat of the army of the Crusader kingdom of Jerusalem at Hattin in 1187 was followed by his capture of Acre, Jerusalem, and other fortress garrisons that, without a supporting army, were in too weak a position to hold out and felt vulnerable.

The most famous Crusader castle, Krak (or Crac) des Chevaliers, was originally built to guard the route from Tripoli to Hamah. In turn, the Crusaders developed the fortifications under the Count of Tripoli, but the castle that survives was totally rebuilt by the Hospitallers (Knights of St. John) after they obtained it from the count in 1142. It successfully held out against Saladin in 1188, ensuring that it was one of the few remaining Crusader castles in 1190. The defenses were strengthened at the start of the thirteenth century following a devastating earthquake and included a massive talus, which not only increased the strength of the castle's inner walls but also made it resistant to further earthquakes. The outer wall was strengthened by semicircular protruding towers. The nature of the site made mining (i.e., the undermining of the walls) difficult. The multiple character and interlocking strength of the defenses ensured that, once the outer walls had been penetrated, it was still necessary to advance along overlooked corridors and ramps, exposing attackers to fire and ambush. The defense was layered. The outer walls included shooting galleries, box machicolations, and the walkway, while the inner castle had slits in the walls and at the top openings for bigger weapons in the shape of large catapults. Castle architecture reflected the role of specialists in fortification technology.[15]

Despite this, the fortress fell to the Mamluks after a siege of scarcely more than a month in 1271 as they rolled up the remains of the Crusader world. Sultan Baybars used deception: the defenders were sent a forged document telling them there would be no relief and advising surrender. The Mamluks captured Acre in 1291 with a determined assault after its defenses had been weakened by trebuchets (they brought more trebuchets than most armies) and, more significantly, by mining, which brought down a large chunk of the south wall. Krak itself was a hideout for rebel troops in the Syrian conflict of the 2010s and was bombarded by Syrian and Russian aircraft, bringing down some of the outside walls. So also with devastation to other medieval fortifications, notably in Syria at Aleppo, but also in Lebanon. Krak is one of the most impressive surviving medieval military sites, and the remains can be viewed in drone footage on YouTube. Partly as a result, Krak has for many come to characterize the Crusader castle, even though, by its nature, it is atypical.

EUROPE

Fortifications and sieges were important to conflict in medieval Europe.[16] As in earlier periods, this helped ensure that common soldiers (i.e., infantry) played a major role in warfare.[17] As always with fortifications, more than the fortresses themselves was at stake. Instead, castles, like other fortifications across the world, were particularly effective as part of a combined military system. Indeed, European military history in the eleventh to thirteenth centuries in part centered on how the development of knights, infantry, castles, and siege techniques enabled the rulers who employed them to extend their power, both against domestic opponents and on their frontiers. The latter forced the rulers of more peripheral regions threatened with this extension, such as those of Lithuania, Prussia, Scotland, and Wales, to build castles of their own.

As a sometimes overlapping factor, as instruments of conquest, castles were built to consolidate Christian expansion at the expense of non-Christians. This was the case in Spain and Portugal during the lengthy wars with the Moors from the eighth to the fifteenth centuries. During the Reconquista, the Moors in turn built castles opposing those of the advancing Christians. Pretty much every Christian castle was answered by a Muslim one, and vice versa. For example, built in the eleventh century after the surrounding lands were reconquered, Loarre Castle in Huesca Province is ten kilometers from its opposing Muslim castle, each able to see the other.

In the Baltic lands, where the "Northern Crusades" were being staged, castles were built, notably in the lands of the Teutonic Knights. Malbork, which was selected in 1309 as the residence of the grand master, was adapted and strengthened, as was the wider complex, which included impressive walls and fortifications for both the castle and the neighboring town. River features played an important role. In 1410, a Polish siege was repelled after the field army of the Teutonic Knights had been defeated at Grünwald/Tannenberg. In 1457, however, Malbork was sold because the Teutonic Order was unable to pay its mercenaries, again an indication of castles as part of a system.

More generally, castle building was an aspect of the expansion of territorial control. In northern England, the Norman presence was anchored in the eleventh century with the building of castles in Durham (1072), Newcastle (1080), and Carlisle (1092). Newcastle was the linguistic counterpart of Neuburg (German) and Neufchâteau (French), and the frequent use of these, and related names, testified to the significance of the construction of new fortifications. In Flanders, in the early fourteenth century, the French sought to use the construction of castles to advance their interests, as at Lille, a fortified position that remains significant to the present day.

However, castles built to attack or defend in Europe had a power radius of only about fifteen miles. This was a good patrolling journey for a mounted man without killing his horse. The radius of power would be less on rough ground or in mountainous terrain. Within states, castles continued to serve to affirm power. Thus, the Castelvecchio in Verona in northern Italy, built by Canegrande II in the 1350s, bristled with battlements and demonstrated his power over the city. That castle benefited from being built along the river Adige. Other castles sought to use height to their benefit, as with that in Meersburg in southern Germany which was built on a rocky promontory and protected by a fourteen-meter moat. Alongside a twenty-eight-meter-deep well and a subterranean passage to Lake Constance, this was dug in 1334 by the new Prince-Bishop of Constance, Nicholas of Frauenfeld, the papal candidate, when preparing to resist a siege by Emperor Ludwig of Bavaria. The fourteen-week siege failed.

As in other periods, sieges were more common than battles. For example, in the Albigensian crusade in southern France, the Crusaders participated in at least forty-five sieges but fought only four field battles between 1209 and 1218. The positions besieged varied greatly, from walled cities in the plains, such as Toulouse, to isolated hilltop castles. Some of the castles were built on historic sites. The impressively located Château de Puilaurens was on the site of a Visigothic citadel. Negotiation, not assault, settled most of these sieges, and in those, both defensive and offensive capabilities were in large part significant in affecting the terms of negotiation. Both in negotiation and in other operations, siege machines and engineers were less important than luck, resolve, and aggressiveness.[18] Terror was widely used to force surrender.

Aggressiveness proved particularly significant in the seizure in 1204 of Château-Gaillard, a still impressive site on a high position on the banks of the river Seine. Built by Richard I in 1196–98, it was captured from his brother, John, king of England and Duke of Normandy, by the forces of Philip Augustus, king of France. The magnificently strong individual castle was helpless if isolated from its broader political-logistical support system. The castle was isolated by the besieging force, which blocked the Seine and prevented a relief force from reaching the castle. A land force under William the Marshal was also driven off. The castle was eventually starved into surrender. Its seizure left Normandy vulnerable to rapid conquest. The castle was partly destroyed by Henry IV of France in 1603 in the aftermath of the Wars of Religion.

Fortification techniques developed, not least in enlarging the size and raising the height of castle works, and in increasing their complexity. This was especially so in the thirteenth century. Raising the height was important in the pre-cannon era because, alongside mining, major threats to fortifications were posed by scaling the walls, archers, and stone-throwing weapons. Each threat could be lessened by raising the height, which affected fire from within the castle as well. Town walls were also improved and extended. In Grenoble, the Roman wall built at the end of the third century was extended in the thirteenth century, with a further extension at the end of the sixteenth century.

On a smaller scale, a new form of walled town known as a *bastide* was being built in southwest France in the thirteenth century. The *bastides* followed a common design and were self-contained entities, with church, market, homes, and defended gates. Many extant examples are still largely unchanged. The most active founders of *bastides* were Alphonse de Poitiers, brother of Louis IX of France, Count of Toulouse from 1249 to 1271, who built fifty-seven, and Edward I of England, Duke of Aquitaine, who sought to consolidate his hold on the northern borders of the duchy. More generally, walled hill towns remained significant as a means to enhance natural defensive features, for example with the Tuscan town of San Gimignano in which families competed to build the highest tower.

There were also fortifications for religious foundations. In France, the magnificent cathedral at Albi was immensely strong and defendable. The Cistercian abbey of Flaran had a rampart from the fourteenth century.

More generally, there was an interplay of defensive techniques and offensive practices, each at least partially dependent for their utility on the other. This was seen in the Mongol invasion of the Rus' principalities in 1237–38 as the presence now of Mongol siege engineers weakened the value of defensive works, such as with the strongly fortified city of Riazan, which was successfully stormed in late 1237 after a relief army had been defeated by the Mongols. This was followed in 1238 by Rostov, Iaroslav, Torzhok, and Suzdal, although Novgorod was protected by an early thaw, which was a prelude to the city submitting. In 1239, it was the turn of cities farther south, notably Pereiaslavl and Chernigov, followed by Kiev, to fall to the Mongols. No city appeared safe. The majority of the Rus' towns were defended by wooden structures, which made them more vulnerable. The siege engineers were used not only for siege engines but also in the construction of walls around the Rus' cities to prevent the inhabitants from escaping and to protect the Mongol troops.[19]

THE BRITISH ISLES

In England, after the Norman Conquest in 1066, castles were very different from the characteristic feature of Anglo-Saxon fortification, the *burh* or fortified town. In much of the British Isles, castles were built following the arrival of the Normans, a process helped by their adaptability in use and format. However, there was no national "master plan" implementing strategic considerations. The location of castles reflected a number of factors, not only military imperatives, but also local resources and politics. The first castles constructed in the county of Lincolnshire were those of Lincoln and Stamford. They were probably built to control both towns and routes. The reasons why individual castles were built are often unclear, although GIS (Geographic Information System) work on viewsheds has clarified many cases. With GIS, a computer can plot exactly what could have been seen from a castle, given the castle elevation and surrounding terrain. It can even adjust for factors like season, which affects the foliage. The computer can therefore show one of the key ways a castle was sited to fit into (and dominate visually) the local region. Locations served social and economic purposes as well as military-strategic, and this affected their location.[20]

Early Norman castles in England and Wales were generally motte-and-bailey or ringwork (enclosure) forms, earth-and-timber constructions, thrown up in a hurry (although still requiring many man-days to construct), and yet able to give protection against local discontent. Motte-and-bailey forms, essentially wooden stockades atop earth mounds, had a long currency in the British Isles to the thirteenth century, as did ringworks. Cost and the shortage of skilled masons affected the attraction of construction in stone, but not all early Norman castles were built of timber and earthwork. Exeter, London, York, and others had early stone phases.

Castle design, whether of timber, stone, or both, was intended to promote a powerful symbol of the new landholding families in relation to each other. William I, the Conqueror (r. 1066–87), and his successors also maintained castles in the shire towns, such as Oxford (as well as in London), as part of their framework of royal government. Unlike with the *burhs*, domestic control was a key feature in the history of Norman castles, and security against internal rivals was just as important as defense against external threat, notably from Scots and Scandinavians. However, the proliferation of private castles complicated internal security once the Norman aristocracy became a potential threat to royal government. This was true as early as 1075, with Anglo-Saxon troops called out then to threaten these castles.

Many castles, including Cambridge, Chester, and Wallingford, were built over existing towns, devastating their townscapes. With time, there were improvements in castle design. From the reign of William II (1087–1100), many earth-and-timber constructions were replaced by stonework. In London, the great White Tower constructed during the first forty years of Norman rule as the Tower of London, was later surrounded by a succession of walls and defensive towers. Two sets of encircling defenses were added in the thirteenth century. Substantial river defenses and a moat were part of the powerful new complex which has survived to the present. Norwich, built by 1075, was a motte and bailey, but by 1125 the mound was crowned by a strong square stone keep. The castle site was on a large rock outcrop, which further enhanced its defensive potential.

While sieges of castles were ubiquitous in the medieval world, as a separate purpose, castles, such as the White Tower and Windsor for the Crown in England, had a key function as fortified residences. Especially, but not only, in western Europe, there was a major contrast in focus, as well as an overlap, between the situation in which castles were fortifications and many were used as instruments of conquest, and the degree to which the majority of castles were also homes in some sense, however occasional their use as such, as well as administrative centers for the estates (or states) that belonged to their owners. Such contrasts and overlaps reflected the complex nature of the continuum of purpose that can often be discerned across both space and time.

Town walls were intended to control the entry of people and goods. Castles were easier to defend than fortified towns, as the fortifications of the latter had to be related to the towns, while castles could be sited very much for defensive considerations, particularly to take advantage of hillsides and their ability to magnify the problems facing attackers. Thus, many castles were in the most defensible places. Yet, although smaller and therefore requiring fewer defenders, stand-alone castles were not necessarily superior to fortified towns. This situation owed something to the creation of castles as key elements in many town fortifications. Moreover, the location of many castles reflected their social and administrative status and attributes.

In England, references to the sieges of towns were not common between 1070 (after William I's suppression of English rebellions based in towns, notably Exeter) and the thirteenth century. Sieges of castles, however, characterized warfare, as in the lengthy civil war during Stephen's reign (1135–54). Battles, as at Lincoln in 1141 and 1217, were generally related to sieges, whether of towns or of stand-alone castles.

Wales was a prime example of the use of fortresses in territorial expansion. Castles were built both by the English Crown and by Norman aristocrats seeking to expand their power. William I was probably responsible for building Cardiff Castle when he visited Wales in 1081. One of his lords, William fitz Osbern, a close ally of William, had already built a stone castle, the first in Wales, at Chepstow on the River Wye, in 1067–71 and used it as a base for expansion westward into south Wales. Another, Roger of Montgomery, founded a timber castle at Montgomery and advanced from there westward into central Wales. He was also responsible for pressure farther north from the castle at

Oswestry. Hugh of Avranches, "Hugh the Fat," Earl of Chester, pushed his way westward along the coast of north Wales, building castles at Bangor and Caernarfon and, in 1088, at Aberlleiniog on the island of Anglesey.

In a pattern to be seen in the American West during the nineteenth century, where wooden stockades provided defensive posts against Native American attack, castles provided refuge from Welsh attack but could also be easily bypassed. Thus, fortress construction did not fully stabilize Norman control. Instead, the Normans had to rely on light forces of their own to pursue Welsh raiders. Lightly armed cavalrymen linked to castles were one remedy. Fortifications always need active defensive personnel in order to play anything other than a passive defensive role.

Henry I (r. 1100–35) acquired the site of Carmarthen in 1109 at the lowest bridging point on the River Tywi. He developed it as a royal lordship with a castle and a town. Henry also granted the region of Ceredigion to Gilbert of Clare, who conquered it in 1111 and consolidated his position by building a number of castles. However, in the civil war of Stephen's reign (1135–54), the Welsh pushed back, for example capturing Carmarthen in 1146.

The Welsh also built and developed castles. Thus, Rhys (d. 1197), ruler of the principality of Deheubarth, was able to hold off Henry II in the 1160s, capturing Cardigan (1165), Carmarthen (1166), and, in cooperation with Owain of Gwynedd, Rhuddlan (1167), the latter after a siege of three months. Rhys improved Norman castles that he captured at Cardigan and Llandovery and built his own. Similarly, the princes of Powys built Castell Coch—the Red Castle—now Powys Castle, although that was captured by the English in 1196.

In the thirteenth century, the princes of Gwynedd (northwest Wales), Llywelyn the Great (d. 1240) and Llywelyn ap Gruffydd (d. 1282), united the part of Wales outside Norman control and built stone castles, including at Dolwyddelan, Dolbarden, and Criccieth. These were different from earlier earth and wooden structures, such as Dafydd ab Owain's castle at Rhuddlan, because they did not burn. The castles were designed to protect routes through Gwynedd. The size of their garrisons is unclear, but they represented an immediately available force. Compared to the castles built later by Edward I, the Welsh castles had simple plans, but they were an advance on what had come earlier. Dolbarden's round keep was a strong feature, and Criccieth's twin-towered gatehouse was state of the art.

In 1212, Llywelyn the Great, having been recently defeated by the English under King John, rebelled while John was handicapped by serious opposition to his policies in England, and captured the new English castles in Gwynedd. In later conflicts, however, Llywelyn found it difficult to capture English castles, failing at Builth (1222), Montgomery (1228), Caerleon (1231), and Carmarthen (1233). The threat he posed led to extensive English improvements to fortifications, for example those made by the Marshal family at Chepstow, Cilgerran, Pembroke, and Usk (which Llywelyn captured in 1231); by the Crown at Montgomery (which Llywelyn also captured in 1231); and by others at Bronllys, Skenfrith, and Tretower. Llywelyn ap Gruffydd, grandson of Llywelyn the Great, resisted English expansionism, taking Builth Castle in 1260, Brecon in 1262, and Deganwy, the leading castle in north Wales, in 1263 after it had been surrendered by its blockaded garrison. Powis Castle followed in 1274.

In turn, Edward I's conquest of the mountainous region of northwest Wales from 1277 proved decisive. The castles the Welsh built did not deter or delay Edward's armies to any real extent. Having forced Llywelyn to surrender in 1277 and greatly restricted his principality, Edward anchored his position with a major program of fortification at Aberystwyth, Builth, Flint, Rhuddlan, and Ruthin. Llywelyn's brother, Dafydd, started a new rebellion in 1282, seizing the royal castles of Flint and Rhuddlan and the new Marcher castle at Hawarden. The rebellion was overcome, Edward overrunning all of Gwynedd in 1283, taking castles such as Criccieth. The sole significant siege of a Welsh castle was Dryslwyn in 1287, during a rebellion in South Wales. A trebuchet was used at Dryslwyn and was then taken to Newcastle Emlyn in a column of eighty carts. Welsh castles were places of last retreat and did not play a significant strategic role in thwarting Edward.

Welsh revolts in 1287 and, more seriously, 1294–95 encouraged Edward to press on with his own program of fortifications. There were new sites for fortification and a new strategic task because Gwynedd was now Crown property. Edward had seen Crusader castles in the Holy Land in 1270–72 and introduced the concentric style he had seen there from the 1280s. This did not focus on keeps, instead presenting a ring of walls and towers around an open bailey. A strengthened gatehouse was integral. The major new fortresses built for Edward in north-west Wales by Master James of St. George, a Savoyard, especially Caernarfon, Conwy, Harlech, and Beaumaris, were all coastal castles that could be supplied by sea. The castles had fortified towns as an integral part of their design, which helped consolidate the conquest. Most of the heavy building materials for their construction was brought by sea. The construction of these massive stone-built works was a formidable undertaking, costing at least £93,000, a massive sum (roughly equal to £100 million or $130 million in 2017), and using thousands of English workers who were attracted by higher wages than those offered by the Church, which misleadingly complained that its builders had been conscripted. This effort reflected the strength and administrative sophistication of the English monarchy.

The castles remain the most visited fortifications in Britain after the Tower of London and are often held to define the castle for British readers. The castles were a demonstration of power and, in the case of Caernarfon, a fortress-palace, of royal ideology and imperial pretension. At the same time, it is important not to exaggerate ostentatious display and symbolic value at the expense of functional military purposes.[21] Marcher castles were constructed at Chirk, Denbigh, and Holt while, further afield, castles at Llawhaden and Kidwelly were strengthened. The Welsh castles at Criccieth, Dolwyddelan, and Castell y Bere were taken over and strengthened. The castles of Aberystwyth, Beaumaris, Caernarfon, Conwy, Denbigh, Flint, and Rhuddlan were associated with new or transformed towns that were created for settlement by English craftsmen and merchants and that were clearly seen as centers of English influence and culture. Adjuncts to the castles, the towns were protected by walls and were part of the same defensive position.

The castles built in Wales played a key role in confronting rebellions. The castle program, however, did not deter that of 1294–95, which was led by Madog, a member of a cadet branch of the Gwynedd dynasty. The uncompleted castle at Caernarfon was taken and the town walls destroyed, although the castle at Conwy successfully resisted attack. Once Madog was defeated in 1295, Edward pressed on with his program. Caernarfon was recovered and completed, while Beaumaris was begun in 1295 in response to the rebellion. However, after two or three years, in which much was constructed, Edward's attention focused on Scotland, and Beaumaris was never finished.

In a major rebellion, Owain Glyn Dŵr (Owen Glendower), in 1400–08, captured Conwy briefly in 1401, followed by Carmarthen (1403 and 1405), Cardiff (1404), Harlech (1404), and Aberystwyth (1404), but Caernarfon held out successfully in 1401 and 1403. On the whole, Welsh guerrilla tactics and devastation could not challenge the English castle garrisons effectively. Aberystwyth and Harlech were recaptured in 1408 and 1409, and the increasingly unsuccessful Glyn Dŵr disappeared in 1415, probably killed in a skirmish.

English expansionism in Ireland was also marked by the construction of many castles, such as Athlone, Carrickfergus, Coleraine, Dundalk, Kildare, and Trim. Again, these were intended to establish control, to overawe opposition, and to provide fortified residences and centers of government. King John's castle at Limerick controlled a major crossing point on the River Shannon and the entrance to the long inlet at the mouth of the river. This represented a major trade route and allowed for the collection of taxes, as well as providing a center for administration and control.

When William II occupied Cumbria in 1092, he created a town and built a castle at Carlisle. Castles played a major role in successive conflicts between the rulers of England and Scotland. This was especially the case with Berwick-on-Tweed, with the English capture in 1296 a key event as Edward I sought to establish his position. The significance of castles when held by the English led the Scots under Robert the Bruce to slight them (damage them so as to end or reduce defensive capabilities) after capture. This was done in 1314 with Edinburgh, Roxburgh, and Stirling, after the first two fell to assault and the last, besieged, surrendered after the English army, under Edward II, was defeated nearby at Bannockburn. He had advanced in order to relieve the castle. After the convention of the times, the castellan had agreed to a cease-fire and to surrender the castle if it was not relieved by a given date. This common tactic benefited both the besieged and the besieger.

The fate of these castles indicated the vulnerability of isolated garrisons. Instead, as with Roman fortifications, castles were most valuable when used aggressively as a means to support operations.[22] They generally proved less valuable in defense other than as a short-term rallying of the situation or as a way to impose delay.

Within England, castles such as Elmley in Warwickshire, held by the Beauchamps, a major aristocratic family, from about 1130 to 1446, were both a symbol and a reality of regional power. Civil wars also saw castle building. Thus, under King Stephen (r. 1135–54), prominent nobles, such as John the Marshal in Hampshire and Wiltshire, used the conflict to pursue their own interests and strengthen their local power, and many castles were built. Similarly, in 1138, Stephen's influential brother, Henry of Blois, bishop of Winchester, is reported to have begun six castles. Castles built without permission were referred to as adulterine, and their demolition was stipulated in the Treaty of Wallingford in 1153. Much of the conflict involved attempts to capture castles, with Stephen focusing his efforts on besieging those held by opponents. In 1136, he captured Bampton and Exeter, thirst leading the garrison of the latter to surrender. In 1138, Shrewsbury Castle followed, as did Devizes, Sherborne, Malmesbury, Newark, and Sleaford in 1139; in 1140 Ely; in 1142 Wareham, Cirencester, Bampton, Radcot, and Oxford; and in 1146 Bedford. However, Stephen was not always successful. He failed at Wareham (1138), Lincoln (1141), with a relief army defeating Stephen, and at Worcester (1150, 1151). The time taken for many sieges absorbed the dynamic of campaigns. The major political players, such as Earl Randulf of Chester, Earl Geoffrey of Essex, and Earl Robert of Gloucester and the bishops of Bath, Ely, and Winchester, were significant because they controlled castles. Castles also played a major role in the rebellion against Henry II in 1173–74, both in England and in his Welsh dominions. More generally, at the same time as new castles were built, others went out of use.

In the thirteenth century, castles such as Oxford played a key role in the civil war at the close of John's reign (1215–16). In 1215, he successfully besieged Rochester Castle, a notably strong stone castle protecting the crossing of the River Medway, going on to take the castles of his northern opponents in 1215–16, following with Colchester in 1216 and maneuvering to raise the sieges of Windsor and Lincoln. At Rochester, the undermining of one of the corner towers of the keep proved crucial.

The government of the young Henry III (r. 1216–72) benefited greatly in 1216 from the strength of Dover and Lincoln Castles when resisting French and pro-French attacks. The French Dauphin was unable to force the surrender of Dover and was forced to split his forces. At Lincoln, the relief force trapped the besieging army and defeated it. Henry's government restored its authority by sieges of the castles of its opponents, notably at Bedford. Later in the reign, Henry

III did the same after the rebellion of Simon de Montfort, particularly at Kenilworth, a castle notable for its extensive water defenses, in 1266. Its capture was a key element in the suppression of the rebellion which had already been defeated in the Battle of Evesham (1265). The battle was crucial, like that of Lewes the previous year in establishing the initial success of the rebellion, but the siege was necessary to the ending of the rebellion.

Sieges were also significant to the restorations of royal authority in the fourteenth and fifteenth centuries. Battles, not sieges, proved the centerpieces in short campaigns, as in the Wars of the Roses in the late fifteenth, but castles were besieged. For example, Dunstanburgh Castle on the Northumbrian coast was successfully besieged by the Yorkists in 1462 and 1464 and was badly damaged. In 1464, it was subjected to a powerful artillery bombardment, becoming, in some accounts, the first occasion when an English castle fell to gunpowder artillery.

Control over castles was seen as a key way to demonstrate power and maintain support. Thus, Sir William Herbert of Raglan Castle, a major supporter of the Yorkists, was made chief justice and chamberlain of South Wales and Lord Herbert in 1461 and was granted the castle, town, and lordship of Pembroke, as well as being made steward of Brecknock Castle in 1461, constable of Carmarthen and Cardigan Castles in 1467, and constable of Conwy in 1468. He captured Harlech that year. There were also developments in the character of fortifications. Henry, 2nd Duke of Buckingham, was made constable and steward of all the royal castles in Wales and the Marches by his ally Richard III in 1483, only to fall out, rebel, and be executed that year.

Built by the town from 1481 to 1494, with an allowance from customs revenue, Dartmouth Castle was the first in England to be designed to have guns as its main armament, although other towns, such as Southampton, had built gun towers into their defensive walls. Both possessed properly conceived gunports that could cover their respective estuaries.[23]

During the War of the Roses, a revival of fortified features in the houses of the elite testified to concerns about safety.[24] Lord Hastings's brick-built castle at Kirby Muxloe, complete with gunports at ground level, was a good case in point. However, as elsewhere in the world, these features were also a mark of status.

CANNON

In the fifteenth century, across much of Eurasia, fortifications increasingly had to respond to the threat or apparent threat of cannon, although the process of change was often gradual. Prior to cannon, gunpowder had played a role in sieges, with the gunpowder attached to devices such as balls and sticks, fired from siege engines, or used for sapping under the walls. Gunpowder was employed as an incendiary device, both against fortified positions and, conversely, from their walls in order to destroy wooden ladders and towers used in siegecraft. The Chinese use of thick earthen walls limited the impact of cannon when they were introduced, although they helped the Ming capture Shaoxing in 1359. The Mongols, or certainly the people they conscripted, played a significant role in the diffusion of gunpowder.[25]

More generally, across Asia, walls tended to be made of rammed earth. This was the case for example with the city of Abdullah-Khan Kala constructed in the Merv oasis at the beginning of the fifteenth century by Timur's son, Shah-Rukh. The defenses were strengthened by towers, bastions, and a citadel. These strong defenses, however, did not stop Safavid invaders from defeating the Uzbeks in 1510 because the latter allowed themselves to be lured out of the city to their defeat in battle. In a period that cannot be accurately dated, but which was probably from the end of the fifteenth century into the sixteenth century, the defenses were adapted to enable the use of cannon and muskets. This entailed a number of stages. In the first, an additional wall was added in front of the main line of fortifications, while the main wall was provided with battlements with vaulted cannon ports. Subsequently, the walls were heightened, and then the fortifications were strengthened with the construction of eight bastions built with mud bricks in order to provide artillery platforms that enjoyed height over the artillery of the besiegers and that also provided lateral fire. The fortifications of the city were abandoned in the nineteenth century.[26]

In India, forts did not tend to fall to cannon, in part probably because of the major improvements in fortifications that had taken place over the thirteenth and fourteenth centuries, with walls made thicker, the building of round (as opposed to square) towers and of strong projecting bastions to minimize the threat from mining, and adaptations to the walls to enable the installation of defensive artillery. Moreover, forts were increasingly built on steep, rocky hills and in the midst of forests, both of which hindered attack. Such positions were difficult to capture by storm or siege, which led to an emphasis on blockade, a lengthy process in which the exhaustion of the fort's supplies was countered by the strains on the larger besieging army. As a result, there was a stress on obtaining surrender by bribery, which was a major aspect of the more general use of conciliation in order to incorporate new territories and to sustain control over existing ones.

In Europe, improvements in the production of iron, making it possible to manufacture larger cannon and cannon that took heavier charges, were important, as was the replacement of stone by iron cannonballs, the use of more effective gunpowder, changes in the transport of cannon, and the development of the trunnion (supporting cylindrical projections on each side of cannon), which made it easier to alter the angle of fire and increased mobility and rates of firing. Thanks to finding a rapidly burning mixture with a high propellant force, gunpowder was transformed from essentially an incendiary into a stronger explosive device. The use of potassium sulfate, rather than lime saltpeter, possibly from about 1400, helped limit the propensity of gunpowder to absorb moisture and deteriorate. Moreover, around 1420, "corned" powder was developed in western Europe, the gunpowder being produced in granules that kept its components together and led to its being a more effective propellant, providing the necessary energy but without dangerously high peak pressure. As well as being easier to handle, this gunpowder was safer to use. The employment of improved metal-casting techniques, which owed a great deal to a different but related activity, the casting of church bells, and the use of copper-based alloys, bronze and brass, as well as cast iron, made cannon lighter and more reliable. They were able to cope with the increased explosive power generated by corned gunpowder, while improved metal casting also permitted trunnions to be cast as an integral part of the barrel.[27]

All of these factors increased the effectiveness of artillery. As a result, the stone-throwing trebuchets went out of fashion relatively quickly after cannon were deployed in western Europe, with only a few appearing after 1415. Less bulky, cannon eventually offered a greater mobility and accuracy. Moreover, located on the ground, cannon were far less vulnerable than siege towers to the counterbattery fire from the cannon in the besieged fortresses. Cannon were also transported complete, so that in most cases they were ready to fire within hours. In contrast, ballistas and trebuchets were in many cases built on-site, with the use of certain prefabricated pieces. This took manpower and time and meant that the gunpowder siege engines were ready much faster than non-gunpowder weapons. In comparison to cannon, siege towers, while able to respond to firepower, were cumbersome. Battering rams were a very short-range, line-of-sight projectile weapon, which were made obsolete by the increased range of cannon. Also, the increase in the rate of fire was significant, even though cannon were front loaded.

As a consequence, the methods of siegecraft and, often, the results changed. For example, the methods employed in the sieges of Calais in 1346–47, in which the English used ten cannon but had to rely on (eventually effective) starvation, and 1436 were very different. The failure of the second siege was not because the cannon were ineffective but because the Flemings fell out with each other and left the siege, taking their cannon with them. Duke Philip the Good of Burgundy, whose ancestor Philip the Bold (r. 1363–1404) had developed an impressive artillery train, could not keep the Flemings at peace, and he did not have enough of his own cannon to continue without them. In the meanwhile, there had been a marked increase in the use of cannon.[28] Stone is resistant to compression but less so to violent impact. Philip the Bold was among the first to prove the value of cannon in siege warfare. In 1377, he besieged the English-held fortress of Odruik, near Calais, with a siege train that, according to Froissart, contained seven cannon firing projectiles of two hundred pounds/ninety kilograms. The garrison surrendered when it witnessed the destructive effect of the shot on its walls. This presaged a marked increase in the use of cannon.

In England, it was under Henry IV (r. 1399–1413) that the major change occurred, with the development of large cannon for attacking purposes, rather than the earlier use of cannon primarily on the defensive. Royal forces using cannon successfully besieged Warkworth and Berwick Castles in 1405, helping to end a rebellion by Henry, 1st Earl of Northumberland. Contemporaries attributed the success of the royal forces to the cannon. Cannon were also used by Prince "Hal" (Henry), the future Henry V, in the sieges of Aberystwyth (1407–08) and Harlech (1408–09) Castles after they had been captured by Welsh rebels under Owain Glyn Dŵr, but the cannon did not succeed and it was necessary to rely on starvation.

In 1415, the English used cannon as a key force enabler in capturing the French town of Harfleur during Henry V's invasion of France. This was the first occasion on which the English used gunpowder weaponry extensively in a siege, and it encouraged a change in method, although in 1415 other factors played a role as well in the town's surrender, not least the danger of an assault and the lack of any prospect of relief. The latter was generally a key element in sieges. Harfleur was well fortified, including with the gates protected by bulwarks from which guns could be fired. The use of cannon by the attackers was in part important in the suppression of fire by the defenders. The English thereafter did not always place reliance on artillery, starving Rouen, the capital of Normandy, into surrender in 1418. Nevertheless, the focus on artillery increased, as in the siege of Meaux, with its extensive water fortifications, in 1422.[29]

In 1449–51, the fortified positions in English-held Normandy and Gascony fell rapidly to Charles VII of France's stronger army, not least his impressive train of cannon. This had been developed and was commanded to great effect by the Bureau brothers, who displayed their skill in the last siege of the war, that at Cherburg in 1450. The cannon were placed by the brothers on the sands so that they could cover the sea-facing wall of the fortress. The cannon were carefully left in place when the tide came in, only to be ready for reuse when the tide receded. Charles essentially relied on intimidation. In the Hundred Years' War between the kings of England and France from 1337 to 1453, this method was common when garrisons were small and the chance of a relief force showing up unlikely. An attacker would negotiate the surrender of the inhabitants, usually in two weeks' time. If a relief army arrived, or the defenders could anticipate that one would arrive, then there was no surrender, and the attackers would resort to bombardment. If surrendering, the garrison could leave with its belongings, promising not to fight for two or three months. If not, then the garrison would forfeit their lives once the fort was taken. This system usually worked: Henry V did this across Normandy and the Ile de France in 1417–19 (only Caen, which was stormed after it was heavily bombarded and its walls breached in 1417, Falaise, and Rouen did not surrender within two weeks), as, in opposition, did Joan of Arc and the Bastard of Orléans along the Loire in 1429. In their case, Jargeau did not surrender and had to be taken by force, but Meung and Beaugency surrendered. The latter was particularly important as it contained the sole bridge across the Loire between Orléans and Blois, a bridge that had twenty-six arches. The English from 1415 and the French in 1429 both had impressive artillery trains. The English failure at Orléans in 1429 reflected a lack of manpower, which ensured that the siegeworks were incomplete and allowed the French army under Joan of Arc to break the siege.

Charles VII's successor, the adroit Louis XI (r. 1461–83), further developed an effective system. The increased ability, thanks in large part to cannon, to operate rapidly and to purpose in fortified regions, such that it was possible to overrun an entire region in one campaign, increased strategic options and the political threat posed by war,[30] although this argument has to be used with care, as implementation was more difficult than this formulation might suggest.

The use of cannon spread. By 1494, Italian cannon founders had established a casting yard in Moscow, but it was not until 1514 that Russian artillery was sufficiently powerful to help determine the fate of a siege, that of the major, Polish-held fortress of Smolensk.

There is no mention of the Ottomans (Turks) having cannon when they besieged Constantinople in 1396, and they used them unsuccessfully in the siege of 1422. However, their cannon played a role in the capture of Constantinople in 1453, although not a crucial one, and they proved less effective at Belgrade in 1456 and Rhodes in 1480.[31] The fall of Negroponte (1470) owed much to breaches made by Ottoman cannon. Ottoman failure at Rhodes in 1480 and that of the Neapolitans to regain Otranto the same year were probably due to limitations of the artillery, which was inflexible and had a slow rate of fire due to a lack of skill in the founding and use of gun barrels, reflecting their relatively late deployment by the Ottomans. In both cases, the fortifications were "pre-bastion" in design. The Ottoman advance encouraged threatened powers to improve their defenses, as the kingdom of Hungary did along the rivers Danube and Sava.[32]

Cannon also played a role in the Spanish conquest of the Moorish fortresses of the kingdom of Granada in the 1480s–90s, not least by outgunning the defenders; but Spanish military capability was not simply a matter of firepower, and divisions among the defenders were significant. Malaga resisted bombardment in 1487 only to surrender as a result of hunger, which, in many respects, was also the fate of Granada.[33]

In turn, in response to cannon, fortification architecture developed, part of the process by which improvements were countered.[34] From the 1410s to the 1450s, the Teutonic Order reinforced the outer ring of the fortifications of its headquarters at Malbork, including building a bulwark with well-protected gates designed to resist firearms. At Meersburg, the northeast defense tower had shooting slits for the use of firearms, the upper level ones wide in order to provide a good overview, and those on the lower floor narrow to provide better protection.

Cannon and fortifications were in a counterpointed tension, with effectiveness in part dependent on developments in the other, although the use of gunpowder weaponry by the defense was also important.[35] Thus, the fortress of Alexandria built by the Mamluks in 1479 had many cannon.[36] The Mamluks employed cannon in their captures of 'Ayntāb (1471), Andana (1471), and Zamanti (1472) in their war with the emir of Dhu'l Kadr. In the event, Egypt fell to Ottoman attack in 1517 after the Mamluks were defeated in battle and their ruler was killed. The Ottomans did not need to rely on sieges.

At the same time, fortification and siegecraft involved far more than responses to cannon,[37] points more generally true with the history of both. For example, fifteenth-century sieges in Italy indicated the importance of the spirit and commitment of the combatants and the availability of good infantry for storming the breaches, rather than gunpowder weaponry. The same has always been the case. A celebrated passage by the Florentine historian Francesco Guicciardini emphasized the impact of the horse-drawn cannon used by Charles VIII of France when he successfully invaded Italy in 1494–95.[38] However, some of the bolder claims on behalf of this enhanced capability have to be questioned. In 1494, the key Tuscan frontier fortresses attacked by the French— Sarzana and Sarzanello—repulsed the attacks, and the French were able to advance only as a consequence of a treaty negotiated by Piero de' Medici. The following January, Montefortino near Valmontone was stormed and sacked, without any apparent use of cannon. A bombardment did make a crucial breach in the walls of Monte San Giovanni, permitting its storming that February, but the bombardment of the Castel Nuovo in Naples, still an impressive position, was not as effective. Ten days of cannon fire inflicted only limited damage, the French ran short of iron balls and gunpowder, and the surrender of the garrison reflected exhaustion and division rather than the inexorable pressure of cannon fire.[39] As opposed to cannon, mining also remained important and benefited from gunpowder, which greatly increased the effectiveness of the technique.[40] Thus, the impact of gunpowder varied greatly.

FIELD FORTIFICATIONS

There are several possible routes to "modernity" in fortification, although the concept itself is problematic other than as a description of the current situation. For example, the wagon forts of the Hussites of Bohemia in the early fifteenth century,[41] that used unsuccessfully by the Teutonic Knights at Grünwald/Tannenberg in 1410, and those seen in the Islamic world in the sixteenth century, as used by the Ottomans (Turks) at Chaldiran against the Safavids (Persian) in 1514, may appear an anachronism that looks back to the Hittites of Antiquity and to the use of such techniques by the Helvetii fighting Julius Caesar in 58 BCE and by the Goths at Adrianople (378). There had been prominent instances in the meantime. At Mohi in 1241, the Hungarians retreated to their wagon fort after the Mongols had driven them back from their defensive position at a bridge on the Sajo River. In the initial clash, the Mongols had used their siege weapons. The tactical dimension rewarded the rapid establishment of defendable structures to anchor a defensive formation. This was the case whether or not firepower was involved. The Mongols left the Hungarians a way to escape their wagon fort, and the Hungarians were then destroyed in the open field while retreating. The Mongols pressed on to storm the cities of nearby Buda and Pest. Later examples of wagon forts, for example as used in the American West or by the Boers in South Africa, both in the nineteenth century, may support an analysis of such techniques focused on their apparent anachronism.

However, these wagon forts may also be presented as forerunners of more recent field defenses, providing both an obstacle to charges and protection from arrows, as well as "pop-up" forts, with a mobility and cost that avoided many of the issues with fixed fortifications while also offering a solution to the problem of slow-firing gunpowder weapons. Aside from the issue of fitness for purpose in determining the value of particular forms, a major conceptual, methodological, and historio-graphical problem is presented by the marked preference for discussing fixed fortifications as opposed to their alternatives. In western Europe, field fortifications were employed extensively, including by the condot-tieri at the end of the fourteenth century; by the French at Castillon in 1453; by the English during the Wars of the Roses at the battles of Ludlow, Northampton, and Second St. Albans; and by the Burgundians, in conjunction with their extensive artillery, at Grandson (1476) and Morat (1476).

In practice, there was a continuum as far as fixed and field fortifica-tions were concerned, and one that should prevent any radical differen-tiation in the discussion. Moreover, the balance between fixed and non-fixed, however defined, was far from static. Utilitarian and cultural fac-tors both played a role. Again, both were on a continuum. Each was a response to the perception of military, political, and environmental challenges and opportunities.

At Chaldiran (1514), the Ottoman defenses blocked the attack by the Safavid cavalry, providing opportunities for the deadly defensive fire of Ottoman infantry and cannon. Sultan Selim I, "the Grim," won a major victory as a result, although it proved impossible thereafter to overthrow the Safavids. Ottoman tactics at Chaldiran were similar to those used successfully by the Ottomans at Baskent (1473), Raydaniyya (1517), and Mohacs (1526), at the expense of the Turkmen, Mamluks, and Hungarians respectively, as well as to the Mughal tactics at Panipat (1526) and Kanua (1527) and the Safavid tactics at Jam (1528). In each case, victory was obtained. The winning side used a deployment known in Turkish as *tábúr cengí*: a row of carts linked by chains was arranged across the center to block the advance of the opposing force, and be-hind it, both artillery and infantry were deployed. Mounted archers were placed on the wings.

The vital Ottoman addition to the notion of a wagon fort, long famil-iar to the Turko-Mongols of Central Asia, was firepower. Babur, the Mughal conqueror of northern India in the 1520s, borrowed the tactic, as did Ivan IV (the Terrible) of Russia, helping to lead him to victory over the Crimean Tatars, a cavalry army, at Molodye in 1572.

Tactical, operational, and strategic elements played roles in the de-ployment of wagon forts and in their persistence. There was a continu-ing recognition that the defender could not control the mobility of his opponent in the encircling terrain and could not build in short order stout, defensive works. The American army's firebases in South Vietnam during the Vietnam War had elements of the earlier wagon forts.

THE AMERICAS AND AFRICA

Outside Eurasia, there were forts in what was to become Latin America, as with those built by the Olmecs, Mayas, [42] Incas, and others. These forts indicate traces of sophisticated defenses, such as the Inca fortress of Sacsayhuaman near Cuzco built in about 1440. Bastions have been found in Peru, Mexico, and Brazil.

There were also significant defensive sites in North America. At Cahokia in Illinois, the fortifications built in about 1100 contained what have been presented as projecting bastions. Fortified villages in North America could also have bastions, for example, upper Missouri sites. These bastions provided opportunities for archers to provide flanking fire on attackers. While its new defenses were being constructed, the Crow Creek site in South Dakota was captured in about 1325. On a steep bluff near the Missouri River, it was protected by a bastioned wooden palisade fronted by a ditch. Between 1110 and 1300, most large villages in northeastern North America were protected by palisades, and some had ditches. The process had begun earlier. In southern Ontario, the spread of settlement had led by 800 to the construction of villages protected by palisades and, eventually, by double palisades, which created a series of defendable cul-de-sacs. [43] By the seventeenth century, sources indicate that palisades were backed by platforms from which archers could provide defensive fire. [44] Baffled gates were frequent in the Americas.

The Mississippian culture had sites with some defensive structures. Occupied from about the 1100s to the 1600s, and the center of a large chiefdom, Etowah, a fifty-four-acre site, had a large encircling ditch protecting the town. Inside it was a wooden palisade, which contained rectangular bastions or towers located at regular intervals. [45] So also with defensive structures at Ocmulgee, a settlement that thrived between 900 and 1150. The journals of the Spaniard Hernando de Soto, who traveled around the region in 1540, mentioned a number of sites. [46]

The understanding of temporal and geographical fortification patterns is difficult, as evidence is generally indirect.[47] However, research in particular areas can lead to conclusions of more general applicability. For example, research on East Timor in the East Indies where, in 1100–1700, there was a major shift toward fortified settlement sites in the shape of stone-walled structures on hilltops and cliff tops, has linked this to climate change in the shape of the El Niño–Southern Oscillation. Decreasing and unpredictable rainfall was the key context, leading as it did to differing areas of "drought tolerance" and "tolerance in space." A lack of constant weather patterns would lead to an emphasis on granaries and their defense. At the same time, as a reminder of the dynamic nature of research and, at times, what may appear the intrusion of exogenous political desiderata, there has been skepticism about climate-based accounts and an argument for the redating of sites and for the possibility that the profits of sandalwood exports and other external factors were crucial in the process of fortification. Contrasting interpretations serve as a reminder of the active character of scholarship in fortification history, both in terms of fieldwork and with reference to post-fieldwork analysis. This underlines the difficulties of developing and adopting global models and the problematic nature of supposedly definitive accounts. In contrast, for example, to East Timor, in the Pacific Northwest of North America, the focus was on coastal positions where salmon congregated.[48]

Knowledge of fortification in Africa is affected by the nature of archaeological survival and research. As elsewhere, environmental factors were highly significant. Where timber was common, the focus was on wooden palisades. Where stone was workable, as in Abyssinia (Ethiopia) and Zimbabwe, it could be used. Stone-walled enclosures were important in the empire of Great Zimbabwe, notably in the thirteenth century. The impressive walls were long, high, and thick.[49] Sun-dried mud bricks were important in the Niger valley, notably in the cities of Mali and in what is now northern Nigeria.

CONCLUSIONS

The Western view of medieval conflict is highly influenced by castles. They played a key role in subsequent story making about the period, whether in novels, television programs, or films. For example, castles were central sites and images of control and/or oppression in Walter Scott's novel *Kenilworth* (1821), in the various accounts of Robin Hood of Sherwood Forest, and in more recent uses of medievalism in imaginative fiction, ranging from *The Lord of the Rings* to *Game of Thrones*. In *The Lord of the Rings* (1944–45), one of the volumes is titled *The Two Towers*, and one of the central battles is the siege of Helm's Deep. So also with online war gaming and other approaches. With many medieval castles having been converted to palaces, or later palaces built to resemble castles, the notion of a "castle" in the popular imagination is at variance with what a "proper" medieval castle looks like. Pictures of the Bavarian nineteenth-century palatial mock castle Neuschwanstein appear in books that are supposedly about the real thing, and a search on Google for "castle" yields some amusing results.

Castles were indeed impressive, but they did not exhaust the repertoire of fortification in the period. Indeed, as in other periods, a range of fortified features, methods, and purposes was significant. To the south of the forest of Fontainebleau near Paris in the fourteenth century, an area of about 1,050 square kilometers had fifty-five fortified places, roughly one for every nineteen square kilometers. These included twenty-eight fortified churches, five fortified towers, and four fortified manor houses. This range of structures is even more apparent if a global perspective is adopted. However, although the form and setting of fortifications might vary, the standard defensive features of ditches, defended gates, and bastions remained crucial. They were found for example in Eurasia, Africa, the Americas, and Oceania.[50] In much of the world, archaeological and other work is still necessary to understand basic information about the dating, location, and use of castles as a whole or of individual castles. Analyses of distribution can offer suggestions, as in Okinawa where "most of the castles are located close to ecotones [transition areas] between different types of soil."[51] The integration of detailed work from around the world remains a necessary task.

As with other periods, the focus on scholarly attention tends to be on battles, not sieges. However, the latter were not only important but were also seen as important and glorious by contemporaries. In 1496, the Spanish commander Gonzalo de Córdoba gained great renown by being one of the first into the breach in the walls of French-held Ostia.

Sieges were also brutal. Brutality was not restricted to any particular group or nation. The Crusaders massacred the populations of Antioch and Jerusalem indiscriminately, killing not only Muslims but also Syrian Christians and Jews without distinction of age or gender. The Mongols followed a deliberate policy of total annihilation toward those who resisted them but were lenient to those who surrendered without a fight. The mountains of skulls they erected outside Baghdad and Aleppo were replicated by Timur. Troops who had been repulsed attempting to assault the walls of a city or fortress had to be incentivized to encourage them to resume the attack. Pillage and its attendant rape were the incentives. In the Morea in southern Greece in 1460, Sultan Mehmed II, after his troops were repulsed in their first attack on Kastrion, addressed his troops: "he promised splendid rewards to those who should fight well, and stated that the fortress would be pillaged. Then he gave the order to attack." The women and children of the captured town were enslaved. In 1462, one-third of the population of captured Mitylene was enslaved and distributed to the soldiers, while all the captured Italian mercenaries were killed.[52]

3

THE SIXTEENTH CENTURY

The continuing role of cities in political legitimation and government, and the urban-based nature of trade and finance, underlined the value of controlling them by means of fortifications. Thus, for example, in Central Asia, campaigning revolved around the major cities, notably Merv, Herat, Samarqand, Kandahar, Kabul, and Meshed. After his victory over Babur, the Mughal leader, at Sir-e-pul in 1501, the Uzbek ruler, Muhammad Sahybni, attacked Samarqand, finally starving the city so as to force Babur to abandon it. Similarly, Delhi and Agra were key points of contention in northern India. Although goals did not change, the spread and increasing sophistication of cannon became much more of a factor in the attack on fortresses and their defense in the sixteenth century, although, as usual, the situation varied greatly across the world. For example, when the Spaniards arrived in Manila Bay in the Philippines in 1572, the local communities were defended only by a bamboo stockade at the entrance to the Pasig River, and only one stone fort is known to have existed in the Philippines before the Spaniards arrived. Conversely, the stone-built Spanish fortifications in the Caribbean proved vulnerable to attack, initially by Huguenot (French Protestant) corsairs and subsequently by English warships.

NEW DEFENSES

In Christian Europe, in a very different context, cannon were most effective from the fifteenth century and, even more, the sixteenth against the stationary target of high stone walls. As a result, many fortifications were redesigned to provide lower, denser, more complex, and therefore more difficult and uncertain targets. There were important developments and adaptations to resist cannon prior to the better-known *alla moderna* system of anticannon artillery fortifications. Notably these included inserting gunports and adding masonry reinforcements to existing towers and adding sloping skirts at the base of walls. The *alla moderna* system was a development of the boulevards used earlier in Europe, as at the siege of Orléans in 1429. These were earth-and-timber outworks constructed to keep the besiegers from running their cannon close to the walls. However, fortifications designed to cope with artillery were first constructed in large numbers in Italy, including by the Ottomans who enhanced the defenses of Otranto after capturing it in 1480. Italian architects were instrumental in spreading new ideas across Europe. The use of earthworks proved a relatively inexpensive way to strengthen defenses. At Otranto, freestanding interior earthwork ramparts proved significant. A new ditch and a defending rampart were created opposite the breach caused by the Neapolitan siege train. In addition, two thousand stakes linked by chains prevented a cavalry breakthrough into the town, while heavy enfilading fire across the face of the breach inside the walls turned the area into a carefully organized killing ground. Freestanding interior earth ramparts helped protect Pisa in 1500 and Padua in 1509 from storming.

In the system known recently, but not at the time, as the *trace italienne*, bastions, generally quadrilateral or pentagonal, angled, and at regular intervals along all walls, were introduced to keep the besieger from the inner walls and to provide gun platforms able to launch effective flanking fire against attackers. The bastion developed from the 1450s, with important work by Francesco di Giorgio Martini (1439–1501) and the Sangallo family. Cannon were placed on the ramparts, which helped ensure that the defense could be active. The use of planned fire zones by the defense was more important than the strength brought by height, whether of position or, on top of that, of walls. There was a complex relationship between fire zones and fortification changes. Defenses were lowered and sunk in ditches, obliging the attackers to expose their batteries, and the defenses, strengthened with earth to minimize the impact of cannon fire, were slanted to help deflect and defeat cannonballs. These improvements in fortifications were designed to lessen the impact and decisiveness of artillery in siegecraft. There were similar designs in Japanese castles.

In small part drawing inspiration from idealized radial city plans offered in Renaissance art and utopian political tracts,[1] new-style fortifications were built in Italy at a number of places, including at Civitavecchia, the port in the Papal States, in 1515, Verona from 1527, Florence in 1534, Ancona (in the Papal States) in 1536, and Genoa in 1536–38. In Siena, the medieval walls were modified from 1527 with the construction of powerful bastions near the gates. From 1549, in addition a citadel was built by the occupying Spaniards. Outworks there provided cover for cannon.[2] In 1513, the city of Lucca also began to review and rebuild its defenses, but the cost as well as developments in ideas about fortification meant that the work continued in stages throughout the century and was not finally completed until 1650. Whereas castles in Europe had often been on hilltops, looking down on the countryside, and remote from towns, modern fortifications were generally on the flat and frequently near towns or on the edge of them, as with Turin, where, having regained the city from France, Emmanuele Philibert of Savoy-Piedmont built a citadel *alla moderna* from 1564. The citadel was separate from the more general defense works of the city.[3] The intensity and length of the Italian Wars encouraged investment in fortifications.[4]

Many fortresses, however, were a continuation of earlier works. Thus, in Bari, Spain added bastions to a Norman fortress built over a Roman fort and strengthened in the early thirteenth century by Emperor Frederick II. In Trieste, the Roman fort was the basis for a fifteenth-century castle begun by Frederick of Habsburg and finished by the Venetians.

Taking forward some of the points made in the last chapter, the often-cited idea that cannon brought the value of medieval fortifications to an end, and thus brought the medieval military system to a close, requires qualification. Even when cannon were brought up to take part in sieges, itself a difficult process given the limited transport system of the age, they were sometimes only marginally more effective than previous means of siegecraft. Indeed, cannon initially failed to achieve the fall of a fortress more often than they succeeded, and many times a castle instead fell to treachery or negotiation rather than to bombardment. A study of four Italian sieges in 1472–82 demonstrates this point. Volterra in 1472 fell to negotiation, Colle di Val d'Elsa accepted terms in 1479 after a siege of two months, and Otranto did so in 1481 after a siege of four and a half months. Ficarola fell in 1482 as a result of treachery. Artillery was important throughout all four sieges but was not decisive in its own right.[5] In addition, stormings, rather than sieges, were also important, as, during the Italian Wars (1494–1559), when the French stormed the Venetian-held fortified city of Brescia in 1512. Such fortified cities were very important to conflict in northern Italy.

Fortifications *alla moderna* spread so that, by the 1560s, twelve Netherlands towns had a complete circuit and another eighteen a partial circuit.[6] Prior to the rise of gunpowder and earth fortifications, the northern Netherlands, which lacks stone, were not particularly well fortified. Thus, gunpowder and fortification *alla moderna* were critical factors in the independence of the Dutch Republic.

With the demise of the siege tower and the battering ram, siege operations in 1550 were different from those of a century earlier and were far more focused on cannon. At the successful English siege of Boulogne in 1544, over 250 pieces of heavy ordnance were deployed, including mortars firing exploding cast-iron balls. Similar numbers were used by the French against the English occupiers of Le Havre in 1562 and by the Turks against Malta in 1565. The deployment of artillery, by both attackers and defenders, had implications for the management of operations including for fortification design. This required adaptation, not least of existing fortifications, as was done after the English captured Boulogne in 1544 and Le Havre in 1561.[7] They only held the first until 1550 and the second until 1562.

The introduction and effects of gunpowder weapons were gradual processes, more akin to evolution than the much overused term *revolution*. Indeed, the notion of an early modern European military revolution, which in many respects was an orthodoxy from the late 1950s to the 1980s,[8] has since been subject to serious criticism. Particular flaws have been found with the account of the position in the Middle Ages, with the use of the concept and term *revolution*, and with the assessment of what are presented as crucial changes in Europe. The relationship between the system *alla moderna* and the size of armies, the former leading to more widespread siegeworks, and thus to larger forces, is a matter of controversy.[9]

The critique, however, does not mean that the gradualness of the spread of gunpowder weaponry should become an anachronistic reading back of the role of cannon. This reading back was seen in plays, including the works of William Shakespeare, and clearly his anachronism worked with contemporaries. In Shakespeare's *King John* (1596), cannon play a major role in the struggle between John's forces and those of King Philip Augustus of France in the early 1200s, notably in the fate of Angers, a walled city which the French, indeed, successfully besieged in 1204–05. In practice, cannon did not play a role in the rapid French conquest then of Normandy, Maine, and Anjou, although it had done so in Normandy in the closing stages of the Hundred Years' War in 1449–50. Conversely, Shakespeare deliberately puts his reference to battering rams in the Ancient world in the play *Troilus and Cressida* (1608), a play set during the siege of Troy, with Ulysses referring to "the ram that batters down the wall." In *Macbeth*, the evil protagonist declares,

> Hang out our banners on the outward walls;
> The cry is still, "They come"; our castle's strength
> Will laugh a siege to scorn. Here let them lie
> Till famine and the ague eat them up.

The discussion of fortifications in, and after, the Renaissance looked back to Classical sources, although empirical observation of Roman fortresses was also significant. Battista della Valle's *Vallo Libro Continente Appertinente à Capitani, Ritenere e Fortificare una Città con Bastioni*, a very popular work on fortifications that went through eleven editions from 1524 to 1558, drew heavily on Classical sources. Published in Lyon in 1554, Guillaume Du Choul's study of Roman fortification and military discipline appeared in new editions in 1555, 1556, and 1567. Mathematics was also a key element. The concern with fortifications can be seen in a range of publications, including two by Girolamo Cattaneo (d. c. 1584), who settled in Brescia, a town in the Venetian empire, where he published *Opera Nuova di Fortificare, Offendere, et Difendere* (1564) and *Nuovo Ragionamento del fabricare le fortezze; si per prattica, come per theorica* (1571). These were frequently reprinted. The architect and mathematician Pietro Cataneo wrote *I Quattro Primi Libri di Archittectura* (1569), while Carlo Teti, who spent much of his career in Munich where he taught the art of war to the future Duke Maximilian of Bavaria, published *Discorsi di Fortificationi* (1569), with a greatly expanded edition in 1575. The military architect and engineer Antonio Lupicini, who worked in Vienna, published his *Architettura Militare* (1582), and in 1583 Girolamo Maggi and Giacomo Castriotto published *Della Fortificatione delle città* (1583). Buonaiuto Lorino, a Florentine who designed fortifications for Venice, France, and Spain, published *Le Fortificationi* (1596). The role of Italian talent is notable.

Publications were important in developing and strengthening the consciousness of a specific military tradition. Printing spread techniques far more rapidly than word of mouth or manuscript, encouraged the sharing of information, and permitted a degree of standardization.[10]

Adopting a wider perspective, Niccolò Machiavelli (1469–1527), a onetime senior Florentine official, notably in organizing a militia for the republic in 1506–12, in his *Il Principe* (*The Prince*), written in 1513, addressed the question of the usefulness of fortifications as a means of maintaining control. Machiavelli emphasized the importance of circumstances and, in particular, the value of popular support:

> Princes, in order to hold their dominions more securely, have been accustomed to build fortresses, which act as a curb on those who may plot rebellion against them, and which provide a safe refuge from sudden attack. I approve of this policy, because it has been used from the time of the ancient world.

Having then discussed three cases of rulers destroying fortresses, Machiavelli continued:

> So we see that fortresses are useful or not depending on circumstances; and if they are beneficial in one direction, they are harmful in another . . . the prince who is more afraid of his own people than of foreign interference should build fortresses; but the prince who fears foreign interference more than his own people should forget about them . . . the best fortress that exists is to avoid being hated by the people. If you have fortresses and yet the people hate you they will not save you; once the people have taken up arms they will never lack outside help.[11]

In his *Arte della Guerra* (*Art of War*), written in 1520 and published in 1521, Machiavelli sought to revise Classical military thought, not least to take note of the lessons offered by the Italian Wars which had begun in 1494. The impact of artillery was a major theme:

> Towns and fortresses may be strong either by nature or by art . . . those situated upon hills that are not difficult of ascent, are deemed weak since the invention of mines and artillery. Hence, those building fortresses in these times often choose a flat site and make it strong by art.
>
> For this purpose, their first care is to fortify their walls with angles, bastions, casemates, half-moons, and ravelins, so that no enemy can approach them without being taken in both front and flank. If the walls are built very high, they will be too much exposed to artillery; if they are built very low, they may be easily scaled.

Machiavelli's response, a high wall with a ditch on the inside backed by artillery, was not a brilliant one, but he correctly argued the need for a multisector defense in the shape, in particular, of covering the gates with ravelins (outworks with two faces forming a salient angle), and also keeping the area beyond the fortifications a bare firing zone.[12]

In response to gunpowder, the change to fortification was largely gradual. Indeed, there were a number of much cheaper ways to enhance existing fortifications than the *alla moderna*, and these other methods were used much more extensively. Linked to this, the *alla moderna* system did not develop in a vacuum.[13] As is always the case, most positions were not fortified at the scale and expense of the best-fortified locations. The decision by Venice to rebuild totally the defenses of Nicosia in Cyprus in 1560 was relatively unusual, as, even more, was the scale of the work, with a three-mile walled circuit and eleven fully angled bastions.

Most sieges did not match the major and lengthy efforts mounted against the best fortified locations. Examples of such efforts included the Ottoman sieges of Rhodes in 1522 and of Famagusta in 1570–71, as well as the eventually successful efforts mounted by Spain, in opposing the Dutch Revolt, against Antwerp in 1585 and Ostend in 1601–04, both well defended as well as strongly fortified. These, however, were not the standard for successful sieges.

Determination was a crucial element in both attack and defense. Charles V's unsuccessful siege of Metz in 1552 was a key episode in his war with Henry II of France. His artillery, about fifty siege cannon, breached the city's walls, but the French had constructed new defenses within them and the harsh winter proved deadly for Charles's army, leading him to abandon the siege, not least when his main mine had been countermined by the French. Unsuccessful at Metz, Charles lost the initiative, which instead was grasped by his opponents, both Henry II and the German Protestant princes. Determination was also crucial in the case of the resistance of Malta to Ottoman attack in 1565.

Again, as a reminder of variety and of the need to be wary of adopting both a characterization in terms of an ideal type and a teleology of development accordingly, the largest new fortifications in Europe, those at Smolensk in Russia constructed between 1595 and 1602, were built in the traditional fashion, with a stone wall 6.5 kilometers long and 8 to 13 meters high, strengthened by thirty-eight towers.[14] The Russian emphasis was on a strengthening of stone walls and an increase in the number of firing positions. The vulnerability of high stone walls, however, meant that such fortifications were increasingly regarded, notably by non-Russians, as anachronistic. Indeed, after a twenty-month siege, Smolensk's walls were breached by the besieging Poles in 1611 (after which the city was stormed) and by the Russians when they recaptured it in 1654.

Moscow, which fell to the Poles in 1610, itself had multiple levels of defenses. The royal, religious, and governmental heart of the city was the inner walled Kremlin (from *kreml'* or "citadel," a term that dates from the fourteenth century when the Kremlin was enclosed by a white stone wall in 1367) and its later, connecting *Kitai-gorod*, meaning "the city enclosed by an earthen-basket wall," the walls of which were built in 1535–38. To the east, north, and west was the "white town" (*belyi gorod*) stone wall, so called because either the stone was white or the enclosed part contained tax-exempt settlements. Earthen reinforcement was an important component. Five miles long and with twenty-eight towers, these walls were built in 1583–93. Surrounding that was a wooden palisaded area, and beyond that an outermost earthworks and wooden wall with twelve major gates, constructed in 1591–92 and known as *zemlianoi gorod* ("earthen city"). Over two centuries the authorities constructed four concentric defensive rings showing a variety of techniques.[15]

SIEGES AND CAMPAIGNING

In general, as also in other periods, fortifications were of most value when combined with field forces able to relieve them from siege. Indeed, many campaigns revolved around attempts to mount sieges and, in response, to relieve besieged positions. As a result of the latter, sieges led to major battles. Examples included Ghajdenwān (1514), Jam (1528), Pavia (1525), Mons (1572), Ivry (1590), Nördlingen (1634), and Rocroi (1643). These were victories respectively for an Uzbek relief army over the Safavids, the Safavids over the Uzbek besiegers of Herat, Habsburgs over the French, Habsburgs over the Dutch, Henry IV of France over the (French) Catholic League, Habsburg forces over the Swedes, and French forces over the Spaniards. Each was a victory that was more significant than the accompanying siege. Ottoman victory over the Mamluks at Marj Dabiq north of Aleppo in 1516 led to the abandonment of the citadel of Aleppo, while the Ottomans also readily captured Damascus. So also with the Ottoman victory near Cairo in 1517. In 1520, Janbirdi al-Ghazālī, the rebel governor of Damascus, besieged Aleppo, which was the key point in northern Syria if an Ottoman counteroffensive from Anatolia was to be blocked. The cutting off of the water supply of Aleppo was a typical tactical move in sieges in the Islamic world in this period, but he had to return to Damascus to repel an Ottoman force en route from Egypt. Al-Ghazālī was defeated and killed outside Damascus, and the city then fell.

Sieges were frequently determined not by the presence of wall-breaching artillery but instead by the availability of sufficient light cavalry to blockade a fortress and dominate the surrounding country. In doing so, the cavalry took a crucial role in a war of posts and raiding.[16] Supply issues, however, were not simply a problem for defenders. Sieges accentuated the logistical problems that were so difficult for contemporary armies, as besieging forces had to be maintained in the same area for a considerable period, thereby exhausting local supplies. The besieging army faced problems maintaining a close line of control around the city under siege. This was combined with a heightened state of alert for either a breakout or a break-in by a relief force. The besieged had to maintain their force in a state of alert, but the process was less taxing.

In the Mediterranean, besiegers had to control the surrounding sea area of their target port in order to ensure unhindered logistical support for their own force and to thwart relief attempts. This was significant at Rhodes, Tunis, Bonifacio (in Corsica, besieged by a Franco-Ottoman force in 1553), Tripoli, Djerba, Malta, and Famagusta.

Other factors were also involved in fortification and in the campaigning linked to it. In terms of the significance of power, the demonstration of force by means of fortifications could be more important than the specific usefulness in action of such fortifications. So, moreover, in attacks on fortresses. Indeed, many sieges ended not with a fight to the finish but with a surrender in the face of a larger besieging army. This was a relationship that could be almost ritualistic in its conventions, although the conventions varied, notably between Christendom and Japan.

In turn, ignoring the conventions could lead to harsh treatment of the defenders, and deliberately so in order to encourage other surrenders.[17] Defenders who went on resisting after the walls had been breached risked being killed or harshly treated if captured, as with Oliver Cromwell's operations in Ireland in 1649 at Drogheda and Waterford. At Drogheda, where Cromwell's impressive train of siege artillery enabled him to fire two hundred cannonballs in one day, the garrison of about 2,500 was slaughtered, the few who received quarter being sent to work the Barbados sugar plantations as, in effect, slave labor. Spaniards in the Low Countries in the early 1570s displayed great savagery, for example at Oudewater in 1575. Taken by storm, it was brutally treated, with all the soldiers and militiamen killed, as well as over half the population. The ferocity of the Spanish treatment even of cities, such as Haarlem in 1573, that had not been breached and stormed but had actually surrendered reflected a response to rebels and heretics and to the fact that they had continued to resist after the batteries had been "planted," so that they had no reasonable prospect of success. The policy of sack and massacre was a deliberate one of the Duke of Alva, but neither Don John of Austria nor the Duke of Parma agreed with it, and the policy was discontinued.

FIELD FORTIFICATIONS

Field fortifications became more significant in response to the deployment of artillery, in part in order to protect forces from bombardment. As a result, the entrenchment of camps was recommended,[18] a process eased by having Roman precedents. Separately, these fortifications provided opportunities for defending forces, notably to help protect them against attack, whether from cavalry, pikemen, or fire from musketeers. Field fortifications countered the slow rate of fire of the cannon and their lack of mobility.

A good example was provided by the Spanish use of field fortifications as a key element in their victory over the French at Cerignola in 1503. In this respect, the field fortifications served as an element in a combined-arms army. They also provided a substitute for pikemen. At Cerignola, the Spaniards, from behind a trench and earthen parapet, stopped three attacks by the French cavalry, exposing them, and the Swiss pikemen in support, to heavy Spanish fire from musketeers (the Spaniards lacked pikemen). Gonzalo de Córdoba's revival of the art of field fortification thereby transformed tactical possibilities. However, as a reminder of the difficulty of judging the reasons for success, and thus of assessing capability, this was possible largely because the French attacked rapidly and without due care, failing to bring up their artillery against the Spanish fieldworks, which would have been vulnerable to cannon. In practice, the effectiveness of cannon was strongest against a static defense because it was easier to decide and calibrate targeting and cannon fire was slow. Yet to respond to these factors against field fortifications, it was necessary to bring up the artillery expeditiously.

In India, at the First Battle of Panipat in 1526, the Mughal invaders under Babur delayed the advance of his more numerous and more mobile Lodi opponents by deploying a line of wagons, linked by ropes of hide and breastworks, while digging a ditch to strengthen the forest cover for his flanks. The Lodi were driven to attack due to logistical problems, but, as with the successful English archers at Crécy (1346) and the French at Castillon (1453), the strength of Babur's position magnified the impact of his firepower. Similarly, at Kanua in 1527, Babur used a ditch and wagons linked by chains against the more numerous attacking Rajputs. The capability of commanders and troops to construct improvised fortifications became an important factor in their capability both in battle and to fight a siege, either in or outside the besieged city.

WESTERN EXPANSION

Outside Europe, Western expansion was anchored on land by fortresses. This was seen across the oceans and with the major eastward expansion of Russia. In the latter case, forts were established at Samara and Ufa in 1586, and then, across the Urals, at Tyumen in 1586 and at Tobol'sk on the river Ob in 1587. In their expansion, the Russians did not face fortresses in Siberia, instead using them as a tool of their offensive.

However, the Russians faced fortresses when, turning south and southeast, they attacked Islamic opponents, notably the khanate of Kazan. This was a key target for Ivan IV, "the Terrible" (r. 1547–84). Kazan was long an opponent of Russia, not least as a source of slave raiding by light cavalry and as competition for the fur trade to the east. The city stood on a high bluff overlooking the Volga River. It had double walls of oak logs covered over with clay and partially plated with stones. These were formidable defenses even if they did not match fortifications constructed *alla moderna*, but it should not be assumed that the latter were necessarily better. There were fourteen stone towers with cannon and a deep surrounding ditch. Such ditches posed an obstacle to attackers, accentuated the height of the defensive walls, and made it much harder to undermine them. This factor remained a constant with fortifications.

The garrison of Kazan consisted of thirty thousand men with seventy cannon, comprising the main army of Kazan, which was a strong force, although there was also a light cavalry army, about twenty thousand strong, that sought to harass the besiegers. Ivan attempted two winter campaigns against Kazan in 1547–48 and 1549–50. These, however, failed because the Russian army had no fortified bases in the region, had to leave its artillery behind because of heavy rains, and ended up campaigning with an exclusively cavalry army that was of no use in fixing a presence or in investing the fortress of Kazan.

But for the third campaign a base was secured. In the winter and spring of 1551–52, the Russians prefabricated fortress towers and wall sections near Uglich and then floated them down the river Volga on barges with artillery and troops to its confluence with the Dviiaga, twenty-five kilometers from Kazan. Here, the fortress of Sviiazhsk was erected in just twenty-eight days, providing a base. That summer, siege guns and stores were shipped to Sviiazhsk, and a Russian army, allegedly 150,000 strong with 150 siege guns, advanced, reaching Kazan on August 20. The Russians constructed siege lines from which cannon opened fire, and they also used a wooden siege tower that carried cannon and moved on rollers. The ditch surrounding the city was filled with fascines, and sappers tunneled beneath the walls. The mines were blown up on October 2, destroying the walls at two of the gates, and then the Russian army, drawn up into seven columns, attacked all seven of the gates simultaneously. They soon broke through, and Kazan fell with a massive slaughter of the defenders.

The Islamic khanate furthest north had thereby fallen. Ivan exploited his success by moving down the now-vulnerable Volga valley to install his candidate in the khanate of Astrakhan in 1554 and then to displace him and capture the city. As a result, in 1556 Russian power was established on the Caspian Sea. Thus, the capture of a major fortress had major and lasting strategic consequences for Russia and its neighbors, not least the permanent loss to Islam of its most northerly state.

In turn, the Ottoman (Turkish) plan in 1569 to drive the Russians from Astrakhan failed, which was unsurprising as it was a problematic operation, mounted at the margin of Ottoman power. The Ottoman plan for a canal from the Don to the Volga so that ships could convey siege artillery proved too ambitious. Ottoman troops advanced overland, but, short on artillery, the siege of Astrakhan was soon abandoned, and food and water shortages claimed part of the army on its arduous return journey to Azov.[19]

Farther west, the Russians began the construction of fortified lines to thwart the large-scale northward raiding attacks by the Crimean Tatars. The construction of successive lines, each farther south, also provided a way to consolidate and demonstrate the Russian position in the steppes. Thus, defensive lines both served as a substitute for natural features when, as in the steppes, they were not available and also acted to even the situation with attacking cavalry. An early line was built along the river Oka, while fortresses were founded at Kursk and Voronezh in

1586 and at Belgorod soon after. After completing the Belgorod fortified line in 1654, Russia unleashed that year what became the Thirteen Years' War with Poland (1654–67). This was another example of the strong correlation between the progressive installation of fortifications and offensive field operations.

Overseas, the European powers were similarly dependent on fortifications. This was the case with both Portuguese and Spanish expansion, and subsequently with that of England, France, and the Dutch. With limited manpower, the Portuguese empire, which established the pattern in the Indian Ocean, depended on the combination of fortified positions, notably citadels at ports, such as Goa (modern India), Malacca (Malaysia), Mombasa (Kenya), Mozambique, and Muscat (Oman), with warships that used these ports. Portuguese fortresses could be attacked by local rulers, as were Goa and nearby Chaul in 1571, but, without naval strength, it was not possible to block the naval relief which proved crucial in these cases.[20]

So also with Spain, although, alongside fortifications at ports, such as Vera Cruz (Mexico), Havana (Cuba), and St. Augustine (Florida),[21] more of its fortifications protected inland centers of government, such as Mexico City. The Spaniards responded to threats, especially from the French and the English, and this led them to fortify key points in their maritime system. The destruction by the French in 1555 of the original, rather modest fort in Havana led Spain in 1577 to build the Castillo de la Real Fuerza with its thick stone walls. Subsequently, to protect the entrance to the harbor, the castles of San Salvador de la Punta and El Morro were built on its opposite sides between 1589 and 1630. Although the improved fortification of the Spanish Main was successful against the raid in 1595–96 by Sir Francis Drake and Sir John Hawkins, in 1598 George, 3rd Earl of Cumberland, captured the heavily fortified San Juan de Puerto Rico that had previously repelled Drake.

Spain also responded to native opponents as in 1601 when Alonso de Ribera built Fort Talcahuano to defend Spanish settlements near Concepción in Chile. In the Philippines, the Spaniards benefited from the limited and weak nature of local fortifications and, in turn, fortified their own positions. The value of this was shown in 1574 when an attack on Manila by Lin Feng, a Chinese pirate, was driven off.

OTTOMANS

That the Ottomans (Turks) did not have a fortification reevaluation equivalent to that of the western Europeans, in expenditure or style, was not so much due to a failure to match Western advances as because the Ottomans scarcely required such a development as they were not generally under attack. Moreover, the Ottoman emphasis on field forces and mobility, as well as their interest in territorial expansion, ensured that they were less concerned with protecting fixed positions. Ottoman artillery proved particularly effective.[22]

In contrast, Western losses of fortresses to the Ottomans early in the sixteenth century, such as the Venetian fortress of Modon in Greece (1500), the Hungarian fortress of Belgrade (1521), and that of the Knights of St. John at Rhodes (1522), as well as a lack of confidence in mobile defense, encouraged the introduction of the new angle-bastioned military architecture. Weakly defended Belgrade surrendered after a short siege. A longer siege of five months led to the capitulation of Rhodes, one assisted by the refusal of Venice, mindful of its relations with the Ottomans, to permit the dispatch of supplies. The Knights of St. John had strengthened Rhodes since the siege of 1480. Successive grand masters had built large bastions that provided effective enfilade fire along the ditch, although they were not angled ones. Their most significant innovation was the strengthening and widening of the walls to create a terreplein, which allowed them to move their artillery easily along the walls. They resisted assaults and bombardment with great determination, inflicting very heavy casualties on attacking forces. However, the Ottomans made effective use of mining, using gunpowder charges when the mine was exploded. The effect was devastating against the modern, bastioned defenses of Rhodes, despite extensive countermining by the defenders. The Ottomans also used gunpowder to create a smoke screen before launching a major attack on the St. Nicholas Tower. The knights, who were affected by their supplies of gunpowder running out, were given reasonable terms of capitulation.

Relatively affluent thanks to their trading system and fiscal prudence, the Venetians were very quick to use new angle-bastioned fortress architecture in their extensive empire, as in Cyprus, which was greatly exposed to Ottoman attack. Thus, what might appear advanced arose from military weakness. In 1550, Venice sent Michele Sanmicheli

(1484–1559) to report on the fortifications of Famagusta. He recommended and implemented extensive modernizations, including the construction of the Martinengo Bastion in the northwest corner of the city, which proved so strong that the Ottomans never attacked it directly during their siege of the city in 1570–71. Sanmicheli also worked in Dalmatia, Crete, and Corfu and on the Venetian terra firma, as well as building a fort on the Venetian Lido in order to protect the city from the sea.

The Ottomans deployed twenty-two cannon and two mortars against Modon in 1500, firing 155 to 180 shot daily. In 1529, they were less successful when they attacked Vienna, the walls of which were three hundred years old. Niklas von Salm conducted a vigorous defense, showing how fortifications could be rapidly enhanced and expanded in times of need. The energy and skill with which this was done was a key element in any successful defense and should not be detached from discussions of fortifications or treated as inherently secondary. Salm blocked Vienna's gates, which were the most vulnerable position in any fortified position; reinforced the walls with earthen bastions and an inner rampart; and leveled any buildings where it was felt to be necessary. This defense exacerbated the problems the Ottomans already faced by having to begin the siege relatively late in the year, which was a consequence of the distance the Ottoman forces had to advance from Constantinople, a distance far greater than that to Belgrade in 1521 or, indeed, to Rhodes. Having successfully withstood the assault in part with an improvised defense, the Habsburgs afterward constructed massive, purpose-built, encircling fortifications for Vienna. These long retained their value and were instrumental in the successful defense of the city in 1683.

In 1565, Malta was invaded by Ottoman forces in a campaign in which the strength of the defensive positions, some recently enhanced,[23] proved a key element in the Ottomans' failure. Most notably, it took over a month (as well as heavy casualties) to capture Fort St. Elmo, a secondary fortress, and not the anticipated three days. And yet there were many other factors, not least poor and divided command (which contrasted with the attack on Rhodes in 1522 for which Suleiman the Magnificent had been present)[24] and the determination of the defense. The close proximity of Sicily and the presence of Spanish troops and galleys there was a crucial moral factor, as they held out the

possibility of relief. Two relief forces landed, the first at a vitally important time, on June 25, the day Fort St. Elmo finally fell. With good
leadership and the good luck of a fortuitous mist, the force of forty-two
knights, twenty-five gentlemen volunteers, and six hundred veteran
Spanish infantry entered Birgu without loss. Their arrival so disheart-
ened the Ottoman commander that he offered the grand master terms,
which were refused. Due to bad weather and the caution of the Spanish
fleet commander, the second relief force, nine thousand strong, did not
land until September 7. It proved decisive in lifting the siege.[25] In 1563,
Spanish forces had also broken a blockade of Oran.

In contrast, the Ottomans were far more successful when, based
nearby, they invaded Venetian-ruled Cyprus in 1570–71. Far larger
than Malta, and therefore more of a task to defend, Cyprus had modern
fortifications, notably at Nicosia,[26] but no supporting field army or fleet,
and the Ottomans were able to direct the pace of operations. Relief did
not come, unlike in Shakespeare's play *Othello*, when the Moor is sent
to Cyprus to provide protection against a projected invasion that is, in
fact, destroyed by a storm. Landing fifty thousand troops on July 2–4,
1570, the Ottomans rapidly overran the island. In the center of the
island, Nicosia, which had plentiful good artillery, had no hope of relief
from the sea, and it fell on September 9, largely due to poor leadership.
The commander of Girne (Kyrenia), which was a small but powerful
modern fortress, surrendered shortly afterward, after he had been presented with the heads of the commanders of the Nicosia garrison as a
warning to accompany the offer of a safe evacuation of himself and his
garrison. They left safely for the Venetian possession of Crete where, as
a punishment for surrendering, the commander spent the rest of his life
in prison. Such actions established and affirmed conventions of behavior.

A substantial garrison of about 8,500 troops and ninety cannon
under Marco Antonio Bragadin continued to hold Famagusta, despite
the demand for surrender being accompanied by the head of Niccolò
Dando, the lieutenant general of Cyprus, who had been killed at Nicosia. Larger than Kyrenia and with sea access, Famagusta was a tougher
proposition than the other two fortresses, its defenses were probably
superior to those of Malta, and its commanders were of exceptional
courage and ability. Although gunpowder stores ran down, Venetian
relief vessels broke through with supplies. Ottoman cannon failed to

breach the walls, and the Ottomans had been forced to commence mining operations, which took time. Had the garrison realized that the Ottomans would not honor the terms of their surrender, it is unlikely that they would have done so, although they were starving and running critically short of gunpowder. The unusual and brutal refusal of the Ottomans to honor the terms owed much to anger with the success of the garrison in inflicting such heavy casualties during a siege of eleven months. All the remaining Christians in the city were killed, and Bragadin was flayed alive.

There were other Ottoman successes against major targets. In 1574, an Ottoman expedition captured La Goletta at the mouth of the Bay of Tunis, which Spain had fortified at great expense, followed by Tunis. The two positions were too far apart to assist each other, the Ottomans received support from the local population, and there was no prospect of any relief.

When the Ottomans needed fortresses, they built them, for example along the Damascus–Cairo and Damascus–Mecca roads, in order to protect travelers on these important routes from attacks by Bedouin Arabs. Both routes were long protected by fortifications and garrisons. The Ottoman frontier moved southward to the First Cataract on the Nile near Aswan around 1555 and, by the early 1580s, to the Third Cataract. A number of fortresses garrisoned by Bosniak troops marked the advance of Ottoman power, notably Qal'at Sai. In 1582, a chain of seven fortresses were built on the Red Sea coast from Suakin to Massawa in order to consolidate its capture from Ethiopia. Frontier zones were both defined and protected by fortifications. In the seventeenth century, there were also to be important Ottoman fortifications in Yemen. Fortifications in this area served as a deterrent to a repetition of the Portuguese attacks launched in the 1510s. In the Van region of eastern Anatolia, an area threatened by the Safavids of Persia (Iran), the Ottomans heavily fortified a line of towns around the lake. These fortifications both held off the Safavids and also served to overawe the Kurds.[27]

Farther south, the Jawazir tribe unsuccessfully besieged Basra, the main Ottoman position in southern Iraq, in 1549, 1566, and 1596, but in turn Ottoman campaigns against the tribe failed. In 1584, there is reference to an Ottoman riverboat armed with cannon bombarding a mud-brick fort held by the Jawazir. The Ottomans had a system of forts throughout Iraq, but between them stood many other mud-brick forts built and maintained by different tribal groups that frequently were in rebellion.[28]

Much effort was invested in fortifications against the Turkish threat, notably in the Austrian-ruled section of Hungary[29] and along the coasts of Naples and Sicily, for example at Trapani. At Gibraltar, the privateering attack in 1540 made by the Algerine clients of the Ottomans was successful in part because the position was protected from the north, but not from the south, the direction of attack. As a result, Charles V ordered new bastioned fortifications to protect the settlement from the south. Built in the 1550s, these were designed by Italian engineers, first Giovanni Battista Calvi, and from 1558, when Philip II ordered the work to continue, by Giovanni Fratino.[30] Elsewhere along the southern coast of Spain, watchtowers were built. In southern Italy, Charles V had the twelfth-century Norman tower in Lecce surrounded by modern fortifications and also improved those elsewhere, including at Bari, Otranto, and Trani. At Le Castella in Calabria, the seaside fortifications were on a site originally fortified in the fourth century BCE in order to protect the nearby town of Crotone.

JAPAN

Fortresses played a role in Japan where the extent of instability and civil warfare in the sixteenth century encouraged their building and maintenance. However, the need for fortifications fell as cohesion and unity were imposed by force and through battle and siegecraft. Japanese castle building responded to gunpowder by combining thick stone walls with location on hilltops of solid stone, which gave the fortresses height and prominence and blocked mining. Unmortared and angled stone block at the base guarded against earthquake damage as well as besiegers. Toyotomi Hideyoshi, the unifier of Japan in the 1580s and 1590s, proved successful in siegecraft, as with the fall of Odawara and other Hojo fortresses in eastern Honshu (the main island of Japan) in 1590. Cannon became more important from the 1580s, but Hideyoshi's success in sieges owed much also to other factors, notably the use of entrenchments to divert the water defenses offered by lakes and rivers, a technique also employed by other powers, for example the Mongols (successfully) against Baghdad in 1258. These entrenchments threatened fortresses with flooding by rising waters, or with the loss of the protection by water features on which many in part relied. This reliance was true of many fortresses, not least because of their role in protecting crossing places across rivers. This was a function that remains significant to the present day, as crossing places are particularly vulnerable.

INDIA

In India, Akbar, the expansionist and highly successful Mughal emperor (r. 1556–1605), anchored his position in northern India with a number of fortresses, especially Agra, Allahad, Lahore, Ajmer, Rohtas, and Attock. His victory at the Second Battle of Panipat in 1556 brought control over Agra and Delhi because cities were vulnerable militarily to whoever commanded the countryside and could blockade them and because there was no political logic to support the defeated. Sieges

Figure 3.1. Matsuyama Castle, Japan

were also significant to Akbar's repeated military and political success. Logistics played a major role in them, while negotiations frequently accompanied sieges as part of the process by which the display of power was intended to produce a solution.

Not always, however. In 1567, Akbar declared a jihad against Udai Singh, *rana* of the Rajput principality of Mewar. Initial attacks on the Mewar fortified capital of Chittauragarh (Chittor), which stood high on a rock outcrop above the Rajastan plain, were repulsed, and Akbar resorted to bombardment and the digging of mines: tunnels under the walls filled with explosives. The latter were especially helpful in producing breaches in the walls, although the construction of a *sasbat* (or covered way) to the walls to cover an attack was also very significant. After a nighttime general attack, the city fell in 1568, with all the defenders and twenty to twenty-five thousand civilians killed in hand-to-hand fighting. The fortress was then destroyed. In 1569, the major fortress of Ranthambor, held by a vassal of Udai Singh, surrendered after a bombardment by fifteen enormous siege guns that had been dragged by elephants and bullocks to a commanding height. Hilltop locations in India reflected the major value of topography to the defense and also the political message of overawing offered by fortresses.[31] Fortification *alla moderna* was introduced to India by the Portuguese, who were also probably responsible for circular bastions in India, but the diffusion of these techniques was limited.[32]

In India, there was an increased emphasis on the use of cannon both in fortifications and in siegecraft.[33] Large cannon were mounted on bastions and made effective by the use of trunnions and swivel forks, providing vertical and lateral movement. This innovation has been seen in forts from the late 1550s. As a result, bastions were rebuilt in the 1560s, notably by the rulers of Bijapur, creating massive platforms which in turn were protected by a masonry wall. The resulting positions enjoyed a 360-degree sweep and had considerable height.[34] At the same time, not all rulers followed this practice. In southern India, pre-gunpowder systems of defense continued into the late eighteenth century,[35] contributing to the fall of the city and state of Vijayanagara in 1565, although the earlier defeat that year of the army of its ruler, Rama Raya, at the Battle of Talikota was also crucial.

CHINA

In China, the military strength of the Ming empire (1368–1644) lay more in fortifications than in firearms. The majority of the army served against the Mongols along the vulnerable northern frontier where there was a series of major garrisons in the complex known as the Great Wall. This provision became increasingly important as Mongol attacks became much more serious in the mid-fifteenth century. So also with the fortified nature of Beijing. The failure of the Mongols in the early 1450s to capture Chinese cities, including Beijing, encouraged a new Ming emphasis on fortifications, first to protect strategic passes. Later, especially in the 1470s, the Great Wall of the first Qin emperor was reconstructed, and there were also new fortifications. In 1550, Mongol raiders under Altan Khan breached the Chinese frontier defenses northeast of Beijing, going on to besiege the city and loot the suburbs. However, the Mongols had no artillery to breach the walls and instead left swiftly with their spoils. The Mongol attacks ensured considerable improvement in the Great Wall, which became higher as well as containing room for cannon, troops, and munitions in the wall itself; being adapted for cannon and musketeers; and being strengthened with an impressive network of watchtowers, beacons, and fortified camps. Korea, a Chinese tributary state, used fortifications as a form of active defense in the early fifteenth century against the Jurchens who were based in what is now Manchuria and the Russian Far East. The Koreans established a chain of defensive positions to consolidate the frontiers, using settlement as part of the process.

Settlements were more generally part of the process of defense against nomadic attack and were frequently linked to fortifications, walls, and military colonies. Soldier colonies continued to provide the Chinese with a means to support fortifications in the holding of territory. Much of the army was based in military colonies, mostly near the frontiers, where soldier-farmers, provided by the government with seeds, animals, and tools, produced food while also manning the fortified strongholds that the colonies contained, strongholds that, in turn, protected the storehouses and granaries. In the fifteenth century, however, this system deteriorated, in part because of the impact of Mongol attack, but largely because the officers tended to take over the colonies, using the soldiers as a labor force. Thus, focused on fortified settle-

Figure 3.2.   The Great Wall of China

ments, the military came to approximate the system of land in return for military service found in many other states, for example much of the Ottoman Empire.

The importance of the Chinese northern defense system resumed in response to what were ultimately successful Manchu attacks in the early seventeenth century. The Chinese sought to cope by relying on walls and on garrisons at strategic passes. As a result, terrain and topography were to be aided by fortifications. Separately, as a response to the arrival of Portuguese warships in Chinese waters from 1521, China built coastal fortifications as well as deploying fleets. In addition, the Ming protected positions and deployed forces to maintain authority and defend against rebellions,[36] and also in the 1590s the Ming intervened in Korea in support of the Koreans against two Japanese invasions. These invasions involved sieges, as did the process of driving back the Japanese.

Numbers were crucial in Chinese siege techniques. The earlier use of gunpowder in China ensured that their fortified cities had very thick, tamped-down earth walls capable of withstanding the artillery of the sixteenth century and earlier. Breaches of the walls were uncommon. As a consequence, assault, focusing on the gates, rather than bombardment, was the tactic used against fortifications, as with the capture of Suzhou in 1367. This tactic was appropriate to the large forces available. The risk of heavy casualties could be accepted, a matter both of pragmatic military considerations and of cultural attitudes toward loss, suffering, and discipline. Sieges had to be brought to a speedy end because of the serious logistical problems of supporting large armies, problems which encouraged storming attempts. If, however, those failed, then it was necessary to rely on blockade.[37]

EUROPE

Over a long period, many European castles fell into ruin. Social elites, notably across much of western Europe, tended to look to the crown in the early sixteenth century and, in doing so, to abandon earlier tendencies to resist unwelcome policies by violence. Alongside improvements in fortification techniques in particular areas, there was also a destruction of fortifications, deliberate or by neglect. The latter proved especially important, particularly with the rotting of wood, the slippage of earth and stone, and the filling in of ditches and moats by debris. Wood was the most fragile of these materials. It was prone to rot, notably in response to rain, surface water, and the capillary action of subsurface water. There were no damp-proof courses.

There was also the neglect seen in deciding not to enhance fortifications, notably to counter new developments in artillery. In large part, this neglect reflected financial pressures or calculations of strategic need and priority. Not everything could be improved or maintained. As a separate factor, governments actively sought to weaken the military resources of real and potential domestic adversaries. As a result, building fortifications became a questionable step for the latter, because they led to a focusing of state action.

The fortifications of the sixteenth century and later might provide lodgings for their garrisons, but they were generally not private and domestic in the medieval tradition. Instead, although there were different patterns, notably in Poland, they were usually instruments of the state, as earlier in the Roman period. The medieval castle had been different in many of its applications. In the United Provinces (Dutch Republic), alongside the maintenance of town walls, new fortified positions in the seventeenth century were concentrated in frontier regions, as, in particular, at Breda. In contrast, ruined castles were recorded by painters, for example Jan van der Croos's *Landscape with Ruined Castle of Brederode and Distant View of Haarlem*. Town walls could be maintained as another aspect of state provision, not least as many state functions were diffused in what in practice were governmental structures that had a strong delegated character.

The Knights' War in the Empire in 1522–23 was symptomatic of a more general shift in power toward rulers who had more resources and could better afford both cannon and to modernize their defenses. The Rhineland Imperial Free Knights were led by Franz von Sickingen, a Lutheran with a long-standing feud with the archbishop-elector of Trier. However, his siege of Trier was unsuccessful. Forced to raise the siege, Sickingen retreated to his castle at Landstuhl, which in April 1523 succumbed to bombardment. Sickingen suffered a mortal wound from a stone splinter.

In both the sixteenth and the seventeenth centuries, civil wars, such as the German Peasant's Revolt of 1524–25; the Dutch Revolt against Spanish rule, which began in the 1560s; and the French Wars of Religion, which also began in the 1560s, put a continuing value on fortifications, although sometimes encouraging their destruction. Fortifications could thwart or delay attacking forces and thus have a major operational, even strategic, impact, which was the case in all three of these conflicts. In 1514, the rebel peasant army in Hungary lost impetus when it focused on the siege of the powerful castle at Temesvár. In France, the fortifications of the Protestant-held town of La Rochelle successfully resisted royal attack, wrecking the impetus of the royal advance in the mid-1570s, although, in the face of a greater and more sustained effort, it was to fall in 1628. In 1589, Henry III of France was assassinated while besieging Paris, from which his forces had been driven by the Catholic League the previous year in the "Day of the Barricades," in which barrels (*barriques*) had been filled with earth and stones. The French Wars of Religion in the 1560s–90s saw important sieges of Amiens, Dieppe, La Rochelle, Paris, and Rouen. Civil war generally ensured that more fortresses were involved in conflict than in any war on the frontiers. Significantly, the eventual peace treaty, the Edict of Nantes of 1598, guaranteed the Huguenots (French Protestants) the possession of a number of fortified positions. This was a key restriction to royal authority and power, with the two being linked.

In the Dutch Revolt, sieges played a key role from the early 1570s, as with the Spanish success in the capture of the fortified cities of Mons, Mechelen, Zutphen, and Naarden in 1572 and Haarlem in 1573, but with failure at Alkmaar in 1573 and Leiden in 1574. To save Leiden, the Dutch breached the dykes, flooding the region and forcing the Spaniards to retreat. Sieges affected the civilian population in many ways, not least when some were driven out of the besieged position in order to cope with food shortages, as at Sancerre in France in 1572–73, a Protestant-held town that eventually surrendered to the Royalists, and Middleburg, which the Dutch starved into surrender in 1574.

In the late 1570s and 1580s, the Spanish Army of Flanders under Alessandro Farnese, Duke of Parma, displayed great skill in a series of successful sieges, most prominently of Antwerp in 1585, but also of Maastricht and 's-Hertogenbosch (1579); Courtrai (1580); Breda and Tournai (1581); Oudenaarde (1582); Dunkirk, Eindhoven, Nieuwpoort, and Zutphen (1583); Bruges, Ghent, and Ypres (1584); Brussels, Geertruidenberg, and Mechelen (1585); Deventer and Reuss (1587); Bonn (1588); and Rheinberg (1589). The pace of operations was greatly aided by the extent to which the superiority of the Army of Flanders prevented any real chance of relief for the fortified positions, thus generally encouraging the defenders to take the better terms that a swift surrender ensured. Siegecraft was important, but so also was dominance in the field and the political and military weakness of Spain's opponents. The siege of Sluys in 1587 should have been broken by an English relief fleet, but Robert, Earl of Leicester, bungled the attempt.

The Spanish sieges used up many men and greatly increased the length and cost of the struggle, ensuring that it can be presented as a war of attrition, and one in which fiscal problems caused mutinies in the Spanish army. However, the run of success from 1579 demonstrated an ability to achieve predictable results with an effective army, although in 1588 Parma's attempt to use the force of twenty-four thousand men that had been assembled for the Armada campaign, by besieging the strategic town of Bergen-op-Zoom, came to nothing. Despite his best efforts to suborn the garrison, Parma was outwitted by the English commander, Lord Willoughby, and was obliged to retreat with the on-set of winter. By securing his border with France, his lines of communi-cation along the Rhine, and the coastal ports, Parma created a solid base area. His steady, remorseless, systematic advance had the potential to strangle the center of Protestant resistance in Holland and Zeeland, and might have done so but for the strategic decision by Philip II to intervene in France from 1590 to prevent the collapse there of the Catholic League. As a result, the Dutch were able to regain the initia-tive.

BRITAIN

Castles continued to resonate in the politics of Britain. In England, Edward, 3rd Duke of Buckingham, began the construction of Thorn-bury Castle in 1511 when he was high in the favor of Henry VIII, but they fell out in 1521; Buckingham's construction of the castle was one of the charges in the indictment that led to his execution. The castle had six towers with machicolations and a gatehouse on the late medieval pattern. Before he was arrested and executed in 1549 for treason against Edward VI, Sir Thomas Seymour was fortifying Holt Castle at a key crossing point on the river Dee. A medieval foundation as part of the conquest of Wales, this castle had also been the basis for resistance and disaffection in 1387, 1393, 1495, and 1536.[38] Also in the reign of Edward VI (1547–53) and following the victory over the Scots at the Battle of Pinkie in 1547, the English sought to consolidate their control of Lowland Scotland with a series of earth forts. The most significant of these were built around the village of Haddington and followed a mod-ern design with angled bastions. The fortress was subsequently be-sieged by a Franco-Scottish force. It was eventually evacuated as it was proving too costly to maintain. A similar policy of building earth for-tresses was also adopted in Ireland in the Nine Years' War of 1594 to 1603.

In England, however, there was a shift, and notably in the second half of the sixteenth century, from castle keep to architecturally self-conscious stately home. This was symptomatic of an apparently more peaceful society and a product of the heavy costs of castle building. Although they could be retained as residencies, as with Kenilworth, castles appeared to be militarily redundant in the face of royal armies, as with the suppression of the Northern Revolt against Elizabeth I in 1569. The rebels lost dynamism as a result of their siege of Barnard Castle, but it was the advance of a large royal army that proved decisive in that campaign. In the aftermath, rebel castles, such as Warkworth, were seized or weakened.

In part due to a reliance on the navy, most fortifications in England were in a poor state. There had been an extensive abandonment of castles, in some cases from the 1470s, and far more actively under the Tudors who came to power in 1485. Dunstanburgh Castle was already much ruined in 1538, and Dunster Castle in 1542, as a consequence of a lack of maintenance for decades. In 1597, a survey found that Melbourne Castle was being used as a pound for trespassing cattle, and it was demolished for stone in the 1610s, as many monasteries had been earlier due to the Reformation. John Speed described Northampton Castle in 1610: "gaping chinks do daily threaten the downfall of her walls." When, in 1617, James I visited Warkworth Castle, he found sheep and goats in most of the rooms. Bramber Castle, formerly a Sussex stronghold of the Howards, was in ruins.

The major fortresses built in England during the sixteenth century were for frontier defense, not for mounting or resisting rebellion. In particular, on the pattern of the Saxon Shore fortresses built by the Romans, Henry VIII responded to the alliance in 1538 between Emperor Charles V and Francis I of France—and the consequent fears of invasion—by building in the 1540s a series of coastal fortifications on the south coast of England, as at Sandgate, Deal, and Walmer, the "Castles of the Downs." These mounted cannon in order to resist both bombardment by warships and attack by invading forces. The form of a semicircular multigun platform was to become the standard solution for coastal defense, as it permitted engagement with ships from whichever direction they approached and, if not sunk, as they passed. Thus, the designs of these coastal forts influenced those built by the English in Bermuda in the early seventeenth century.[39] More generally, the anchorages on the south coast of England, for example the Solent, Exe, Dart, Plymouth, and the Fal, were to be protected by fortifications as with the building of artillery forts at Southsea, Portland, Hurst, and Calshot and at Pendennis and St. Mawes at the mouth of the Fal. The defenses at Dartmouth were improved, notably with Lamberd's Bulwark in 1545. Henry VIII also spent money in 1539–41 on maintaining and modernizing the fortifications of Calais and, especially, nearby Guines Castle. The medieval towers and walls were lowered and widened to take artillery, and new bastions were added. The boggy nature of the ground made construction difficult, and the redesigned central keep and a protruding bastion, Henry's own innovation, had to be altered to compensate for the soft foundations.

The speed of the diffusion of new ideas was apparent between the design of the coastal fortifications in the early 1540s and the angled bastion designs proposed for the English fortifications in the Boulonais following its capture in 1544.The biggest single new fortified position in England in the sixteenth century was Berwick-on-Tweed, the principal fortress intended both to protect northern England from invasion and, more particularly, to provide a base from which attacks could be mounted on Scotland and notably on the capital, Edinburgh. The fortress also protected the anchorage in the estuary of the river Tweed. The modern new defenses of Berwick were very different from the castellated medieval ones there. A bastioned system was constructed between 1558 and 1569, following the fall of Calais. Work began under Queen Mary and continued until the threat from Scotland subsided.

These defenses were not used under Elizabeth I (r. 1558–1603), but that did not mean they were not a factor in strategic equations of strength. Berwick both threatened Edinburgh with attack by providing English forces with a base for any such advance and also was an obstacle to any Scottish advance southward along the coast. The other major new fortification was the fortress of Upnor, guarding the River Medway and its naval anchorage, which was begun by Elizabeth in 1559. In 1588, in response to the threat from the Spanish Armada, and again in 1596 when another invasion was attempted, there were hasty preparations—cannon were mounted on the walls of Corfe Castle near the Dorset coast and at Portland, Carisbrooke Castle, and Pendennis—but there were few strong fortifications,[40] and the defenses of England primarily rested on the fleet and the army. As the army was largely poorly trained, it was the navy that was crucial. The fortifications on the south coast built under Henry VIII were essentially gun platforms. The bastioned enceinte was added during Elizabeth's reign as part of the anti-invasion measures.

In Wales in the sixteenth and early seventeenth centuries, many castles were abandoned or, as with Beaumaris and Conwy, fell into disrepair, while others were enhanced not with fortifications but with comfortable and splendid internal "spaces," especially long galleries, as at Raglan, Powis, and Carew.

CULTURAL FACTORS

Cultural factors were important to fortification. This was clearly seen in Southeast Asia, where most cities, for example Aceh, Brunei, Johore, and Malacca, were not walled in the medieval period. However, in response to European pressure, construction of city walls spread in the sixteenth century, for example in Java. Nevertheless, the notion of fighting for a city was not well established culturally in Southeast Asia. Instead, the local culture of war was generally that of the abandonment of cities in the face of stronger attackers who then pillaged them before leaving. As in parts of Africa, captives, not territory, were the usual objective of operations. European interest in annexation and the consolidation of position by fortification reflected a different culture. Within Europe, a focus on jurisdictional-territorial goals probably led not only to an emphasis on the gain of particular territories (rather than territory as a whole, let alone the destruction of the opponent's army) but may well have encouraged sieges of the cities that were the centers of jurisdictions, for example Lille and Perpignan, irrespective of their abstract military value.

Thus, the role of fortifications in part depended on cultural factors, a point that is more generally the case with conflict. This was the case not only with the prudential value of these fortifications but also with their symbolic significance. At the same time, this issue requires much more research before processes of cause and effect are fully understood, and cultural "essentialism" is too readily discerned. The political and military contexts within which cultural aspects can be noted and should be discussed were far from fixed. The fixed expenditure represented by fortifications ensured that they were less readily changed than armies in the field. As a result, fortifications could, and can, more easily be labeled as anachronistic and, therefore, to a degree as representative of past cultural factors. Yet this approach can be queried with reference to the continued value and use of fortifications and the way in which these could be adapted to enhance their value.

It is important not to think of cultural factors as only occurring in non-Western societies. They pertained in the West, both in discussion and in practice, for instance in the conduct of sieges. Manuals were scarcely "value free," insofar as such a concept has any meaning. For example, Albrecht Dürer's *Etliche Unterricht, zur Befestigung der Städte, Schlosser und Flecken* (Instruction on the Fortification of Cities, Castles, and Towns, 1527) sought to improve the environment of German artisans.[41] A significant aspect of the cultural dimension was provided by the extent to which fortresses were seen as an acceptable and effective means of overawing opposition. This question had a cultural as well as a functional aspect. Images of strength were significant.

GOVERNMENTAL CONTROL

Political acceptability was a key element in military impact. Fortresses continued to demonstrate power, but the context was one in which this demonstration was more clearly associated with sovereignty. The control of towns was a military and governmental process within states, one seen most clearly when town walls were breached and when town militia were subordinated to royal garrisons, the latter frequently based in a separate citadel within the urban fortifications.[42] To take the example of the Low Countries, rebellious Rotterdam was starved into surrender by Habsburg forces in 1489, and rebellion by Ghent was overcome in 1492 and 1540, the second followed by the construction of a citadel. The city of Groningen acted as a center of regional opposition, resisting Habsburg attempts to bring it under control in 1505–06 and 1514 and that by Duke Karel of Gelderland to take control. A popular revolt in the city of Utrecht in 1525 won support from France and the Duke of Gelderland. After the revolt was suppressed in 1528, in large part because of troops and money provided by the province of Holland, work began on a large citadel, the Vredenburg, within the city walls. It was designed to intimidate the city guilds, but the fortress was to be demolished in 1577 as part of the rejection of Habsburg control.

Similarly in Italy, Cosimo de' Medici, ruler of Tuscany in 1537–74, built three citadels around Florence, each under the command of a non-Florentine. This overawing of the city was important to the consolidation of his power, and in 1569 Cosimo became the first Grand Duke of Tuscany. After Pope Paul III suppressed a tax revolt in Perugia in 1540, he had a citadel built there. Pier Luigi, Duke of Parma (1545–47), built a citadel at Piacenza as part of a campaign to establish his power that also saw moves against the castles of the aristocracy; he was assassinated.

Having regained Amiens from Spanish forces in 1597, Henry IV of France ordered that a citadel be built there to establish royal power. Earlier in the year, the city had refused to accept a royal garrison, as they claimed the right to rely on their militia for their defense, but this refusal helped the Spaniards seize the city. The relationship between political and military factors appeared very clear. The capture of Amiens, as of Antwerp by the Spaniards in 1585, showed that, despite an impressive defense, major fortresses could still be taken in the West. However, the resources and time required to mount successful sieges, four months in the case of Maastricht by the Spaniards in 1579, placed a heavy burden on states.

Alongside the destruction of town walls or the process of making them subordinate to citadels came a more general maintenance and garrisoning of such walls as part of a process of cooperation and loyalty. The insertion of royal garrisons could also be significant.

CONCLUSIONS

The frequency of sieges reflected the continued significance of fortifications. There were many instances at the level of individual positions, and not only in Europe. At Herat, now in western Afghanistan, the Uzbeks launched lengthy and unsuccessful sieges in 1525–26 and 1528, only to capture it in 1529 before the Safavids regained it in 1530. The Uzbeks besieged Herat in 1532–33 but lacked the capability for breaching walls shown by the Ottomans, and in 1533 the Safavid ruler Tahmasp I relieved the city. In 1535, a fresh Uzbek attack succeeded due to support from the governor, Tahmasp's rebellious brother, but in 1537 Tahmasp advanced, seizing the city, which was abandoned by his opponents.

The strength of such fortified positions was important in the wider context of politics and alternative commitments and in part reflected this context. Thus, the Safavid focus in 1529 on suppressing a revolt in Baghdad and in 1535 on the Ottoman advance in Iraq were both important to the fate of Herat. It is not appropriate to abstract fortifications from a major part in the military and political history of the period, but, equally, fortifications need to be assessed in that context.

4

THE SEVENTEENTH CENTURY

THE WRITERS OF THE TIME

The trends seen in the previous century continued. Improvements in intellectual understanding and in education continued to be significant. The use of military engineers who helped ensure the standardization and spread of Western patterns of fortification within the Western world was significant. For example, Guillaume Le Vaseur, Sieur de Beacuplar, a French military engineer, served in Poland in the 1630s and 1640s. Mathematics was a key knowledge in the design of Western fortifications, in large part because of the need to work out covering angles when considering the layout of bastions and the location of cannon. Samuel Marolois's *Fortification ou Architecture Militaire* (1628) was first published in 1614 as part of his *Oeuvres Mathématiques*. The English mathematician Jonas Moore (1617–79) became a surveyor and then advised on the fortification of English-held Tangier (part of the dowry of the Portuguese princess Catherine of Braganza when she married Charles II) before becoming surveyor general of the ordnance. In 1673, Moore published *Modern Fortification, or Elements of Military Architecture* and in 1683 a translation of Tomaso Moretti's *Trattato dell 'artigliera*. Among the many works that followed, Sebastián Fernández de Medrano's *L'Ingenieur Pratique ou L'Architecture Militaire et Moderne* appeared in Brussels in 1696. Another mathematician, Nikolaus Goldmann (1611–55), a Leiden mathematician born in Breslau (modern Wrocław), published *La nouvelle fortification* (1645), while André

Tacquet's study of fortifications and siegecraft was translated into English, becoming part of Thomas Venn's *Military and Maritine* [*sic*] *Discipline in Three Books* (1672).

Writers on fortification and siegecraft were often practitioners. Thus, Francesco Tensini (1579–1638), who in 1624 dedicated his *La Fortificatione guardia difesa et espugnatione delle fortezze esperimentata in diverse guerre* to the doge and Senate of Venice, carried out works at Bergamo, Crema, Peschiera, and Verona. Published in 1630, his book was followed by a second edition in 1655. More than functional considerations were involved in the discussion and presentation of fortifications. Military architecture also played a role in the presentation of idealized images of cities, and thus of civilization. This was the case not only in Europe.[1]

The literature on siegecraft included the republication of material from the Classical world, notably Caesar's *Gallic Wars*, with its description of his successful siege of Alesia in Gaul (France) in 52 BCE, which was the central episode in Caesar's history. The siege was presented by Caesar as the key success in overcoming opposition. The literature of the seventeenth century also made reference to the Classical world, as in Jacques Ozanam's *Traité de Fortification, contenant les methods anciennes et modernes pour la construction et la deffense des places* (1694). In other cultures, such as China and India, there was also much reference back to earlier military episodes.

FORTIFICATION AND ABSOLUTISM

Fortifications were designed not only to deter other states but also to contain domestic disaffection, a situation seen in states across the world. In 1606, French cannon played a major role in persuading the rebel Duke of Bouillon to surrender his fortified town of Sedan rather than face a siege. The artillery was seen as sufficiently important by Henry IV's leading minister, Sully, for him to retain the post of Grand Maître de l'Artillerie.

Governments sought to dominate and used the process of fortification and built specific fortifications accordingly. Thus Louis XIV of France (r. 1643–1715) built the citadel of St. Nicolas at Marseille in 1660 as part of the process of consolidating royal authority and power after the rebellions of the Frondes. Similarly, after the serious rebellion of the city of Messina in Sicily was suppressed in 1678, Carlos II of Spain imposed a substantial garrison in a new citadel. When the States of Holland sought to save money by reducing the size of the Dutch army after the Peace of Westphalia (1648), William II of Orange sent his cousin, William Frederick of Nassau-Dietz, with a ten-thousand-strong army to seize Amsterdam, the leading city, by force. The city was warned in time to fortify, and bad weather foiled the campaign, but, having seen the seriousness of William II, Amsterdam changed policy and agreed to support the army, averting a proper siege.

In turn, if possible, the fortified positions of aristocrats and towns that resisted government were weakened or destroyed. In France, the terms of the surrender of the Huguenot city of La Rochelle in 1628, at the end of a bitter siege, included the demolition of its fortifications, and in 1629, Cardinal Richelieu, the leading minister of Louis XIII, oversaw personally the destruction of the walls of Huguenot towns in the province of Languedoc. At Montauban, which submitted under the threat of a siege, Richelieu both celebrated a Te Deum, an affirmation of Catholic triumph, and watched as the first stone was removed from the town ramparts. In 1632, the castle and ramparts of Les Baux-de-Provence, long a center of aristocratic opposition to royal control, were demolished.

The transition from city walls protected by an urban militia to cities dominated by citadels garrisoned by central government forces was a common occurrence during the century, for example in Prussia under Frederick William, the Great Elector (r. 1640–88), as in Königsberg (now Kaliningrad): a city that had been the center of the identity of Ducal Prussia became the regional basis of state power. This transition was also an aspect of the move from earlier medieval walls to Baroque-era fortifications. This was seen in Munich where Maximilian I of Bavaria built a belt of modern fortifications beyond the earlier medieval walls which had briefly fallen to the Swedes in 1632. In India in 1665, Mughal forces pressured the rebellious Maratha leader, Shivaji Bhonsla, to accept an agreement that conceded most of his fortresses, only for the latter to assert his independence by recapturing the fort of Sinhagad in 1669.

The value of fortifications was enhanced by the customary inability of rebel forces to mount sieges. They tended to lack artillery and assured supplies. Thus, Kalenderoghlu Mehmed, who led a large-scale rebellion in Anatolia, was able to defeat Ottoman forces in 1607. However, he could not take the town of Ankara or the citadel (as opposed to the town) of Bursa.

EUROPE, 1600–1617

Conflict in Europe in the early years of the seventeenth century indicated the significance of sieges, but also how far these sieges reflected issues of general military effectiveness. The war between Spain and the Dutch, which continued until a twelve-year truce was negotiated in 1609, largely focused on sieges in this period, as indeed it had done since the early 1580s. The Dutch failed at Nieuwpoort in the face of a strong garrison and lacking the necessary supplies. In 1602, however, when Maurice of Nassau, the Dutch leader, besieged Grave, the attempt by Francisco de Mendoza to threaten the siege was preempted by Maurice's skill in preparing his defenses, while the Spanish army was affected by a lack of experienced troops and drivers for the artillery, as well as by a shortage of pay and food that led to mutiny. Grave fell. In 1604, the new Spanish commander, Ambrogio Spínola, captured Dutch-held Ostend after a siege that had lasted over three years. Artillery bombardment was important, but so also was the willingness to storm positions, such as the outworks on the west side in 1603 and on Sand Hill in 1604, the last decisive episode of the siege. The Dutch had kept Ostend resupplied from the sea, but the Spaniards gained control of the coastal sand dunes, enabling them to mount batteries to dominate the harbor entrance. Spínola forced the fate of the siege by his willingness to sacrifice troops in determined assaults. Artillery was a key element for both sides. For example, Maurice made much use of cannon in his sieges: ten thousand cannonballs were fired by the Dutch in their successful two-month siege of the fortified city of Groningen in 1594.

THIRTY YEARS' WAR, 1618–1648

Although settled by battles, fortifications and sieges played an important role in the Thirty Years' War of 1618–48 that engulfed most of the European powers, and also in the British civil wars of the 1640s and 1650s. There were clear variations by combatant and campaigning area. In the Low Countries, where, at the end of the truce, the Spaniards fought the Dutch from 1621 to 1648 and the Spaniards fought the French from 1635 to 1659, sieges were far more important than they were in Germany or for the Swedes. Campaigns in the Low Countries focused on sieges, as when the Spaniards captured Breda in 1625, a success celebrated in print and also on canvas by Rubens and Velasquez. In turn, the Dutch advanced by means of sieges, such as those of 's-Hertogenbosch in 1629, Maastricht and Venlo in 1632, Breda in 1637, and Hulst in 1645, all of which were successful. It was scarcely surprising that these years also saw the development of a distinctive Dutch style of fortifications, which owed much to Simon Stevin, Adam Freitag, and Christian Otter. Published in Amsterdam in 1631, Freitag's *Architectura militaries nova et aucta* was translated into French. Otter's study followed in 1646. In Germany, sieges were particularly important in the Rhineland, where there were many fortified towns, but, relatively speaking, less so farther east where the density of urban settlement was lower.

Alongside set-piece major sieges in Europe, such as those of Breda, there were numerous smaller-scale ones. Complete lines of circumvallation designed to cut off relief required many troops and were generally found only in the case of major sieges. Similarly, only a minority of towns were comprehensively fortified.

FIELD FORTIFICATIONS

In addition to fortresses and fortified towns and positions, for example abbeys, field fortifications could be highly significant. From the beginning, such fortifications were often a central part of the waging of war by the Swedes under Gustavus Adolphus (Gustav II Adolf, r. 1611–32). The Swedish soldiers were digging when not marching, and this was a key to the survival of the Swedish army. In turn, in 1632, the Swedes were thwarted when their Austrian opponents under Wallenstein established a heavily fortified position at the Alte Veste near Nürnberg where the Swedes could not make effective use of their cavalry. With the impetus of success gone and the accompanying logistical benefits of the advance lost, the Swedish army confronting this position suffered seriously from desertion, which owed much to the supply problems posed by the devastated countryside.

There were other instances in which field fortifications helped prevent battle, although evidence on this point is often elusive. In 1602, Maurice of Nassau advancing into Brabant found the outnumbered Spaniards under Francisco de Mendoza entrenched near Tirlemont and unwilling to engage him in open battle. This removed the operational advantage from Maurice, who withdrew, feeling that Mendoza was too strong to attack but too powerful to leave in his rear. In 1605, Maurice established a camp at Biervliet, only for the Spaniards under Spínola to take positions in the Dutch rear, which forced Maurice into action.

Field fortifications could also be important in battle, as at Lützen in 1632. In this major battle, Wallenstein remained on the defensive against Swedish attack, deepening a ditch to the front of his position. The Swedes eventually won, but at a high cost, with Gustavus Adolphus among the casualties. Such ditches were important features in many battles, as they limited or constrained advances by opposing forces. Thus, at the battle of the Paitan River in India in 1616, a ditch in front of the Mughal army broke the cavalry attack by the forces of Malik Ambar of Ahmadnagar. Ditches were not the sole important element. In 1691, at the Battle of Aughrim, the Irish made good use of field boundaries as breastworks in their ultimately unsuccessful resistance to the advancing Williamite forces.

A very different type of field fortification was demonstrated in the use by Galdan Khan, the Zhungar leader, of felt-armored camels in campaigning against the Manchu Kangzi emperor of China in the late seventeenth century. The camels were trained to sit down, and the cannon they carried were taken off. The camels became a form of wall, with the felt providing protection against arrows and the cannon firing from behind them. These camels were used at the battles of Ulan Butong (1690) and Jao-Modo (1696), although they did not bring success.

Field fortifications featured in publications, such as Simon Stevin's work on castrametation, the laying out of camps, and John Cruso's *Castrametation, or the Measuring Out of the Quarters for the Encamping of an Army* (1642). Of Dutch descent, Cruso settled in Norwich and played a role in military life. The publication of his book reflected the onset of civil war in England.

BRITISH CIVIL WARS

In the British civil wars of 1638–52, battles were crucial, but sieges proved highly significant as well. For example, in 1643, the storming of the walled city of Bristol was important to the Royalist advance, but, conversely, Royalist sieges of the towns of Gloucester, Hull, and Plymouth that year all failed, the first ending when a relief army arrived. The naval dimension was important to sieges, either to support them or to bring relief.[2] Alongside the sieges of major positions, there were numerous small sieges.[3] The year 1639 saw the publication of Richard Norwood's *Fortification or Architecture Military*, the earliest full-scale work in English on the topic.

Towns like Parliamentarian Northampton and Royalist Worcester supplemented surviving medieval walls with new fortifications, notably earth embankments designed to provide protection against artillery. Northampton was given a new curtain wall that contained bulwarks, flankers, and mounts to provide covering fire. There were outworks at the gates and new batteries. Castle walls were similarly improved, as in Northamptonshire at Rockingham Castle.[4]

In Worcestershire, Dudley and Hartlebury Castles were major Royalist sites. Castles provided good bases for garrisons, and many were brought back into habitation and use. From Northampton, the Parliamentarians competed for control of the southwest of the county with Royalists from Banbury Castle, which had been refortified and established as a garrison to protect the Royalist capital of Oxford. Its Royalist counterparts in the stately homes of Ashby de la Zouch and Belvoir Castle brought much devastation to Leicestershire. Sieges often led to the building of new forts to support the besiegers, as by the Royalists outside Plymouth in 1642–45. Always intended as temporary, these forts generally do not survive at all. For that reason, illustrations of past sieges can be very significant.

Defenses that were not tested could be important, as with those of London that were hastily improved in 1642–43 in response to the threat of a Royalist attack that in practice did not come. Thanks to a formidable effort, allegedly including both twenty thousand citizens working without pay as well as special taxes to cover other costs, an eleven-mile-long earthen bank and ditch supported by, and supporting, a series of twenty-eight forts and two outworks batteries were built. This was very different from the London of its earlier fortifications, notably earlier walls and the Tower of London, for the wider perimeter encompassed a more far-flung city. Moreover, the Tower, a medieval royal castle, was no longer a central part of the defensive equation.

The new fortifications of London provided a vital advantage of defense in depth and gave the Parliamentary forces a greater freedom to maneuver. In the event, having failed to reach London in 1642, when they were held nearby to the west by a larger Parliamentary army in the indecisive Battle of Turnham Green, the Royalist forces did not advance so close to London thereafter. It is unclear what would have happened had they done so. The defenses were strong, but their length ensured that the Royalists only had to find one weak place to break through, as at Bristol in 1643. This was a more general point with fortifications.

Rather differently, although some towns held out in these circumstances, notably the Parliamentary strongholds of Hull, Lyme Regis, and Plymouth, many eventually fell, as Hereford did to a Parliamentary siege in 1646. Moreover, holding towns or castles could prove fruitless in the event of defeat in the field. Thus, in 1645–47, as total defeat appeared increasingly apparent, Royalist castles in Wales fell to the remorseless pressure of superior Parliamentary forces: Beaumaris, Caernarfon, Chepstow, and Monmouth in 1645; Aberystwyth, Conwy, and Raglan in 1646; and Harlech and Holt in 1647. So also in the West Country, with Dartmouth stormed in 1646. In 1651, General George Monck followed up Cromwell's victory at Dunbar the previous year by taking Tantallon and Blackness Castles. Tantallon, a Douglas stronghold from c. 1350, was severely and definitively damaged in Monck's bombardment. The wars saw publications on fortifications and siegecraft, as in David Papillon's *A Practical Abstract of the Arts of Fortification and Assailing* (1645),[5] and also literary references to both.[6]

During and after the wars, the victorious Parliamentarians "slighted" fortresses. For example, at Kenilworth, the north side of the keep was demolished, and parts of the outer curtain wall were destroyed. Corfe, Dunster, Oxford, and Winchester Castles were also among the many to be slighted. All had been important medieval castles. In turn, after the Stuart Restoration in 1660, the walls and defenses of major towns that had backed Parliament, such as Gloucester and Northampton, were slighted. London did not retain its new defenses. Instead, the protection of London from foreign attack focused on the navy, which was greatly developed from the 1650s, while the Tower, which had a garrison, remained the key point in the city itself.

The rapid overthrow of James II of England, Wales, and Ireland (and VII of Scotland) in 1688–89 in the Glorious Revolution by William III of Orange and his Dutch invasion force did not lead to any sieges in England, but it was followed by a civil war as most of Ireland backed James. Battle and siege were intertwined. William's victory at the Battle of the Boyne in 1690 led the Jacobites to abandon Dublin without fighting there. William then advanced on Athlone, a major bridging point over the River Shannon, only to be thwarted when the bridge was broken. He moved downriver to Limerick, unsuccessfully trying to storm it when the fortifications were still largely intact. In this attack, William suffered over two thousand casualties. This showed the costly nature of the often narrow margin between success and failure. Needs drove the process, notably the consequences of attempts to force a rapid close to a campaign so that it could have the desired place within a wider conflict, permitting the movement of troops to other fronts. In contrast, the following month, Cork surrendered to an amphibious force after its fortifications were breached by a bombardment from higher ground and the Jacobite outworks were overrun. In 1691, Athlone fell after hard fighting and a very heavy bombardment, with more than twelve thousand cannonballs fired. William's forces, under Godard van Reede de Ginkel, a Dutch general, were then able to cross the Shannon. The two armies met at Aughrim, with a major Irish defeat swiftly followed by the surrender of Galway and Limerick and the end of the war in Ireland.

CHINA

In general, it was struggles between states, not rebellions, that tended to be the key element in the use of fortifications. This was seen with the Manchu conquest of China in the 1640s and 1650s and with Mughal expansion in India. In China, Manchu success depended on breaking through the Chinese defenses in the north. This proved difficult, largely due to the strength of the forces deployed by the Ming to protect the fortified positions, notably the Great Wall.

The Manchu failed to storm the fortress of Ningyuan in 1626, in part due to Ming cannon, but the fortress of Dalinghe fell in 1631 after Ming relief attempts were defeated. Cooperation with Chinese elements helped the Manchu, as in the capture of the fortified cities of Shenyang in 1619 and Liaoyang in 1621.

Manchu success ultimately depended on a fracturing of the opposition. The unsuccessful defense of a very different fortified position played a major role in this fracturing: while the bulk of the Ming forces were deployed to protect the northern frontier, the rebellion by Li Zicheng led, in 1644, to the defeat of the weak forces protecting Beijing, to the fall of the capital, and to the suicide of the emperor. Li seized power and moved against Wu Sangui, the commander of many of the forces on the Great Wall, only for the latter to defect to the Manchu. The Manchu then conquered China with the assistance of former Ming generals. Without the support of field armies, the fortified cities fell relatively rapidly to the Manchu, prefiguring the Communist conquest of much of China in 1949 after they had been victorious in the north.

INDIA

In India, the major Deccan sultanates of Bijapur and Golconda were annexed in 1685–87 by Aurangzeb, the Mughal emperor, following successful sieges. These were massive enterprises in which strongly walled positions with substantial garrisons fell to large armies, the supply of which was a formidable undertaking. Aurangzeb besieged the city of Golconda with its four-mile-long outer wall in 1687. Two mines were driven under the walls, but they exploded prematurely. The fortress finally fell to betrayal as Mughal forces entered through an opened gateway. The same factor also operated elsewhere, as with the Zhungar storming of Lhasa in 1717. Mughal art celebrated the victory, which represented a major southward extension of Mughal power.

Similarly, Kandahar, the gateway for the Persians (Iranians) to southern Afghanistan and, beyond it, the Indus valley, was the fortress that played the key role in conflict between Persia and the Mughals. Lost by the Mughals in 1622 to the expansionist Abbas I of Persia, Kandahar had been regained in 1638 when the Persian commander surrendered, fearing execution by his ruler. Helped by Mughal weakness in the aftermath of an unsuccessful campaign in Afghanistan, Abbas II recaptured the city in 1648. Mughal attempts to regain it in 1649, 1652, and 1653 failed. It was difficult to campaign effectively so far from the center of Mughal power in northern India, and success had to be obtained before the harsh winter set in. Mughal siege cannon was of poorer quality and less accurate than the Persian cannon, which inflicted heavy casualties on the besiegers. In 1653, three specially cast Mughal heavy guns left breaches in the walls of Kandahar, but the onset of winter and logistical problems made it impossible to exploit them.

Fortresses came in a variety of scales but were particularly found in frontier areas. Faced with serious Pathan revolts in the 1660s and 1670s, Aurangzeb built new fortresses on what for the British in the nineteenth century was to be the North-West Frontier of India. Farther south, in the province of Sind, a network of small forts manned by cavalry and musketeers extended Mughal power.

In western India, the Mughals faced Maratha forts in a bitter struggle in the late seventeenth century. The Maratha advantage of mobility was lost when they defended forts, which provided clear targets for the Mughals and their effective siege artillery: the Marathas lacked comparable artillery, and their siegecraft was poorly developed. Yet, on both sides, there was only limited comparison with the siegecraft developed in Europe. For example, the Mughals for long used stone, rather than iron, cannonballs. Most Mughal siege artillery was not especially sophisticated by European standards and was made of wrought iron as opposed to the less rigid cast iron of Europe.

The Marathas were swayed by the view that forts were necessary for the symbol and reality of power and to provide security, but Aurangzeb was able to conquer a whole series of these forts, most of them hill fortresses, frequently of considerable antiquity. The massive hill fortress of Jinji held out against siege until 1698. In 1699, Aurangzeb launched a systematic attack on the hill fortresses: thirteen fell, most after the bribery of their commanders. Maratha armies were not strong enough to relieve the fortresses, and Aurangzeb covered his siege forces with mobile field armies, as Louis XIV did in Europe. Nevertheless, despite his successes, Aurangzeb failed to conquer the Marathas, while the war was costly and the impression of failure it created was damaging.

JAPAN

In Japan, the end of internal conflict in the early seventeenth century ensured that castle building became far less important, although castles were constructed or improved in the last decades of conflict as at Matsuyama (1603), Iwakuni (1608), and Kochi (1603). In 1603, Nijo Castle was begun as the official residence in the city of Kyoto of the first Tokugawa shogun (key political and governmental figure), Ieyasu. He rewarded his son-in-law, Ikeda Terumasa, with Himejī Castle, and in the 1600s the latter added moats around the castle and built a large, towering keep which provided a potent symbol of the family's power. Ieyasu did the same on the island of Shikoku where he granted the castle of Takamatsu and the fiefdom around it to his relatives, the Matsudira clan, thus ensuring control over the entry port for the island as well as of a newly constructed castle.

In 1614–15, Ieyasu successfully besieged Osaka Castle, defeating Hideyori and bringing stability to Japan. The last large-scale campaign prior to the nineteenth century, the suppression of the Shimābava Rebellion, led to the siege of Hara Castle in 1638. Nijo Castle was completed in 1626 by the third Tokugawa shogun, Iemitsu, with the addition of some structures transferred from Fushimi Castle. Nijo Castle overawed Kyoto, a city that was the residence of the emperor. Thus the castle demonstrated the new power relationship the then largely honorific emperor had had to accept. The vulnerability of Japanese castles was shown by the burning down in 1750 of the five-story castle tower after it was hit by lightning, while in 1788 another part of the castle was destroyed in a major fire.

In Edo (Tokyo), the shoguns also demonstrated an emphasis on fortification. The city as a whole was open, but a castle town was built around Edo Castle, which was the residence of Ieyasu and of later shoguns. In contrast, in China, traditional models of city design ensured that the city was systematically built in layers, with the Forbidden City at the center, next the Imperial Palace, and then the entire city surrounded by the outer walls.[7]

RELIEF FORCES AND BATTLE

The larger armies that were created in many states, notably Mughal India and the European states in the second half of the seventeenth century, required a system of logistical support that had operational consequences. This support owed much to fortresses.[8] In turn, assured supply routes meant that it was inadvisable for advancing forces to bypass fortified positions. This situation was further encouraged by the need to move artillery trains: cannon, their crew, supplies, and draft animals. These could not readily go across country but were generally restricted to roads or rivers. The consequence of the blocking position of fortresses was a focus on sieges. The capture of major positions demonstrated control and thus affected the arithmetic of peacemaking, as territorial possession was the key currency in negotiations.

The availability of relief armies or fleets was a crucial factor in sieges. In 1603, in the Low Countries, Maurice of Nassau besieged 's-Hertogenbosch, but the Spaniards were able to reinforce the city, and Maurice abandoned the siege. Generals were cautious about attacking nearby entrenched forces. In 1604, the States-General decided to relieve Ostend by sending Maurice to feint toward Sluys in order to draw the Spanish army besieging Ostend into battle. Averse to the risk of battle, Maurice instead preferred to besiege Sluys. The Spaniards eventually tried to break through the Dutch lines to relieve Sluys, but they were fought off and the garrison surrendered the next day. Ostend, in turn, fell to the Spaniards. As so often, operations in the field (either a battle or the decision not to engage) helped determine the fate of a fortress, as the garrison now had no hope of relief.

The Spanish relief of Alessandria in northern Italy, in 1657, when it was besieged by the French, demonstrated the same point, as did the

Manchu success in holding off the siege of Nanjing by Ming loyalists in 1659, and that of the Austrians in surviving the Turkish siege of Vienna in 1683. The walls of Vienna had been breached, but the defenders were still holding out when the city was relieved by a German-Polish army under John Sobieski, king of Poland, which totally defeated the besieging force. Conversely, the failure of relief armies could also be crucial, as in England with the fall of Royalist-held York in 1644 after the Parliamentary victory over a relief army at the Battle of Marston Moor (on the pattern of the fall of Stirling to the Scots after the defeat of the English at Bannockburn in 1314), and in India with the Mughal capture of Maratha fortresses. So also with sieges in Japan.

French sieges in the Spanish Netherlands were ultimately dependent on battles, notably Condé's victory over the Spanish Army of Flanders at Rocroi in 1643, that of Turenne over the same at the Battle of the Dunes (1658), and successive French victories over William III of Orange at Seneffe (1674) and Mont Cassel (1677). The Battle of the Dunes arose from the Spanish attempt to relieve besieged Dunkirk and was followed by the French capture of Dunkirk, Gravelines, Menin, and Ypres. Mont Cassel arose from a failed effort by William to relieve St. Omer, while the Battle of St. Denis in 1678 was a result of his attempt to relieve Mons. In the Rhineland, the French siege of Rheinfelden in 1676, begun after a battle nearby, ended when Duke Charles V of Lorraine appeared at the head of an Austrian force and the French retreated.

In turn, sieges depended on blockade, bombardment, and storming in very differing ratios. Techniques varied. In 1621, Gustavus Adolphus of Sweden captured Riga after a siege in which he benefited from the small size of the garrison and the absence of an effective relief army. Gustavus also allegedly employed creeping barrages (systematically advancing artillery bombardment), although this seems implausible, given the need to realign cannon after the recoil following each shot. At Philippsburg, the principal German fortress on the middle Rhine, French cannon prevailed in 1688 over those of their opponents, and the outworks were taken by storm. This successful siege was a crucial accretion of prestige for the French commander, the Dauphin, the heir to Louis XIV, who was in nominal command of the siege army.

Betrayal was also a way to gain control. In 1611, in Russia, Novgorod fell to the Swedes when a gate in the walls was opened by a traitor. In contrast, attempts to storm the city of Tula failed, but the damming of the Upa River flooded it.

Sieges continued to provide a cause for battles, as with French attempts to relieve Paris during the Franco-Prussian War of 1870–71 and the British attempt to relieve positions during the Boer War of 1899–1902.

THE OTTOMANS AND THEIR OPPONENTS

Fitness for purpose is a crucial concept when judging the applicability of fortifications. For example, features deemed necessary to withstand a major siege in western Europe, where appreciable numbers of large cannon could be deployed, were generally more than were necessary for eastern Europe, and far more than were required to defeat a rebellion.

However, specifications were not the key element. During their Thirteen Years' War with Austria (1593–1606), the Ottomans were able to capture many of the fortresses recently modified by the Austrians using the cutting-edge Italian expertise of the period, including Győr (Raab) in 1594, Eger in 1596, Kanissa in 1600, and Esztergom (Gran) in 1605. As more generally, defenses were only as good as their defenders and logistical support. The campaigns focused on control over fortresses, the capture of which served as a demonstration of success, as also with the Persian capture of Baghdad from the Ottomans and the Ottoman determination to recapture it. Attempts to relieve sieges also provided an opportunity for battle or for deciding not to launch an attack. In 1600, for example, the Ottomans captured Kanissa and then successfully resisted an Austrian siege of it the following year, whereas in 1601 the Austrians captured Dzékesfehérvar, blocking a relief attempt, only for the Ottomans to capture the fortress in 1602. Also in 1602, the Austrians captured Pest and, as in 1598, unsuccessfully besieged Buda on the other side of the Danube River. In 1603, an Ottoman attempt to regain Pest was defeated, but, advancing in strength, the Ottomans gained Pest and Vac in 1604 and Esztergom in 1605. The significance of the forts on the Danube emerged repeatedly.

As external pressure on the Turks from the Christian powers—notably Austria and Russia—increased from the late seventeenth century, they maintained many fortresses, including about 130 of various sizes to guard Hungary,[9] and built some impressive fortifications, many of which only fell after lengthy sieges. River crossings were key sites, but generally as part of a protection of the major centers of population. These fortresses included Belgrade, Buda, and Vidin on the Danube, Temesvár on the Tisza, Khotin and Bender on the Dniester, Ochakov and Kinburn controlling the Dnieper estuary, and Azov on the Don. The mouths of rivers were also important sites for fortification. At these mouths, transshipment between river and sea vessels was sometimes necessary. More significantly, these sites were important as controls over access to the river systems. Aside from their military purpose, fortified riverside positions served to police river trade and to levy tolls. Although technically not as impressive as the fortifications that were built in Christian Europe, the Turkish positions fulfilled the same purpose: in general, they absorbed considerable effort before they fell. They also reflected (and indeed protected) the resources available to the Ottoman state. The Austrians indeed initially found it difficult to follow up their essentially defensive success in defeating the Turks at Vienna in 1683.

Rather than focusing on border forts, the Turks, under Grand Vizier Kara Mustafa, in 1683 marched directly on Vienna, which they surrounded on July 16. This date was fairly late in the year for a successful campaign, not least as the defenses, ably improved by Georg Rimpler, were not suited for a general assault but required a siege. While a relief force gathered, the Ottomans began building siegeworks, using both bombardment and mines to weaken the defenses. The mines were especially threatening and were designed to create breaches that would prepare the ground for assaults. The garrison suffered heavy casualties in its defense as well as losses from dysentery. In turn, the Ottomans, who were poorly prepared for a siege of such a powerful position with a very deep moat and large ramparts, suffered similarly; but, during August, the city's outer defenses, where not covered by water features, steadily succumbed. Lacking heavy-caliber cannon, the outgunned Ottomans relied on undermining the defenses, which they did with some success, leading to breaches in which there was then bitter fighting. On September 4, the garrison fired distress rockets to urge the relief army to action. On September 12, this army attacked and routed the poorly prepared Ottoman army: the badly commanded Ottomans failed to configure their forces to resist attack. Michael Mieth, who took a major role in the defense of Vienna, also published that year his *Artilleriae Recentior Praxis*, which was reprinted in 1684.

In 1684, the Austrian commander, Duke Charles V of Lorraine, besieged Buda, the key to Hungary, but the fortress was a strong one with powerful cannon. Disease and supply difficulties hampered the four-month siege, which was eventually abandoned. In 1686, however, when a new siege was mounted, a shell landed on the main powder magazine, blowing open a breach in the walls, and repeated assaults then led to the fall of the city. The Austrians captured Belgrade in 1688, only to lose it to a Turkish counteroffensive in 1690: treachery by a French engineer, timorous command, and explosions in powder magazines have all been blamed. The strength of fortifications made progress difficult in the Danube valley, while local sources of supply were depleted by frequent campaigning, and fighting in marshy, fever-ridden lowlands weakened forces. The Austrians captured Belgrade in 1717, after a dramatic victory by Prince Eugene over the relief army, and lost it in 1739. In each case, victories in battle, and not the siege itself, determined the fate of the fortress. Austrian victory at Mehadia (1789) was followed by the successful siege of Belgrade, the city finally surrendering after a particularly heavy bombardment. There was considerable continuity in the sites of conflict.

In Greece, conflict between Venice and the Turks saw Venetian amphibious forces capture a number of fortresses in the 1680s and 1690s, including Athens in 1687, a capture that involved major damage to the Acropolis. In turn, the Turks rapidly regained them in 1715, only to fail when they pressed on in 1716 to attack Corfu, where they had also failed in 1537. In the eighteenth century, the Turks increasingly used Europeans to design fortifications.

In the seventeenth and eighteenth centuries, in response to amphibious attacks, notably by Venice, Maltese privateers, and assorted pirates, the Turks constructed and strengthened coastal fortifications, both in the Aegean islands and along the coasts of modern Lebanon and Israel. Many of them were improvements on older castles, including Venetian ones in the Peloponnese, as well as Seljuk, Byzantine, and Crusader structures, but new defenses were also constructed. The quality varied, but the Ottomans devoted some effort to plans to modernize fortifications, especially in the mid-eighteenth century.

Their allies, the Crimean Tatars, built defenses across the Isthmus of Perekop at the northern approach to Crimea, and these thwarted a Russian invasion in 1689. The defenses were part of a broader strategy of creating difficulties for any Russian advance south, one that included setting the steppe alight and other measures that hampered Russian supplies. As a result, Russian advances failed in both 1688 and 1689. Instead, after initial failure in 1695, a more peripheral target, Azov, was captured in 1696, largely because the Russians were able to use the river Don as a transport route and thus support a siege.

FRANCE AND VAUBAN

Under Louis XIV (r. 1643–1715), France proved particularly assiduous in constructing and improving fortresses to protect its borders and, in doing so, to entrench Louis's conquests, a policy already advocated in the *Testament Politique*, compiled in the late 1630s by Cardinal Richelieu, the leading minister of Louis XIII. A key role under Louis XIV was played by Sébastien Le Prestre de Vauban, a master of siegecraft as of fortification, although his ideas and work built on the experience and publications of earlier experts, for example Antoine de Ville, who became military engineer to Louis XIII (r. 1610–43) in 1627. His *Les fortifications . . . contenans la maniere de fortifier toute sorte de places tant regulierement, qu'irregulierement* (Lyon, 1628) was reprinted in 1640 and 1666 and used by Vauban. This provides an instructive instance of the interrelationship of developments in the two halves of the century. De Ville also published *De la charge des gouverneurs des places . . . un abrégé de la fortification* (Paris, 1639). In 1626, Honorat de Meynier, a retired military engineer, published *Les Nouvelles Inventions de Fortifier les Places*. The title page announced that the book had been presented to Louis XIII, a presentation that reflected both credit on the book and also a sense of what was appropriate patronage by a king of France.

Under Louis XIII, there were major fortifications, for example at Pinerolo on France's Alpine frontier, although nothing that compared with the systematic attempt to defend vulnerable frontier regions with new fortifications that his son, Louis XIV, supported. At Lorient on the south coast of Brittany, a citadel had been constructed by Cristobal de

Rojàs, a Spanish military engineer, as Spain intervened on behalf of allied Catholic League forces. This bastioned fortification was in part demolished when the Spaniards left in 1598. The fortress was rebuilt and strengthened by Marshal Brissac, with five new bastions added in 1616–22 and the citadel completed in 1637 by a demi-lune.

Under Louis XIV, a double line of fortresses was created to defend France's vulnerable northeastern frontier. Appointed commissioner general of fortifications in 1678, Vauban supervised the construction of thirty-three new fortresses, such as those at Arras, Blaye, Ath, Lille, Mont-Dauphin, Mont-Louis, and New Breisach, and the renovation of many more, such as Belfort, Besançon, Landau, Montmédy, Strasbourg, and Tournai.[10] The challenge posed by Habsburg forces that advanced into France in 1636 led to a determination to block any recurrence.

These fortresses proved of lasting worth. Captured from Spain by France in 1667 in a siege directed by Vauban, and retained under the Peace of Aix-la-Chapelle in 1668, Lille was refortified by him: four hundred men worked on the citadel for three years, creating a base for 1,200 troops. The principal entrance, the Place Royale, was built at an

Figure 4.1.   Fortification built by Vauban, Villefranche-de-conflent

angle to the drawbridge to avoid direct hits. Although it was to fall to the British in 1708 (being returned at the subsequent peace), the still-impressive citadel did not do so in 1744 or 1792, to the British and Austrians respectively. In 1940, the firm, albeit ultimately unsuccessful, defense of Lille delayed the German advance toward the English Channel, providing more opportunity for the evacuation of forces (British and French) from Dunkirk. It did not have this function in 1944 when the Germans retreated ahead of advancing British forces.

In essence, Vauban's skillful use of the bastion and of enfilading fire represented a continuation of already familiar techniques, particularly layering in depth. These were techniques that looked back to the age before gunpowder and that had been much used during it, for example by Venetian and Dutch engineers. Vauban placed the main burden of the defense on the combination of fortifications and artillery, again not a new approach. Instead, it was the crucial ability of the French state to fund such a massive program that was novel. For example, New Breisach, built to control an important Rhine crossing, to offer a route into southern Germany, and to compensate for the loss of Breisach to the Austrians in the 1697 Treaty of Rijswick, cost nearly three million livres to construct between 1698 and 1705. There was a "show" aspect to these fortifications.

Vauban also played a role in the fortification of France's naval bases. This was an aspect of the major buildup of the French navy under Louis XIV, and also a response to the threat of attacks on the bases. Indeed, both Brest and Toulon were unsuccessfully attacked during Louis's reign (by the English in 1694 and 1707 respectively), as Rochefort was by the English under his successor in 1757. The defense of naval bases and other ports was a major aspect of fortifications. It was made more necessary by the wealth produced by transoceanic trade and also by the extent to which attacking warships could bring considerable numbers of cannon to bear, as well as carrying the necessary ammunition. Thus, the Swedes fortified their new naval base at Karlskrona.

Vauban's reputation led to the publication of his works well into the eighteenth century, even outside France. The fifth edition of his *New Method of Fortification* was published in London in 1748, while an edition of his collected works was published in Amsterdam and Leipzig in 1771. To this day, Vauban remains the best-known fortress designer and is the name most associated with fortifications, alongside the Roman emperor Hadrian, after whom the wall in northern England is named, although the most famous individual fortification is the Great Wall of China. The prestige of Vauban ensured that French architects played a major role in fortress design over the following century. Thus, in 1746, the design proposed by Louis Godin was selected by the Spanish government for the Real Felipe fortress in Callao, Peru.

The focus on Vauban is important to the construction of the orthodox Western-centric account of what fortification means. In large part, this account is a reflection of the significance of France within the conventional history of warfare and, in particular, of the, in part misleading, counterpointing of Louis XIV (in the example of Vauban) with the French Revolutionaries and Napoleon, and thus of the ancien régime as opposed to "modern" warfare. As far as the ancien régime is concerned, the standard narrative moves from Spain under Philip II to France under Louis XIV, and then Prussia under Frederick II. There is also a contrast between the stress in scholarly work on Louis XIV's reign on fortifications and a different emphasis in work on German and American military history on attacking armies. That Vauban fortresses survive, in accessible areas, and recognizably look like fortresses is an important part of the equation. It is scarcely necessary to turn to archaeology to understand them.

Fortresses were designed by Vauban not only to defend frontiers but also to facilitate new gains by safeguarding bases for operations, notably the crucial accumulation of stores. In 1689, Louis indicated that he wanted to retain possession of Casale, a fortress on the Italian side of the Alps he had gained in 1681, as it provided a base for operations in Spanish-held Lombardy. Similarly with Strasbourg, also captured in 1681. This crossing point over the river Rhine served for the French as a means to advance east into southern Germany and also as a protection for the acquisition of Alsace in and after 1648. There was strategic as well as operational reasoning in the location of fortresses. For example, Novara, Alessandria, Tortona, and Valenza were seen as links in a chain aimed at the defense of Spanish-ruled Lombardy from attack from the west by Savoy-Piedmont.[11]

On a global scale, Louis XIV had, on his northeastern frontier, a deep fortress belt on a relatively narrow front. This reflected geopolitical factors, notably high population density, a good resource base, excellent river communications to move heavy artillery and supplies, and the proximity to Paris of hostile powers based in modern Belgium.

Vauban was also a master of siegecraft, as at Luxembourg (1684), Mons (1691), Charleroi (1693), and Ath (1697). He showed in the siege of Maastricht in 1673 how trenches could more safely be advanced close to fortifications under artillery cover by parallel and zigzag approaches. The garrison capitulated after a siege of less than a month, as also did those of Valenciennes (1677) and Ypres (1678), while Limbourg fell in 1676 a week after the trenches were opened. The pace at which the French took fortresses reflected their competence in siegecraft and included Dôle and Besançon in 1674; Dinant and Hay in 1675; Condé, Bouchain, and Aire in 1676; Cambrai, St. Omer, and Freiburg in 1677; and Ghent and Kehl in 1678. Dôle and Besançon were in the province of Franche-Comté, which France was ceded in the subsequent peace, that of 1678. In his *Traité des sieges de l'attaque et défense des places fait pour l'usage de Monsieur Le Duc de Bourgogne* [Burgundy], grandson of Louis XIV, Vauban argued that the greater number of fortresses placed an increased premium on siegecraft:

> One can say that in it alone today is the means of conquest and defense, because the gain of a battle only brings temporary acquisitions unless the fortresses are seized . . . a war waged by sieges exposes a state least and gives the most chance of conquests, and today it is most practiced in warfare in the Low Countries, Spain and Italy, whereas in Germany battles play a greater role because the country is opener and there are fewer fortifications.[12]

EUROPEAN EXPANSION

Outside Europe, fortification remained crucial to European expansion, for example in the Americas and West Africa, but also more widely. Thus, in 1635, Zamboanga, on the coast of the island of Mindanao in the southern Philippines, an area of Islamic opposition to Spanish expansion, was captured by Spain from the native people, and a strong fortress was constructed under the direction of the Jesuit missionary-engineer Melchor de Vera. Fortresses were also crucial to the retention of control. Goa, the major Portuguese base in India, successfully resisted attack by the Sultanate of Bijapur in 1510, 1654, and 1659 and by the Marathas in 1683; and Batavia, the major Dutch base on Java, survived two sieges by Sultan Agung of Mataram in 1628–29.

In Siberia, Russia enforced its position with the construction of a further series of fortresses as it advanced farther east. Forts were established at Yeniseysk on the river Yenisey in 1619, Yatuksk on the Lena in 1632, Okhotsk on the Sea of Okhotsk in 1647, and Irkutsk in 1661. The Pacific itself had first been reached by the Russians in 1639, and a post was then established at the mouth of the Ulya River. Forts maximized the defensive potential of firearms. Attacks on forts, such as that of the native Tungus on Zashiversk in 1666–67, were thwarted by the use of defensive gunfire, although Okhotsk was stormed by the Tungus in 1654. It was speedily rebuilt by the Russians and subsequently resisted local rebellions in 1665 and 1677; in the last, it was besieged without success by one thousand men armed with bows and bone-tipped arrows.

Albazin, the major Russian base in the Amur valley, played a key role in the conflict between Russia and the Manchus of China in 1685–86. The original Russian fort, built of wood, was surrendered in 1685 when the Chinese supplemented their superior artillery by placing firewood against the walls and setting it alight. The position, however, was not then occupied by the Chinese, and the Russians reestablished a fort there, this time with thicker walls based on an earth core and with four protruding bastions. The Chinese attacked anew in 1686 but took heavy losses, notably in unsuccessful attempts to storm the fort. In the end, the Chinese resorted to starving Albazin into surrender, only for the Russian government first to surrender it in order to facilitate peace.[13] The need for the Manchu to deploy major forces to take the fortress acted as a constraint on their operational capability.

In Ukraine, Russia continued a southward advance by means of lines of outposts that were intended both to contain the Crimean Tatars and to bring the Cossacks under control. A line was built at the beginning of the century between the rivers Vorskla and Don and was followed by the Belgorod Line (1635–53), a one-thousand-kilometer earthen wall from Akhtyrka to Tambov that was strengthened by fortifications.[14] These included the Simbirsk Line (1647–54) to Simbirsk on the Volga, and then the Trans-Kama Line on to Mensenlinsk on the Ik River in the Urals. In 1679–80, the Russians began work on the Iziuma Line, a 530-kilometer-long position farther south than the Belgorod Line. Russian activity owed much to the spread of a system of local government, supervised by the Moscow Military Chancellery (Razriad), which greatly eased the necessary mobilization of resources.[15]

Less well-fortified or less strongly defended positions could fall, as with the Portuguese base at Ormuz to the Persians in 1622 and those of Muscat and Mombasa to the Omanis in 1650 and 1698, respectively. So also with Portuguese bases around the Bay of Bengal and in Sri Lanka, which fell to local powers or to the Dutch. At the same time, on a long-standing pattern, the fate of Portuguese positions usually reflected not so much their inherent strength or weakness but rather the possibility of relief or recapture and the interaction of local rivalries with broader patterns of great-power antagonism. The prospect or not of relief was a crucial factor. Fort Jesus at Mombasa was strong enough to resist the weakly gunned Omanis. The siege began in 1696, when the garrison consisted of only fifty Portuguese soldiers and a force of loyal coast Arabs. It was strengthened by relief forces brought by sea in 1696 and 1697, but the garrison eventually fell victim to blockade, hunger, and disease. The Omanis fired corpses into the fort, contributing to the epidemic.[16]

If, in the 1630s and 1640s, the Portuguese lost positions, such as Bahia, Luanda, and Malacca, to attack by the Dutch, they were also able to recapture some of them, notably the first two. Portugal was stronger in the Atlantic, where all Dutch conquests in Brazil were recaptured, than in the (for Portugal) more distant Indian Ocean. However, it was not only Portuguese fortresses that fell. In 1662, the Dutch bases of Fort Zeelandia and Keelung on Taiwan fell to attack by Zheng Chenggong (Coxinga), a Ming loyalist Chinese pirate who benefited from well-sited cannon as well as by betrayal. The Dutch proved unable to relieve or recapture the position.

Attacks on fortresses frequently led to their improvement. In response to the Dutch seizure of St. John's in Newfoundland in 1665, a key support for the profitable cod fisheries, the defenses there were improved by the English, and a second Dutch attack was driven off in 1673.[17] In 1672–87, in response to an unsuccessful attack in 1668 by Robert Searles, an English pirate, the Spaniards constructed at St. Augustine in Florida the Castillo de San Marcos, a massive stone fortress with a permanent garrison. The threat of such attack led to the construction of the Castillo de Jagua to protect the maritime approach to the Cuban city of Cienfuegos. So also with the Castillo del Morro San Pedro de la Roca, designed by the Italian military engineer Juan Bautista Antonelli, whose work can also be seen at Havana, and built between 1633 and 1639 to prevent maritime attacks on the Cuban city of Santiago. During the century, England mounted both a successful (1627) as well as an unsuccessful (1691) attack on Quebec, each of which encouraged the French to improve the fortifications.

In general, European-style features were employed in these and other overseas fortifications, as in Sri Lanka where the Dutch, having conquered the Portuguese bases, built about fifty forts in the seventeenth and eighteenth centuries.[18] Typically, it is only the major positions that have received much scholarly attention or are maintained as sites to visit.

If there could be a degree of adaptation to local circumstances, notably the manpower available, it was less prominent than an attempt to reproduce the standard formula. This process was aided by the ubiquity of the building materials, stone, earth, and timber. At St. Augustine, the oldest masonry fort in North America, the Spaniards built with an unusual composite of stones and shells called coquina. Instead of shattering, this stone was able to absorb cannon fire. It was to hold out against British attacks, notably in 1740. At Acapulco in Mexico, the Castle of San Diego, the town's first permanent fortification, was built in 1615–16, protecting the eastern terminus of the lucrative Manila galleon trade. The fortress was pentagonal in shape, with five bastions, and part of the new defense involved the casting of cannon. The designer was the Dutch engineer Adrian Boot. Previous English and Dutch entrances into the Pacific via the Straits of Magellan had led to earlier plans for the fortification of Acapulco.[19] In Buenos Aires, a fortress was built by the Spaniards, starting in 1596. As the river Plate off the city was shallow, the attacking ships had more trouble not running aground than from the menace of the fortress's guns. On the other hand, the river Plate is deeper on what is now the Uruguay coast. Many fortresses were to be built there in the eighteenth century, another instance of environmental adaptation.

The focus in North America was on fortifying positions against attacks by other European powers. However, it is mistaken to argue that Native Americans were incapable of mounting large organized assaults against well-fortified opponents. This assumption is suggested by the general emphasis on the "skulking Indian,"[20] but in practice there was a range of local fighting techniques. Eastern North Americans had many palisaded villages in the seventeenth century, and, with the introduction of firearms, European-style bastions appeared to defend the Native villages against cross-fire. There was at least one example of a masonry fort in New England. However, the Native Americans usually abandoned their forts when Europeans approached them, especially when the latter had cannon. They had learned that forts could be death traps. The fort of the Fox (or Mesquakie) on the Illinois Grand Prairie had a heavily fortified palisade and maze of trenches that protected the Fox from French gunfire in 1730. Nevertheless, the Fox lacked cannon. More generally, a fort could be a trap or an invaluable equalizer, depending on the overall operational situation and particular tactical factors.

In contrast, European-colonial forts mounted cannon. Yet there was a major difference between the European forts designed to fend off Native American attacks, which were based on simple palisade designs, and the more elaborate fortresses built to resist European-style sieges, such as Charleston and Halifax, where the British followed the models of Vauban's fortifications, or St. Augustine in Florida where the Spaniards held off British attack. Fitness for purpose was the key concept.

CONCLUSION

Alongside emphasis on the rules of war, notably in sieges,[21] it is all too easy to forget the harshness involved in siegecraft. In 1676, visiting the Dutch camp before Maastricht, a fortress captured by the French in 1673, John Ellis found many wounded: "maimed many of them as if they had been in a sea-fight, such scarcity of legs and arms there is amongst them."[22] Later that year, the French sent out a raiding party that burned down houses, took prisoners, and extorted contributions of supplies to support their garrison. The Dutch forbade their subjects to pay these contributions, leading the French to execute the hostages in 1677.

As before, the diversity of fortifications continued. In New Zealand, where there were no firearms, *pā* settlements, fortified with wooden palisades (as opposed to *kāinga*, or open settlements), spread, especially on the North Island. Their number suggests serious competition for the resources of land and sea. Although they are difficult to date, and many would not have been occupied at the same time, over six thousand *pā* sites have been found, and it has been suggested that there may have been about twice that number.[23] In contrast, the Samoans adopted forts with high stone walls and a protective ditch or moat, while Hawaiians did not build fortified villages but relied mainly on natural features for defense. The strength of bamboo stockades was shown by the Ahom in what is now northeast India. Fortified positions based on them could be rapidly established, and they proved a difficult target for the attacking Mughals, who, in a conflict in 1636–38, used both entrenchments and elephants against them, the latter for shock action and the former manned with musketeers and cannon. The use of stockades in Arakan, Burma, Kerala, and Nepal reflected the availability of timber.

Stone was important in Abyssinia (Ethiopia). Thus, in 1636, King Fasiladas founded a permanent capital at Gondar in place of a previous situation of a peripatetic capital. A still-imposing castle was part of this capital.

Adaptation and reconstruction were aspects of a long-standing pattern. Environmental adaptation was a key element in the pronounced geographical variation in the method, technology, and ambition of fortifications. Aside from terrain and building materials, factors of population density and distance were significant for the choice of strategic systems. So also was the chance of attack. In these contexts, the latter was a particular factor in the density of fortifications, as with the contrast between France's northeastern frontier and the western frontier of Russia. Nevertheless, transcending the theme of diversity came the ubiquitous cross-cultural phenomenon of fortification.

5

THE EIGHTEENTH CENTURY

It must be fortified. Well this being agreed to, the fortifications were well planned and immediately carried into execution, and all the time they were employed about this, there were several thousands also constantly at work to take away the hill and blowing it up like fire and smoke. They both come on apace and very soon there will be no hill; but there will be fine fortifications. . . .

All these works put together may be very well defended by 10,000 men, an army sufficient to meet any power in the field that can attack this place; but one may as well fight under cover as not.

George Paterson, secretary to the British naval commander in the region, was greatly impressed by the speed of the work when in 1770 he visited Bombay (Mumbai), the major British position in west India. The British had gained the city (and Tangier) from Portugal in 1662 as part of the dowry of Catherine of Braganza when she married Charles II. Paterson thought the square fort, in which the British had sheltered against Mughal assault in 1686 before buying off the attackers, "by no means fit to sustain a modern attack." However, Paterson noted the more modern fortifications going up, including those on a hill overlooking the city.[1] Bombay was not put to the test of an attack in the eighteenth century, either by the French or by Indian powers. The new fortifications were an important demonstration of strength and may well have deterred attack.

More generally, expanding European control was anchored by fortifications. This could be seen with the Spanish empire, as, in frontier areas, with the fortress at Pensacola in west Florida founded in 1698, or that at Monterey, established in 1770 as the capital of New California, or those along the Bio Bio River in Chile, such as the fortress of Nacimiento. Pondicherry, the major French base in India, and a political and military as well as commercial center, was well fortified, with a rampart with bastions on the vulnerable side facing the land constructed in 1724–35, and a rampart on the less vulnerable coastal side in 1745. However, it was subsequently captured by the British in the Seven Years' War (1756–63) and in the French Revolutionary and Napoleonic Wars (1793–1815 for Britain), in large part due to its vulnerability once the British could employ their naval superiority.

NORTH AMERICA

In North America, forts enhanced the French position in the fur trade on a continuing pattern. In 1665–66, five forts were built along the Richelieu River, establishing control over the route from the St. Lawrence to Lake Champlain. Louis de Frontenac, the governor, strengthened the French position on Lake Ontario by building Fort Frontenac in 1673, as well as Forts St. Joseph (1679), Crèvecoeur (1680), and St. Louis (1682), which consolidated France's presence between Lake Michigan and the Mississippi. The network extended westward, with the foundation of Forts St. Croix (1683), St. Antoine (1686), and La Pointe (1693) south of Lake Superior, and Kaministiquia (1678), Népigon (1679), and La Tourette (1684) to the north. Forts, subsequently, were intended to bring the hoped-for route to the Pacific and thus outflank the Spaniards. Moving westward, Fort St. Charles (1732) on the Lake of the Woods was followed by Fort Maurepas (1734) at the southern end of Lake Winnipeg, Fort Dauphin (1741) established their presence on the western shore of Lake Winnipegosis, and Fort La Corne (1753) was founded near the Forks of the Saskatchewan, a crucial node of native trade routes. As also with other states, the names of forts could reflect their significance. Maurepas was the minister of the marine, the key figure in governing France's colonies. The Dauphin was the heir to the throne.

In turn, the British built forts into the interior. Indeed, competing attempts to establish forts, encroachment and "claim by fort," led to conflict in the Ohio River Valley in 1754, provoking war between the two powers: the French and Indian War (1754–63). This is the North American term for the stages there of what the British term the Seven Years' War (1756–63), a title linked to the formal declaration of war which for Britain and France began with the French invasion of the British Mediterranean colony of Minorca, an invasion in which the key element on land was the successful siege of the British fortress there, a fortress intended to protect the naval base.

Conflict, however, had already begun in North America. Outnumbered and defending a hastily built fort in a wholly unsuitable location, George Washington was forced to surrender at Fort Necessity in 1754. British and French fort building to the south of the Great Lakes was another major cause of dispute, with positions such as Oswego highly contentious. The war in North America focused on fortresses, as with the French capturing Fort William Henry in 1757. More decisively, the British brought their strength to bear to capture Louisbourg (1758), Quebec (1759), and Montreal (1760).

Native Americans adapted by abandoning their traditional fortification systems in the face of Western siegecraft capabilities. They lacked the numbers to man any fortification system, and individual positions could, justifiably, be seen as traps, presenting targets for their opponents' cannon. Natives had come to appreciate that defending any given point against a large force was dangerous. Instead, they developed alternative strategies reliant on the likelihood that the militia would not remain for long. In 1776, when American militia invaded the lands of the Cherokee, the latter largely abandoned their towns to be burned by the militia, disappeared into the mountains, and returned once the militia had departed. However, the militia picked a new target, that of destroying crops and shelter.[2]

EUROPEAN EXPANSION

Europe's transoceanic presence in part rested on an ability and willingness to dig. In 1788, Charles, 2nd Earl Cornwallis, the British commander in India, who had earlier surrendered at Yorktown in 1781, took an interest in the purchase of entrenching tools. Having already ordered "4,000 good iron shovels," he wanted "2,000 iron spades to be made immediately." Spades were important in a tactical sense rather than a strategic one. Native Americans did not have shovel tools.

Powerful European-colonial fortifications were of only limited use against well-commanded European assailants who had clear naval superiority and were not weakened by tropical diseases, as the British demonstrated when they took Louisbourg on Cape Breton Island from the French in 1745 and, for good, in 1758, and Quebec in 1759. The latter surrendered after a French army that had sallied forth was defeated: the fortifications themselves were not damaged and indeed, in British hands, saw off a French siege in 1760 after a similar defeat of a British army outside the walls. In turn, the city was relieved after a British squadron arrived once the ice on the St. Lawrence had melted. In 1762, the British landed successfully on the French Caribbean island of Martinique, "silencing the batteries by the ships' gunfire."[3]

In contrast, the British failed against St. Augustine in 1740. Their naval blockade failed to prevent the arrival of supply ships, the well-fortified and ably defended Spanish position resisted bombardment, and, in the face of desertion and disease, the British retreated. In 1702, St. Augustine had also successfully resisted attack. It was too strong to storm, the British cannon were inadequate, and the warships from Cuba relieved the garrison. In a very different context, the Corsican rising against French occupation in Corsica led in 1768 to the surrender of the French garrison at Borgo after an attempt to relieve it was repulsed, as was the garrison's attempt to break out.

European-colonial fortifications were generally able to resist assailants who lacked the skills, resources, and organization required for a lengthy siege. Lieutenant William Horton wrote of the unsuccessful British-Creek campaign against St. Augustine in 1740: "The Indians are good to fight against Indians, and to waste the Spanish plantations, but not fit for entering breaches or trenches, or besieging a town regularly."[4] In the eighteenth century, most major fortifications erected by European forces survived Native siege or attack. In North Africa, Spanish-held Ceuta resisted Moroccan sieges in 1694–1720 and 1732, and Melilla another in 1774–75. On the other hand, having failed in 1667, 1672, 1675, and 1688, the Algerians took Oran from Spain in 1708, only for Spain to regain it in 1732 with a major expedition.

Minor fortifications could hold out, as shown by the Europeans in West Africa, although the French fort at Whydah was captured by Dahomey forces in 1728. Moreover, the British lost some of their forts in the initial stages of Pontiac's War (1763–64) in North America.

This was also true for sieges of non-Western positions. Thus, reflecting opinion in Gibraltar, John Swinton, a visiting British cleric, observed, "The siege of Fez in 1727 by Muley Hamet Deby's army, which made so much noise in Europe was carried on by an undisciplined rabble, who had only one mortar and three cannon amongst them, and who did not know how to use them."[5]

The major overseas centers of European power did not fall to non-European peoples. No Native Americans could have mounted attacks comparable to those by the British against Louisbourg. Spanish-ruled Manila fell to a British force from Madras (Chennai) in India in 1762, but not to a rising in the Philippines nor to an attacking Asian power. Colonel George Monson recorded,

> An eight gun battery was finished about three hundred yards from the wall the 2nd of October at night, and opened the 3rd in the morning on the south west bastion which immediately silenced the enemy's guns and made a breach in the salient angle of the bastion, the fourth at night batteries were begun to take off the defences of the south-east bastion and of the small bastion on the west side of the town; which was opened the fifth by ten o'clock in the morning and had so good an effect, that the general gave out orders for storming the place next day; which was done about seven in the morning, with very little loss on our side.[6]

However, due to a lack of interest and resources as well as the scale of commitments, many Western fortified positions were weak and poorly garrisoned. In 1710, the wood of the French fortress at Fort Louis (later Mobile), which had been built in 1702, was so rotted by humidity and decay that it could not support the weight of the cannon. The garrison suffered from an absence of fresh meat; from an insufficient supply of swords, cartridge boxes, nails, guns, and powder; from demoralization and desertion; and from the lack of a hospital.[7] So also, in particular, with most of the forts in West Africa that protected European trading positions, notably for slave traders. The fort base of Port Louis was described in 1758 by a critical British observer as "of no strength . . . the wall built with clay and soft brick plastered over . . . only embrasures for twelve" guns. Three years later, the British garrison there was decimated by disease.[8] Captain John Blankett of the British navy was unimpressed by the Dutch fort on Timor that he visited in 1790: "A miserable band, composed of a few German deserters and Malays compose a sort of garrison." He correctly argued that the Dutch maintained their position by exploiting the rivalries of the local rulers.[9] Involved in a disastrous war with the Marathas in west India in 1737–40, the Portuguese lost their positions of Bassein, Chaul, and Salsette and very nearly, in 1739, their major base of Goa.

Logistics was another key problem in sustaining fortresses, especially in sustaining overseas fortresses. In 1729, the British Regency Council had to discuss the shortage of magazines and powder in the garrison on Minorca.[10] In 1778, Patrick Henry, governor of Virginia, justified abandoning an attempt to capture distant Detroit from the British: "A post will be difficult to maintain while the great intermediate country is occupied by hostile Indians."[11]

Once the thirteen colonies became independent in 1783, the Americans benefited in their stance toward the Native Americans from fortifications, such as Fort Washington (now Cincinnati), established in 1789. However, the limited number of American regular troops meant that there were insufficient forces for any widespread garrison policy. Furthermore, there and elsewhere, for example with Russia east of the Caspian Sea, garrisons could only work as part of an expansionist policy if, on the pattern of the Russians west of the Caspian, they were accompanied by the "pacification" of areas brought under control earlier in order to provide operational and strategic depth for fresh advances. If not, expansion simply brought the need for more garrisons.

To protect their position north of Mexico from Native American attack, Spain attempted to create a network of presidios (fortified bases), but the Native Americans traveled between them with no difficulty. Again, the Spaniards were too short of troops to operate an effective defensive campaign of this type. In 1680, Santa Fe had resisted siege in the Pueblo Rising but was then evacuated, being reoccupied in 1692.[12] Relatively low walled, presidios were generally capable of withstanding Native American attack, although that was not always the case for presidios built along the Red River in eastern Texas and along the (later) Arkansas border. From the San Diego presidio to the south-central New Mexican ones, the distance is well over one thousand kilometers. The Spaniards organized their presidios in Texas into three vectors, those in the areas of El Paso, San Antonio, and the Red River, but in the face of Native aggression they had to pull back.[13]

The *Monitor*, a London newspaper, in its issue of January 8, 1763, complaining about the peace terms under which Britain had acquired Florida in return for Cuba, referred to

> the untenable fortress of St. Augustine, in which the Spaniards are cooped up continually by the native Indians, who never submitted to the Spanish government . . . the poor, starving, weak, defenceless, unsafe, depopulated town of St. Augustine, and an uncultivated savage land as far as the Mississippi, to which the Spaniards could never make out any right, further than they could command within the length of their great guns.

EUROPE

Within Europe, sieges were important, as fortified positions, such as Lille, anchored political power, contained military supplies, and controlled communication routes, both roads and rivers. Fortified cities could span rivers, providing automatic bridgeheads, while fortresses protected crossings, as Namur did for the river Meuse, Philippsburg and Rheinfels for the middle Rhine, and Kehl and Breisach for the upper Rhine. In his *Rêveries* (1757), written in 1732, Marshal Saxe, who as a leading French commander in the 1740s focused successfully on a war of maneuver, criticized the cost of Vauban's fortifications but also wrote of

> the usefulness of fortresses; they cover a country; they subject an enemy to the necessity of attacking them, before he can penetrate further; they afford a safe admission to your own troops on all occasions; they contain magazines [supply dumps], and form a secure receptacle, in the winter time, for artillery, ammunition, etc.[14]

Saxe himself is best known for his victories in battle, notably Fontenoy (1745), but he was also responsible for a series of successful sieges in the Austrian Netherlands, as Belgium became after the 1713–14 peace settlements. Sieges had become more formidable undertakings because of advances in fortification techniques, associated in particular with Vauban, and because of the greater size of armies available in western Europe from the late seventeenth century, as states consolidated their power after the mid-century crisis. This situation, to a degree, prefigured that during the late nineteenth century, although not that during World War I.

During the War of the Spanish Succession (1701–14), Louis XIV of France sought to acquire fortresses on or near his frontiers, such as Friedlingen, [Old] Breisach, Freiburg, Kehl, and Philippsburg, and also to acquire those that would aid a strategic advance, for example Villingen, which controlled the route to his ally Bavaria down the upper Danube.[15] It therefore represented a way to protect Bavaria against Austrian attack. In the event, the total defeat of the Franco-Bavarian army at Blenheim in 1704 led to British and Austrian forces overrunning southern Germany and capturing the fortresses there, including Ingolstadt and Ulm. Prior to Blenheim, the British forces had stormed the Schellenberg height at the major fortress at Donauwörth in a difficult exercise that became a major feat in hand-to-hand conflict. Sieges played a major role in campaigns. It was important that, as commander of a Franco-Spanish army, James, Duke of Berwick, captured Barcelona for Philip V of Spain (second grandson of Louis XIV of France) in 1714, and in 1719, as commander of a French army, San Sebastian from him, and so on.

In addition to fortresses, the War of the Spanish Succession saw the development of extensive field fortifications, notably the Lines of Brabant, a line of fortifications and trenches from Antwerp to Namur. To a degree, these presaged the lengthy trench systems of World War I. The British forced their way through in 1705. In 1712, the British again broke through the French lines of Ne Plus Ultra, which had been newly constructed to defend the frontier from Namur to the Channel coast.

WAR AND PEACE

Fortresses played a major role in peace negotiations, giving significance to particular locations. Thus, in 1712, Louis insisted on the retention of Lille, Tournai, Condé, and Maubeuge as part of a peace settlement.[16] They were designed to protect France's vulnerable northeastern frontier from attack by Austria and its allies. The strength and extent of the

French fortification system certainly limited attempts to invade France, as in 1708–11 and 1743. Indeed, in the latter case, Lord Cobham, a veteran, referred to France's "almost impenetrable Barrier of Alsace, Lorraine or the Netherlands." The French did not need to use the extensive double crownworks added to the fortifications at Metz and Thionville by Louis de Cormontaigne, who had become chief engineer at Metz in 1733. However, the British were able in 1713 to insist on the dismantling of the fortifications at Dunkirk.

Louis XIV had not succeeded in gaining Kehl and Philippsburg in the 1714 peace settlement, which meant that the French, when they next operated in the Rhineland, focused on those fortresses. During the War of the Polish Succession (1733–35), Kehl was successfully besieged in 1733 and Philippsburg in 1734. These sieges represented and registered success but were scarcely decisive, whereas in Italy major advances were made in campaigning that included sieges as well as battles. However, in 1735 the campaign came to focus on a siege of Austrian-held Mantua that did not succeed.

Other powers were also concerned by the strategic implications of the availability, or not, of fortresses, and thus by the allocation of fortresses as part of a peace settlement. In 1709, Victor Amadeus II of Savoy-Piedmont pressed the envoy of his major ally, Britain,

> that the demolishing of Monmeillan by the enemy [France] has left all Savoy uncovered, and that upon any rupture with France, how impossible it is to preserve Savoy, or any footing on the other side of the mountains [the Alps], except, upon the treaty of peace, the allies will think of procuring him Briançon or Barreau, or both, which would prove but a bare equivalent of Monmeillan.

The French indeed demolished many of the fortresses of Savoy-Piedmont, notably those toward Lombardy. Britain was determined to hold on to Gibraltar and Minorca, which it had seized from Spain in 1704 and 1708 respectively and been ceded by Spain in the Peace of Utrecht (1713). Thereafter, however, Britain faced attacks, notably unsuccessful Spanish sieges of Gibraltar in 1727 and 1779–84 and, in 1756, a successful French siege of Fort St. Philip, the major British position in Minorca, which fell after a British relief attempt by sea failed. In 1727–35, to threaten Gibraltar and prevent incursions from it, the Spaniards built the Linea de Contravalacion. This consisted of two anchoring forts at each end—Fort Santa Barbara and Fort San Felipe—and a wall in between.

To protect the Low Countries from French invasion, Britain and the Dutch supported the garrisoning of a series of what were termed "barrier" fortresses in what at the end of the War of the Spanish Succession became the Austrian Netherlands [Belgium]. These were to be garrisoned by the Dutch in a complicated arrangement designed to lessen reliance on the Austrians, the new territorial power. However, in 1744, the British diplomat Robert Trevor wrote of the "barrier" fortresses in the Austrian Netherlands:

> I dare not preach up the doctrine of putting their fortresses into an impregnable condition. . . . I had rather see the places secured by an army in the field, and opposed to the enemy; than the army secured in the places. I confess, I am one of those, who cannot understand how a country is the weaker, in proportion to the number of fortified places it has; which must however be the case if they are to absorb, instead of ekeing out, the troops of a state.

At the close of the War of the Austrian Succession in 1748, Britain and the Dutch were determined in the peace negotiations to prevent France from retaining any of the many fortresses they had captured in the Low Countries from Austria and the Dutch, fortresses that included the major Dutch border positions of Bergen-op-Zoom and Maastricht, captured by France in 1747 and 1748 respectively. This goal led the British to support a peace on the basis of a return to the prewar situation, which also meant giving captured Louisbourg back to France.

Compared to the French, the Prussians were poor in mounting sieges. Frederick the Great repeatedly lost momentum by getting stuck in front of fortresses and fortress-cities, although victories in 1741 (Mollwitz) and 1745 (Kesseldorf) were followed by the capture of fortified positions. In 1758, Frederick mishandled his siege of the Austrian fortress of Olmütz. [17]

FORTRESSES AND FIELD ARMIES

Both in war and in peacetime consideration, the relationship between field armies and fortresses remained a crucial issue. In 1781, Sir Eyre

Coote, the talented British commander in chief in India, explained his opposition to the idea of attacking the Dutch base of Negapatam:

> It is a rule which a soldier ought never to lose sight of—if there is an enemy in the field, anywhere near, and in force, to a fortified town or garrison, intended to be attacked, first to beat it, and so effectually as to be himself satisfied that it will not be able to rise again in strength sufficient to molest him while carrying on the operations of the siege.[18]

There was a parallel with the dependence on naval power for the defense of island fortresses, such as (unsuccessfully) British-ruled Minorca in 1756, or indeed Austrian-ruled Sicily in the face of Spanish invasion in 1718, the British navy again providing the power in the last case. Fortresses could inflict delays that were especially serious due to political and logistical factors, as they helped make war appear indecisive.[19] Fortresses, however, were vulnerable to defeat by field armies. Fortresses also acted as the bases for these armies, bases that were particularly important with the need for gunpowder and ammunition. For example, the magazines developed to support French forces under Louis XIV were based in fortresses. Equally, they generally only contained supplies able to support initial operations, which caused problems if the conflict was a lengthy one.

The time factor, notably for sieges, was very much affected by the problems created by poor roads, in particular how they were made worse by bad weather. Poor weather and, therefore, poor roads delayed the French cannon intended for the siege of Trarbach in the Moselle valley in 1734. Commanders frequently commented on the impact of bad weather on the movement of artillery.[20]

The British were able to besiege and capture Lille in 1708 because John Churchill, 1st Duke of Marlborough, had earlier heavily defeated the French army at the Battle of Oudenaarde. Lille was well fortified (it is still an impressive site) and ably defended by a large garrison, and there was the prospect of support from a relief army. A poorly coordinated Allied attack on too wide a front on September 7 left nearly three thousand attackers dead or wounded. John Deane of the British Foot Guards recorded in his diary on September 22, this murdering siege, it is thought, has destroyed more than Namur [1695] did last war, and those that were the flower of the army: for what was not killed or drowned were spoiled by their hellish inventions of throwing of bombs, boiling pitch, tar, oil and brimstone with scalding water and such like combustibles, upon our men, from the outworks, and when our men made any attack. Especially the English Grenadiers have scarce 6 sound men in a company: likewise many other inventions enough to puzzle the Devil to contrive.[21]

The Allied attack was only successful when artillery fire was concentrated, making a number of large breaches, and French diversionary attacks were beaten off. The citadel finally capitulated on December 19, after a siege of 120 days that cost the besiegers fourteen thousand casualties. Similarly, Mons and Ghent, both in the Spanish Netherlands (modern Belgium), were captured in 1709, only after Marlborough's victory at Malplaquet. This was a difficult victory, but a victory nevertheless, not least as it left the British free to advance. In 1734, Spanish victory over the Austrians at Bitonto in southern Italy was followed by the capture of the major fortress of Gaeta.

Similarly with the French in the Low Countries in 1744–48. The Dutch-garrisoned "barrier" fortresses proved too weak to resist. In 1745, the British, under William, Duke of Cumberland, sought to relieve besieged Tournai. As so often, as with the Portuguese victory of Montes Claro (1665), the Battle of Vienna (1683), and the Swedish attack on the Russians at Narva (1700), the attempt to relieve a besieged fortress led to a battle. Saxe's victory at Fontenoy on May 11 was followed by the rapid fall to the French of Tournai (June 19), Ghent (July 15), Oudenaarde, Bruges (July 19), Dendermonde, Ostend (August 23), and Nieuwpoort (September 5). In 1745, the Franco-Spanish defeat of Britain's ally Charles Emmanuel III of Sardinia, ruler of Savoy-Piedmont, at Bassignano on September 27 was followed by the capture of Asti (November 17) and Casale and Milan (December 16). In 1746, the French advanced anew in the Low Countries. Brussels fell to Saxe on February 20 after a surprise advance. Trenches were opened before Antwerp on May 24, the garrison surrendering after a week. Mons fell on July 10 after a month's siege. Charleroi was stormed on August 2 after a brief siege beginning on July 28–29, and the citadel of Namur capitulated on October 1. Many of the places, notably Namur in 1692 and 1695, had already faced major sieges.

In 1747, Saxe outmaneuvered Cumberland when he sought to regain Antwerp and defeated him at Lawfeldt. Saxe's protégé, Count Ulrich Lowendahl, rapidly overran the fortresses in Dutch Flanders that covered the Scheldt estuary: Sluys, Sas de Grand, Hulst, and Axel fell between May 1 and 17. Lowendahl then turned to attack Bergen-op-Zoom, one of the strongest fortresses in Europe, the fortifications of which had been strengthened with casemented redoubts by Menno van Coehoorn. Lowendahl began the siege in mid-July, and a month later a British official commented, "It has certainly been carried on with great fury by the enemy, without regard to the loss of men and every other expense."[22] However, progress was slow, and the French had to resort on September 16 to storming the defenses, a desperate measure. Massacre, rape, and pillage followed.

In northern Italy, Prince Eugene, the Austrian general in the 1700s, did not allow the French emphasis on the defense of river lines and fortified positions to thwart his drive for battle, as with his surprise attack on Cremona in 1702 and the outflanking of one French army that was a vital prelude in 1706 to a major victory outside Turin by Austrian and Piedmontese forces that ended a French siege, a siege in which there had been much fighting underground as mines were used. The besiegers had built fortified lines to limit the chance of any relief. In contrast, the siege of Austrian-held Mantua, the major operation in northern Italy in 1735, failed, in part due to the strength of the defenses (which included prominent water features), but in part due to a major rivalry between the governments of France and Spain whose forces were besieging the city.

The significance of fortresses led in countries where there was a free press to interest in publishing work on them. The Huguenot (French Protestant) exile Abel Boyer, a major figure in journalism, published, in London in 1701, *The Draughts of the Most Remarkable Fortified Towns of Europe . . . with a geographical description of the said places. And the history of sieges they have sustained.* In 1727, the second edition of Jacques Ozanam's *A Treatise of Fortification* was published in London, with the addition of *A New and Exact Plan of Gibraltar with All Its Fortifications* by Herman Moll, the latter plan made topical by the Spanish siege that year. Moreover, the publication of this edition as a whole was a response to the more general international crisis of 1725–27.

BOMBARDMENT AND STORMING

Fortresses could be expected to take a battering in any campaign. In 1761, the British fired seventeen thousand shot and twelve thousand shells from a battery of thirty guns and thirty mortars in their successful siege of the French citadel of Belle-Île on an island off the coast of Brittany, a rate of fire that put enormous pressure on supplies.[23] Twenty years later, Captain James Horsbrugh, British adjutant general in Gibraltar, recorded of a not particularly important day in the unsuccessful Spanish siege during the War of American Independence: "Their fire in the last 24 hours amounted to 203 shot and 33 shells."[24] Fortresses also fired a considerable weight of shot. Besieged unsuccessfully by the Prussians from July 13 to 30, 1760, with two failed attempts at storming, the defenders of Dresden, the capital of the Electorate of Saxony, fired 26,266 cannon shot from their 193 pieces of artillery. Prussian bombardment of the city did great damage, and the heat from the burning buildings made service on the ramparts very unpleasant.[25] In 1762, Francis Browne attributed the collapse of Spanish morale in besieged Havana to British artillery:

> Our new batteries against the town being perfected (which consisted of forty four pieces of cannon), we all at once, by a signal, opened them and did prodigious execution. Our artillery was so well served and the fire so excessively heavy and incessant . . . that the Spaniards could not possibly stand to their guns.[26]

Improvements in ballistics played a role from mid-century, as aiming became better understood and more accurate. Changes between the 1756 and 1774 editions of the mathematician Francis Holliday's *An Easy Introduction to Fortification and Practical Gunnery* included material on the theory of projectiles. The increased standardization of artillery was also important as it delivered a greater predictability in firepower and improved logistical capability.

Storming remained important in taking forts and in all parts of the world. For infantry, cavalry, and siegecraft, there was a consistent tension between firepower and shock tactics. The choices reflected circumstances, experience, the views of particular generals, and wider assumptions in military society; these choices were not dictated by technology. The focus on attack in part represented a cultural imperative in the face of the disincentive provided by the growing strength of defensive firepower, but in practice this strength did not preclude advantages for attacking forces. As a reminder of the variety of factors involved at all levels, strategically as well as tactically and operationally, the prestige of the attack, rather than a reliance on ideas and practices of deliberate siegecraft, could, for example, encourage attempts to storm fortresses. These cultural ideas tend to be underplayed or to be treated as anachronistic. Both approaches are mistaken. They stem from a tendency to treat fortification and siegecraft as technical processes and not, instead, to locate them in cultural contexts, or to regard such contexts as aspects of a more primitive system. The latter approach is often adopted by nonspecialists toward non-Western and also premodern processes of fortification and siegecraft. Separately, there could be a tendency to see fortifications and siegecraft as '"unmilitary" or, rather, less martial than battle.

Storming could also be encouraged by a need for speed, both in order to press on to achieve results elsewhere and also so as to deal with logistical problems, which were greatly exacerbated by lengthy sieges. These factors formed a long-standing mix, as did the impact of the weather: generals preferred not to continue sieges into the winter. In 1714, three storming attempts on Barcelona by Franco-Spanish forces were repulsed, but the outnumbered Austrian-Catalan defenders then accepted terms. In contrast, in 1719, French cannon breached the walls of San Sebastian and then bombarded the citadel into surrender. Bavarian, French, and Saxon forces successfully stormed Austrian-held Prague in 1741, the Russians Willmanstrand in Swedish-ruled Finland the same year, and the Russians Turkish-held Izmail in 1790. With Prague, there was no time for a regular siege, and the siege artillery was delayed because of a lack of horses. There were also major failures, as when the British in 1758 had nearly two thousand casualties in an unsuccessful attempt to storm French-held Ticonderoga.

There was a tactical continuum, as the storming of major positions was generally preceded by bombardment and the deliberate preparation this entailed, including the digging of trenches and the construction of artillery platforms. Moreover, storming had an element of battle, for storming attempts could lead to large-scale and lengthy clashes in the breaches. The storming of lesser positions, in contrast, was not generally preceded by bombardment. Instead, it was frequently an aspect of the rapid moves of "small war," with surprise attacks launched without the delays or concentration of force required if artillery was to be deployed. Belle Isle, a French island off the Breton coast, was captured by the British in 1761 when a second successful landing, achieved by climbing steep cliffs, which were not defended, led to a siege of the French fortress, which was strongly contested. Only after a successful breach was made, and knowing that there was no possibility of reinforcement, did the French surrender. The following year, Colonel William Draper, the commander of the British force that captured Manila from Spain, complained that the small number of troops he had been allocated "will sufficiently evince the impossibility of my acting against the place with the formalities of a siege. My hopes are placed in the effects of a bombardment or *coup de main*."[27]

At the same time, there was interest, notably in France, in new projects for fortification, especially from Marc-René, Marquis de Montalembert (1714–1800). A man of great schemes, but not given to costing proposals, detailed design, or the practicalities of local topography, all facets of other exponents of particular schemes, he advanced a series of bold projects from 1776 to 1797. In a pattern more generally the case with many of the theorists of the period, Montalembert was concerned primarily with the basic design of a structure, which to him determined whether or not a fortification was capable of withstanding attack. For him, reason was independent of nature and dominated it: the accidents of terrain and specificities of location could be subordinated to the theoretical plan. With cause, this approach was criticized by contemporaries, in France by the Corps of Military Engineers. Rather than seeing themselves as individual designers, as Montalembert did, engineers saw themselves as a corps, and this institutional response shaped the possibilities of change. Hostility to Montalembert in part arose due to his opposition to Vauban and his ideas, and the weight of the past that they represented. Conflicting claims about the scientific nature of military engineering (identified as a science of fortification), and about what precisely this science was, gave an appearance of confusion to the whole debate, and it was aggravated by Montalembert's attacks. The emphasis can be on artillerist-engineers as modernizers,[28] but the Enlightenment character of the pre-Revolutionary profession was conservative, not least in being opposed to what it saw as the adventurism of ill-considered novelty. In contrast to the earlier response in France, the Prussians liked Montalembert and, in the nineteenth century, built their fortresses after his designs.[29] The debate testified to interest in improvements, commitment to an explicitly rational solution, and the tensions between planning and practicality.

FIELD FORTIFICATIONS

Eighteenth-century warfare is not generally discussed in terms of field fortifications. However, they could be significant, including in battle. Ad hoc defenses played a major role, as with the Russian defenses against Swedish attack at Poltava in 1709, with the defense of the village of Blenheim in 1704, and with the role of the village of Hochkirch in the battle there between Austria and Prussia in 1756; it was impossible to form "une attaque formelle," and instead columns were used.[30] French victory at Roucoux in 1746 centered on the storming of three entrenched villages by the French infantry. In Lawfeldt in 1747, Saxe was again victorious, with the fighting focused on the village lasting four hours: the British infantry in defense of the village inflicted heavy losses on the attacking French, only surrendering their position on the fifth attack.[31]

In field engagements where far fewer troops were present, fortifications were a variant on a more general search for cover. Thus, at King's Mountain in South Carolina in 1780, the victorious Revolutionaries fought with rifles "in their favourite manner . . . an irregular but destructive fire from behind trees and other cover."[32] Linked to this was contemporary interest in "a portable chevaux de fries," an obstacle behind which infantry could defend themselves.[33]

In 1758, discussing British combined operations against western Europe, Robert, 4th Earl of Holdernesse, one of the secretaries of state, commented,

> As to any attempt upon the coast of Flanders, it would be next to impossible to succeed in it, considering the time that is necessary for disembarking a large body of men and that the enemy would be able to send a superior force to drive us back before it would be possible to throw up any entrenchment to secure our stores and provisions.[34]

Field fortifications attracted the attention of commentators and were handled in publications. In London, J. C. Pleydell's *An Essay on Field Fortifications; intended principally for the use of officers of infantry. . . . Translated from the original manuscript of an officer of experience in the Prussian service* (1768) was followed by Johann Tielke's *The Field Engineer; or Instructions upon Every Branch of Field Fortification: demonstrated by examples which occurred in the Seven Years' War . . . translated from the fourth edition of the German original* (1789). The dissemination of best practice by publication and translation was an established aspect of Western military culture, indeed helping, alongside service in other armies, to create this very culture.

ANTISHIP FORTIFICATIONS

The fortification of naval bases and other ports remained a major goal. So also with fortresses designed to prevent warships from passing through bodies of water. This was seen with Ottoman fortifications at the Dardanelles, at the Bosporus, and at the entrance to the rivers running into the Black Sea. There was no provision on this scale in the remainder of Europe.

Antiship fortifications were also important across the West, notably in the Western transoceanic empires. In Callao, Peru, the Real Felipe Fortress was built in 1747–74 at the cost of three million pesetas to defend the main Peruvian port and the city of Lima from the possibility of British naval attack and from pirates. From 1782, two smaller complementary fortresses were built. In Havana, the failure of the defenses to prevent British conquest in 1762 led to the construction of a complex and expensive defensive system, the Fortaleza San Carlos de la Cabaña (1763–74), which never faced attack.

Ships had an impressive ability to carry cannon, and they were impressively able to take punishment. However, as a base for accurate fire, a ship was quite limited. Permanently installed cannon based on land could be better aligned than ship-based ones.

Not only fortresses were involved. For example, during the American War of Independence, a great chain was stretched across the Hudson at West Point in order to block British vessels. This was one of the longest and largest iron chains ever forged and a considerable technological triumph. In 1778, John Stevens attempted to build "a machine in the river at West Point, for the purpose of setting fire to any of the enemy's shipping that might attempt a passage up it."[35] In inshore waters where galleys could operate, notably the Gulf of Finland, fortifications were part of a defensive system that was integrated with these galleys, particularly by Sweden. More generally, fortifications were stand-alone.

New geopolitical challenges could play a role in fortification developments. In 1792, a Russian request to Japan to open diplomatic and commercial relations led a hostile Japan to order the establishment of coastal defenses, although this never came to anything, in part because the Russians did not pursue the matter.[36]

EASTERN EUROPE

In eastern Europe, where there were far fewer fortifications and no system of advanced fortresses, it was easier for the participants in the Great Northern War (1700–21), than for those in the War of the Spanish Succession (1701–14) in western Europe, to make major advances, as when the bold Charles XII of Sweden invaded Poland in 1701, Saxony in 1706, and Ukraine in 1708. He was defeated in battle by Russian forces at Poltava (1709), rather than being checked in a siege. However, individual fortresses could be important in eastern Europe, not least as the way to secure control of a region. Thus, the capture of Narva in 1704 and of Viborg, Reval, and Riga in 1710, by the Russian forces of Peter the Great I (r. 1683–1725), and of Stettin (1714), Stralsund (1715), and Wismar (1716) by Sweden's western assailants, Denmark and Prussia, were crucial stages in the collapse of the Swedish empire. Charles XII himself was shot dead while besieging the Norwegian fortress of Fredrikshald in 1718, and his death led to the end of the siege.[37]

Similarly, fortresses such as Ochakov and Izmail played a major role in successive Russo-Turkish wars. Moving onto the defensive created serious problems for the Turkish empire, both structurally and in terms of ethos. There was a marked deficiency in preparations for defenses. Nevertheless, key fortresses, such as Ochakov, were improved. This defensive emphasis and improvement to fortifications affected strategy. The greater strength of fortresses, the determination to secure territorial gains, and the need to dominate supply routes all ensured that sieges remained very significant in campaigning north of the Black Sea, as also in the Danube valley where they had for long been to the fore.

In 1736, having failed to capture it the previous year, the Russians seized Azov after the main powder magazine blew up. In 1696, having failed to capture it the previous year, Peter I (the Great) had captured Azov, only to have to return it after his defeat in battle at the river Pruth in 1711. Also in 1736, the Russians invaded Crimea, the center of the power of the Crimean Tatars who were key Turkish allies, storming the earthworks that barred the Isthmus of Perekop at the entrance to the Crimea: after a bombardment, the Russians under General Münnich launched a night attack in columns against the western section of the lines, the troops climbing the wall and gaining control with scanty losses.

Ochakov proved a more difficult obstacle in 1737. As in other lengthy sieges, logistics was a key element. Münnich's advance was supported by supplies brought by boat down the river Dnieper, and thence by thousands of carts. The initial assault failed, but the fortress was successfully stormed after the powder magazine exploded. In 1739, victory at Stavuchanakh was followed by the capture of the major fortress of Khotin. The Turkish fortresses on the rivers athwart Russia's advance into the Balkans, such as Izmail and Silistria on the Danube, played a key role in campaigns, affecting Russian options and mobility.

Battles took precedence. Thus, Count Peter Rumyantsev's repeated victories in 1770, at Ryabaya Mogila, Larga, and Kartal, enabled him to capture Izmail, Kilia, and Braila rapidly. Indeed, Grand Vizier Halil Pasha had advanced north of the Danube to protect the fortresses. At the same time, the collapse of the Turkish military system was crucial, as the garrisons lacked adequate supplies and pay. Victory in the field created options, even if on some occasions, as at Khotin in 1769, the Russians were unable to mount a successful siege. In 1774, Rumyantsev's victory at Kozludji south of the Danube left the main remaining Turkish fortresses, notably Silistria (which had resisted attack in 1773), vulnerable, and the Turks hastily made peace. As a reminder of the need to assess field formations, Rumyantsev advanced on the battlefield with his infantry organized in oblongs, which included mobile artillery able to repel Turkish assaults.

In 1788, in the next war, Ochakov was stormed anew after lengthy bombardment, Izmail following in 1790. At Izmail, the ditches were filled and the walls sealed by ladders. More than a third of the Russian force and two-thirds of their officers were killed or wounded. The prevalence of storming reflected the absence of an equivalent set of rules to those that limited bloodshed in western European sieges, but it was also due to logistical issues. As is so often the case, cultural factors have to be seen as an aspect of a broader set of criteria. The vigorous Sultan Selim III of Turkey (r. 1789–1807) shared in the pride of constructing new fortresses that was shown by many other monarchs. François Kauffer, a French engineer, was asked to produce plans for strengthening fortresses exposed to Russian attack, such as Akkerman and Izmail. For Selim, casting new cannon was part of this process.

With a predisposition to search for signs of decline, Western observers, however, were generally scathing about Turkish fortresses. George Frederick Koehler, a German in the British artillery who inspected Turkish defenses in 1791–92, reported "nothing which can with propriety be called a fortification." Sir William Sidney Smith was similarly critical, while in 1793 George Monro reported of the Dardanelles, "where they have forts, they are so situated as to be nearly useless, either from the construction or from neglect of what is well constructed."[38] Such scathing remarks were also seen in the discussion of fortresses in India and Persia (Iran) by Westerners. In practice, the stone-throwing cannon in the forts in the Dardanelles still posed a major problem in 1807 for British warships seeking to sail through en route to Constantinople.

In the Balkans, fortresses were also important in successive wars between Austria and Turkey. Having captured Belgrade in 1717, the Austrians then refortified it, with a new enceinte (perimeter) of eight substantial bastions. However, defeats in the field and a collapse of confidence led the Austrians to surrender the still unbreached fortress in 1739. Belgrade featured again when the two powers next fought, in 1788–90. Having failed to surprise it in 1788, the Austrians captured the city in 1789 after a massive bombardment and thanks to Turkish defeats in the field. Belgrade surrendered, only to be returned in the subsequent peace.

In Poland, many fortresses were demolished by invading Swedish and Russian forces during the Great Northern War (1700–21). As the

Polish army was greatly reduced in size in 1717, the remaining fortresses lacked the assistance of the army, although they did have some significance in conflicts with Russia in 1733–35 and 1768–72. In 1772, Russia captured Kraków as the result of a three-month siege. The changes in the political situation caused by peace with the Ottomans from 1713 and by growing Russian influence in Poland ensured that many fortresses in southern and eastern Poland were of no more use and became increasingly neglected. Across Poland as a whole, some fortresses were under royal supervision, some governed by the cities, and others in private hands.

RUSSIA

Continuing the seventeenth-century pattern, Russian control was anchored by lines of forts. In the North Caucasus, a rising under Mansur Ushurma, a Chechen Naqshbandi sheik who launched a holy war in 1785, posed serious problems with the defeat of a Russian force in battle, but Mansur failed in his attacks on the forts of Kizliar and Grigoriopolis that year. In turn, he was captured in 1791 when the Russians successfully captured the Turkish fortress at Anapa near the Kuban, a victory eased by success in driving back the local Ottoman field force.[39] The Bashkirs were suppressed to the northeast of the Caspian in the 1720s and 1730s. Russian control was anchored over them by a new line of forts from the river Volga to Orenburg. Orenburg was to hold out when besieged by the rebels during the Pugachev peasant and Cossack rising of 1773–74, as did Yaisk and the citadel of Kazan.

Other lines of forts farther east consolidated Russia's advancing frontiers, defying the Kalmyks and the Zhungars. The southward advances of these fortifications closed the way for nomadic invasions, sealed off regions from hostile reinforcement, and prepared for subsequent successful Russian advances into Kazakhstan and Central Asia in the nineteenth century. Fortresses built on the Irtysh River included Omsk (1716) and Ust'-Kamenogorsk (1719). The Usinskaya Line, based at Troitsk (1743), was constructed along the Uy River to protect the developing agricultural zone to the east of the Urals. The Ishim Line was replaced by Petropavlovsk (west of Omesk, 1752) and its Presnogor'kovskaya Line (1755), in modern northern Kazakhstan. By the second half of the century, a chain of forts, over four thousand kilometers in length, extended from the Caspian to Kuznetsk in the foothills of the Altai Mountains.[40]

In his *Decline and Fall of the Roman Empire*, published between 1776 and 1788, Edward Gibbon presented such fortifications as a vital aid to European civilization:

> Mathematics, chemistry, mechanics, architecture, have been applied to the service of war; and the adverse parties oppose to each other the most elaborate modes of attack and of defence. Historians may indignantly observe that the preparations of a siege would found and maintain a flourishing colony; yet we cannot be displeased that the subversion of a city should be a work of cost and difficulty, or that an industrious people should be protected by those arts, which survive and supply the decay of military virtue. Cannon and fortifications now form an impregnable barrier against the Tartar horse; and Europe is secure from any future irruption by Barbarians.

In practice, these facilities did not stop the flight of the Kalmyks in 1771 or bring victory over the native Chukchi in northeast Siberia, but the general point was correct. The fort at Anadyrsk successfully resisted a Chukchi siege in 1762.

CHINA AND SOUTHEAST ASIA

So also for Chinese advances into Central Asia, notably into and in Mongolia, Xinjiang, and Tibet. Chinese fortification techniques, however, were different from those of the Europeans. The Chinese, who were not seriously threatened at this point, built with earth. These earth forts were to be surprisingly effective against British warships in the nineteenth century. In China's cities, the elite banner units were based in segregated walled compounds. In Lü Hsiung's novel *Nü-hsien wai-shih* (1711), the impact of cannon was condemned:

> At midnight, Moon Queen, together with Instructress Pao and Instructress Man, went and had a look at the situation of Pei-P'ing so she might point out a strategy. She saw the cannon without number had been placed on top of all the city-walls: Red-Barbarians' cannon, shrapnel-cannon, Heaven-exploding cannon and Divine Mechanism

cannon. Moon Queen said. . . . "Such things are not meant for use against people! They turn all who dare to be soldiers into a pulp of flesh. There is no use anymore for the six tactics and three strategies."

Fortifications could also be used by China's opponents, most prominently by the Tibetan minority of western Sichuan, who were known as the Gyalrong or Golden Stream tribes and have also been called Jinchuan. They used strong, well-sited stone fortresses. Such stone towers were also seen elsewhere, for example, from earlier periods, in Sardinia and in the Western Isles off Scotland. It proved very costly and time consuming for the Chinese to take the towers, while bypassing them led to a vulnerability to attack on Chinese supply lines. The 1747–49 war ended inconclusively despite major Chinese efforts. In the second war, that of 1770–76, the Chinese were again hindered by the numerous stone towers of their opponents, which were now strengthened against Chinese cannon by the use of logs and packed earth. Capturing the towers, in which the Chinese used cannon, took much effort but was finally successful. Military technology was important, but so were divisions among the Jinchuan.

In order to control the area, the Chinese then established fortresses of their own in the shape of military colonies staffed with Chinese troops. This was a technique they used on both external and internal frontiers, for example in Xinjiang against the Zhungars, as at Hami. It was a long-standing technique in Chinese history, just as it had been used by the Romans. In response to the Miao revolts in the provinces of Hunan and Guizhou in 1795–97, the Chinese created more garrisons in the region while also introducing military-agricultural colonists, who produced food, and building a wall.

Fortifications and sieges played an important role in conflict in Southeast Asia. The Siamese capital, Ayuthia, to the north of Bangkok, was a major target for attack. Burmese offensives focused on the city. In 1760, disease and the strength of its fortifications thwarted the siege, only for it to be stormed in 1767.

INDIA

In India, there were many fortresses, and Maratha hill forts in west India played a major role in resisting Mughal attack in the 1700s, limiting the impact of Mughal advances. The mobile and decentralized style of Maratha campaigning undermined the logistical basis of their slower-moving opponents' operations. At the same time, alongside logistical considerations, Maratha strategy reflected political and cultural assumptions about place, more particularly the belief that forts were necessary for the symbol and reality of power, a Maratha belief that provided the Mughals with clear targets. Position warfare was different from its maneuverist counterpart; the latter favored the Marathas. In part, Aurangzeb, the Mughal emperor (r. 1658–1707), was successful thanks to his siege artillery. However, on the pattern of his campaigns in the Deccan in the 1680s, exploiting the weaknesses and divisions of opponents proved more useful, notably the bribery of fortress commanders. Moreover, Maratha field forces were not strong enough to break sieges which Aurangzeb covered with field armies.

As elsewhere, the fall of fortifications, sometimes undefended, followed battles. The major victory of Nadir Shah of Persia over the Mughal emperor Muhammad II at Karnal, north of Delhi, in 1739 was followed by the fall of Delhi without resistance.

During the eighteenth century, focused in most cases solely on local control,[41] Indian rulers made little effort to strengthen fortifications by means of adding bastions and reducing the height of high stone walls that were vulnerable to cannon. The standard location for fortresses remained mountains or hills, and the terrain provided a degree of protection not generally seen in Europe. Furthermore, although British officers who had seen service in Europe often remarked how much weaker, irregular, poorly maintained, and lacking sufficient artillery and supplies were the numerous forts that peppered India,[42] the thick walls of these fortresses for long proved resilient.

This was apparent when Gheria and Khanderi in 1718 and Colaba in 1721, forts on the Konkan coast on the Arabian Sea (western India), saw off British naval attacks. However, Gheria was to fall in 1755 to a combined land and sea campaign, with the warships closing in to bombard the position at pistol-shot distance, making a breach for storming, which led to its surrender. Rear Admiral Charles Watson noted, "The walls are very thick, and built with excellent cement, and the best stone I ever saw for such a purpose. We found upwards of two hundred guns . . . had the garrison been provided with men of spirit and knowledge it must have been a much dearer purchase to us."[43]

Western powers introduced new techniques into India. John Corneille noted in 1754 that when Fort St. David in the Carnatic was acquired by the British East India Company, it was "an irregular square fortified according to the Moorish manner, with round towers at the angles," whereas the Company had "modernised the fortifications with a good bastion at each angle, a hornwork before the gateway, two half-moons in the ditch . . . and a well-mined glacis." The Company was fortifying Madras with "several excellent good bastions, and a broad, deep, wet ditch" and at Trichinopoly had replaced a reliance on high battlements and round towers by adding bastions.[44]

Moreover, European and European-trained forces became more significant in India from the 1740s, and the effective artillery they deployed posed a challenge to Indian fortresses. Irrespective of the strength of the fortification, a bold assault or defense could be a key element, as with Robert Clive's successful defense of the fortress of Arcot in the Carnatic against the much stronger local forces of the local nawab in 1750. The fortifications of Arcot had been poorly maintained, but, on behalf of the East India Company, Clive held off a siege that included an assault on two breaches. He took part in the capture of Gheria in 1755.

British attacking tactics relied on opening a breach with artillery and then storming the breach, as in 1791 when the British captured the Mysore hill forts of Nundadroog and Sevendroog, both hitherto thought impregnable,[45] and in 1799 when Seringapatam, the Mysore capital, a formidable position on an island in the river Cauvery, was taken. The rapid breaching of the walls of Ahmadabad, a Maratha stronghold in western India, demonstrated the effectiveness of British artillery and led to its fall on February 15, 1780. The British had arrived on February 10 and on the 12th established a battery for three nineteen-pounders and two howitzers within 350 yards of the wall. The defenders "attempted to disturb the workmen with some small pieces of artillery from towers on the walls, but these were soon silenced by 2 long six-pounders sent down with the covering party." By the evening of the 13th, the cannon had battered a breach one hundred yards wide "besides the defences taken off for a considerable distance to the right and left"; by the evening of the 14th, a level breach 150 yards wide had been made. The fortress was stormed at dawn on the 15th, the defenders being taken by surprise. Many "behaved nobly, drawing their swords and dealing blows around them even after the bayonets were plunged in their bodies."[46] Another force stormed by escalade the fortress of Gwalior, which was generally reckoned impregnable, although that was only so because it was situated on precipitous rocks.

Not all operations were successful, as Lieutenant-Colonel Henry Cosby noted in 1780 when he reported on the consequences of delays in raising ladders:

> By this time the enemy's whole force were collected to oppose us, numbers of blue lights hoisted all along the face attacked and rows of pikes presented through every embrasure so that it now became impossible to enter, as a man no sooner got to the top of the ladder than he was knocked down by a shot or a pike.[47]

Moreover, the Indians were able to deploy artillery to deadly effect against British force. Major Skelly recorded of the British troops hard attacked by Tipu's forces in a redoubt outside Seringapatam on February 7, 1792:

> The enemy now brought three field pieces against us from which, as well as with their musketry and rockets . . . our loss soon became serious . . . the want of water was severely felt . . . these different attacks were still attended with loss on our side, and the redoubt was now become a horrid scene of carnage—many had fallen, and the rest, through heat, exertion, and thirst were almost exhausted. Most of them, however, stood gallantly to their duty, though in a few signs of despondency began to appear.[48]

Indian rulers developed an effective attacking capability in the closing years of the century. In the late 1780s and early 1790s, Mahadji Shinde built up the firepower of his army, and his artillery contributed to the fall of the major Rajput fortress of Chitor in a matter of weeks.

IRAN

In Persia (Iran), the emphasis was on battle, not siege, which often proved difficult. Strong in cavalry, not infantry, the Safavid (Persian) army sent to suppress an Afghan rebellion mounted an unsuccessful siege of Kandahar in 1711 and was heavily defeated as it retreated. In 1721, an Afghan army besieged Kirman in eastern Persia but failed to take the citadel. In contrast, in 1722, advancing into central Persia, the Afghans, after defeating a far larger Persian army at Gulnabad, block-aded the capital, Isfahan, defeating attempts at relief but lacking the numbers to storm the city and the artillery to breach its walls. Famine in the city caused by a seven-month siege finally led to its surrender.[49]

In turn, Nadir Shah, who made himself shah of Persia in 1736, captured Kandahar in 1738 after a nine-month siege, in large part due to help from within the city, which was a repeated feature in South Asian military history, but far less so in Europe. Nadir, however, pre-ferred battles to sieges because the latter posed a major logistical chal-lenge, and it would be difficult to maintain the cohesion and morale of a besieging army composed in large part of tribal levies, a pattern that was very familiar in much conflict. His lack of adequate siege artillery left risky, wasteful assaults or lengthy blockades as the only alternatives when attacking fortified positions. Blockade meant delay and de-manded patience, which did not suit his personality. In advance of his cannon, Nadir arrived at Turkish-held Kirkuk in northern Iraq in 1743 and was unable to capture the town, but once the artillery arrived, a day's bombardment led to the surrender of the fortress. However, he was repelled from Mosul and Baghdad, the major Turkish bases. De-spite the establishment of a siege train, siegecraft was still a capability in which the army was deficient and storming attempts on Mosul failed.[50] In 1776, Karim Khan, who dominated Persia in the 1760s and 1770s, blockaded Turkish-ruled Basra into surrendering after a thirteen-month siege.

In Persia's internecine struggles, control over the cities, notably Isfa-han, Tehran, Shiraz, and Kirman, played a major role. In the late 1780s and early 1790s, the Qajar tribe under Agha Muhammad (r. 1779–97) took over the entire country, destroying the rival Zands. Isfahan was captured in 1785, Tehran accepted Agha Muhammad's power in 1786, Shiraz was relieved in 1792 when attacked by the Zands, and Kirman, besieged, was taken by treachery in 1794, with all the surviving men blinded. Farther east, control over Herat, Balkh, Kandahar, Kabul, Peshawar, and Lahore played a key role in power politics, both within the Afghan state and in relations with its neighbors: Persia, the Uzbeks, the Mughals, and the Sikhs.

BRITISH ISLES

The major fortified British positions were naval dockyards with their munition stores, notably Portsmouth, or overseas bases, notably those in India, the West Indies, and North America, as well as Gibraltar and Fort St. Philip on Minorca. The last, exposed by a lack of naval support, was successfully taken by the French in 1756 and 1782. In Britain itself, fortification was largely pressed on in Scotland to defend against a possible pro-Jacobite rising or invasion. There was not a program of fortification elsewhere in the British Isles. There was no system of citadels protecting major domestic centers of government, no as-it-were policy fortresses for that end.

Indeed, when in 1745 the Jacobites moved from the Scottish Highlands and later invaded England, they benefited from the weakness or absence of its fortifications. Not only did this ensure that the Jacobites did not have to fight their way through a series of positions, losing time and manpower as they did so, but it also meant that the British army lacked a network of bases that could provide shelter and replenish supplies. The campaign revealed the mostly inconsequential nature of fortifications left over from an earlier era of warfare and, linked to this, the extent to which the state was poorly defended. There were fortified positions that affected the campaign, notably Carlisle, Edinburgh, and Newcastle. The last, where there was a large force to protect the crossing of the River Tyne, as well as the possibility of shipping in reinforcements, ensured that the Jacobite advance south did not occur along the east coast. So also with Berwick, where the crossing of the River Tweed was protected by a well-garrisoned fortress where extensive works had been built as recently as 1717–21.

Instead, the Jacobite advance was launched farther west, via Carlisle. Despite fortifications, both Carlisle and, earlier, the city (but not castle) of Edinburgh fell to the Jacobites. Moreover, there was no resistance to their advance in most of the towns they entered. On the western route into England, these included, south of poorly fortified Carlisle which had resisted, successively Lancaster, Preston, Manchester, and Derby, none of which was fortified or contained garrisons. As a consequence, rivers, such as the Ribble and the Trent, on which Preston and Derby respectively sat, were crossed with ease. The defenses of both the castle and the city of Carlisle were in a weak state. The walls were not covered by a system of outworks designed to keep the trenches and artillery of besiegers at a distance, and they were short of gunners. Had it been well defended, it could have been bypassed, as in 1715, for the Jacobites lacked sufficient numbers to blockade it effectively, adequate artillery to bombard it, and experience in siegecraft. Fears of a storming led the militia and the citizens to urge the commander to surrender, and this resulted in capitulation after a siege of less than a week. The Jacobites turned back after capturing Derby, not because of the strength of any fortifications that lay before them but due to reports about British field armies.

When Charles Edward Stuart retreated into Scotland, he left a garrison of 350 men in Carlisle Castle to show that he was determined to return to England and to avoid the necessity of besieging the town on his return. It was hoped that such a force would delay the Duke of Cumberland's pursuit. The defenders, who had only ten cannon, sought to strengthen the defenses with ramparts and iron spikes and burned down houses that might cover the attackers. Arriving on December 21, 1745, Cumberland described the castle as "an old hen-coop, which he would speedily bring down about their ears, when he should have got artillery."[51] He summoned guns from the port of Whitehaven, had batteries constructed for them, and blockaded the defenders, cutting off their water supply. The siege was not without its problems from "the wetness of the season, which makes it difficult to raise the earth, the badness of the ways for conveying the artillery, the want of engineers, ammunition etc."[52] On December 27, the cannon arrived, and their superior firepower doomed the defenders:

> A battery of six eighteen-pounders was perfected the 27th at night, and on Saturday was fixed with good success, but the shot failed a little so that the fire was slacker on Sunday. However, this little loss of time was of no consequence as a supply is received which will be continued as far as there is occasion; and the battery was augmented

that night. Overtures for a surrender were made Saturday night and again on Sunday night, but his R.H. [Royal Highness, Cumberland] would not hearken to anything.[53]

Cumberland set the match to the first gun himself, a symbolically important step, and his guns reputedly fired over 1,100 shots on the 28th. The outgunned defenders saw their fortifications battered and the walls breached in two places. They surrendered on the 30th, unable to obtain any terms other than the promise that they should not be put to the sword but be reserved for the royal pleasure. Cumberland reported, "I wish I could have blooded the soldiers with these villains but it would have cost us many a brave man, and it comes to the same end, as they have no sort of claim to the king's mercy."[54] Many were hanged for treason.

The following month, the Jacobites besieged well-fortified Stirling Castle.[55] The besiegers had little to counter the castle's artillery. An unsympathetic townsman recorded, on January 26, "great firing from the trenches upon the castle with small arms, from nine in the morning till six at night, without any execution." On the 28th, the Jacobites finished their battery, but when, the following morning, they began to fire their three cannon at the castle, the defenders replied with thirteen cannon which "dismounted their guns . . . broke their carriages and levelled their trenches in a sad manner, and a great number of them killed."[56]

Similarly, in March 1746, the Jacobites besieged Blair Castle. As they only had two four-pounders, one of which was inaccurate, and nobody trained in undermining fortifications, the seven-foot-thick walls were impregnable. An attempt to starve the garrison into surrender did not succeed before a relief force arrived. Fort Augustus was also attacked in March. It surrendered after a siege of only two days and the explosion of the defenders' magazine. The Jacobites there pressed on to attack Fort William, but Grant, the siege engineer, who had been so successful at Fort Augustus, was killed by a cannonball, and his French replacement proved incompetent. The defense was helped by having enough supplies as well as a determined commander and was stronger than Fort Augustus. A sally by the garrison destroyed the Jacobite batteries, leading the Jacobites to abandon the siege. Morale fell, desertion rose, and Charles Edward was obliged to retreat, abandoning his guns.

The garrison itself had been running very short of supplies. Soon after, on April 16, the conflict was settled by Cumberland's total victory at Culloden.

Bringing to a close a rebellion that had threatened the total overthrow of Hanoverian rule in Britain, Culloden was followed by pressure for a renewed program of fortification in Scotland, although earlier such orders, as in 1725,[57] had not ensured peace. The victorious general, William, Duke of Cumberland, wrote, "It will be absolutely necessary that new forts be erected here [Inverness], and where Fort Augustus stood." His protégé, William, 2nd Earl of Albemarle, followed up by arguing, "Fort George, Fort Augustus and Fort William should be made strong, defensible, and capable of containing considerable garrisons; the barrack of Inversnaid at the head of Loch Lomond should be made defensible."[58]

A major new fort near Inverness, Fort George, was begun at Arderseer Point in 1749. Costing over £100,000, a sum that was a tribute to the power of the British state, it was a state-of-the-art bastioned fortification protecting Inverness from an invasion via the Moray Firth that remains impressive to this day. That it did not hear a shot fired in anger is beside the point, for the deterrent aspect of fortification was, and is, a crucial one, a point also true of military systems as a whole, whether designed for defense or attack or both.

Ireland was poorly fortified. Henry Conway reported from Dublin in 1756,

> Among the places commonly spoke of as garrisons the greatest part are improperly termed so, such as Dublin, Cork, Limerick etc. which not being in any state of defence are no otherwise to be considered as garrisons than as they want some troops to defend any stores, trade, etc that are in them and to keep the Papists [Catholics] in awe, so that the only places which deserve to be thought of as garrisons to be held against an enemy are almost reduced to Charlesfort and Duncannon Fort now repairing.[59]

Four years later, Commodore François Thurot in command of three ships and six hundred troops attacked the Irish fortress of Carrickfergus. The poorly maintained castle had a sixty-foot breach in the wall, while the cannon were dismounted and unable to respond to the French attack. Nevertheless, the garrison, about two hundred strong, supported by some of the local gentry, resisted both in the town and at the castle until, their ammunition exhausted, they surrendered.

DEMILITARIZATION

This pattern was more generally the case. On and near the frontiers, new fortifications protected newly won and also apparently vulnerable positions. Elsewhere, however, there was a general failure to keep up with the need to maintain fortresses if they were to be fit for purpose other than for maintaining civil order. This was a failure that was understandable in terms of the costs and garrisoning involved and one in part tackled by the use today of police. In Ireland, George, 4th Viscount Townshend, who became lord lieutenant in 1767, focused on domestic order. Supporting the recruitment of Catholics to the army, he also introduced a system of military organization based on well-constructed barracks and magazines.

Private individuals in many states increasingly chose to rely on the state to defend them. In England, Brampton Bryan Castle, a Herefordshire stronghold that had resisted Royalist siege in 1643 only to fall and be sacked in 1644, was replaced by a new brick house built by the Harley family in the early eighteenth century. Castle Howard, the name for the seat of the Earls of Carlisle designed by Sir John Vanbrugh, was no castle, no more than Hearst Castle overlooking the Californian coast was when built from 1919 to 1951.

During the 1745–46 Jacobite rebellion, John, Lord Glenorchy, a supporter of the government and a Scottish landowner, wrote to his daughter, "I have often repented taking out the iron bars from the windows and sashing them, and taking away a great iron door, and weakening the house as to resistance by adding modern wings to it. If it had remained in the old castle way as it was before, I might have slept very sound in it, for their whole army could not have taken it without cannon."[60]

However, in 1762, which was internally more peaceful, and with the French fleet heavily defeated three years earlier, Elizabeth Montagu could reflect, "A virtuoso or a dilletanti may stand as secure in these times behind his Chinese rail as the knight on his battlements in former days."[61] The establishment of militia forces to supplement regular armies further encouraged a move away from fortification for domestic security as, later in the nineteenth century, did the development of police forces.

Most castles continued to fall into ruin. Ludlow Castle, once the headquarters of the Council of the Marches, fell into disuse when the council was dissolved in 1689. In his *Tour* (1724–26), Daniel Defoe wrote, "Very perfection of decay, all the fine courts, the royal apartments, halls, and rooms of state, lie open, abandoned and some of them falling down." Fire could contribute to decay. In 1716, Cloppenburg Castle in Lower Saxony was largely destroyed by a fire. Ruins themselves became picturesque. Richard Wilson, who visited Okehampton Castle in 1771, soon after painted a Romantic vision of the hilltop castle with its ruins silhouetted against the evening sky. Aristocrats might have unprecedented wealth and might live in castles, such as Alnwick (Duke of Northumberland) and Powderham (Earl of Devon), but these had become stately homes and they lacked forces of their own. The role of defensive fortifications had been replaced by a state monopoly.

New stately homes, such as Blenheim, itself built for a famous general, were undefended or, rather, defended in terms of the estate and not to provide protection against an attacking army. Much work was devoted in Britain, as elsewhere, to walls, gates, and lodges that provided bounds to the estate, and in England from the late 1770s, game preserves were increasingly protected by spring guns and mantraps. New houses, in contrast, no longer bore defensive features in the British Isles, while those on old houses were not preserved. Fortification was reduced to fantasy, as in fortified walls for example at Castle Howard, the new seat of the Earl of Carlisle, as described above; to garden follies; and to mock Gothic castles. The approach from the landscaped grounds to the house was easy for people, with the major obstacle being the ha-ha, a ditch to keep the castle away from the house itself. The new neo-Gothic style of the later eighteenth century was not designed to provide strength and was almost a parody. Indeed, castellated features very much became an architectural device that lacked any fortification feature, as, for example, with Cragside in the nineteenth century. In the 1720s, the remains of a castle in Liverpool had been demolished to make way for a church. In Meersburg, the Prince-Bishops of Constance left their medieval castle and built a splendid Baroque-style palatial residence that lacked defenses.

The declining significance of walls was also seen with cities. London's walls fell into decay. Karlsruhe, begun by Karl Wilhelm of Baden-Durlach in 1715, was without walls, although most German cities did not lose their walls until the nineteenth century. In 1771, William, 2nd Earl of Shelburne, decrying the corruption of Genoa, also noted "Fortifications ruinous."[62] In 1781, Joseph II demolished many of the Barrier fortifications.

FITNESS FOR PURPOSE

Fitness for purpose was a key concept and helped direct and reflect a variety in specifications and tasks. Equations of defensive strength and offensive firepower were important in determining the potency of fortifications and the success of sieges, although they should not lead to the discounting of leadership, unit cohesion, and fighting quality. Rather than assuming a perfect state of fortification or system of siegecraft, it is necessary to evaluate systems, not only with reference to the specifications that led to these equations but also within the constraints of manpower and cost. This returns attention from the theoretical and systemic to the particular, specifically to the political character of decision making. The latter could focus on the benefits that might result if resources were employed differently.

Most obviously, apart from the cost of construction, major fortifications required large garrisons and numerous cannon that could not readily be used for other purposes. Those near Susa, designed to protect Piedmont from French invasion along the Alpine valley of the Dora Riparia, were estimated in 1764 to require a garrison of nearly four thousand troops.[63] Such forces could act as an operational reserve, but more commonly garrison forces were smaller, they lacked mobility and flexibility, and, as a result of a lack of training and a process of ossification, they could even be without combat effectiveness. These forces tended to be made up from second-rank units and often older soldiers. Indeed, fortifications were often effective, as in Spanish America, if supported by a local militia. This could compensate for the limitations of regular forces available.[64]

As noted earlier, choices over sieges were not dictated by technology but reflected a range of factors, both contextual and specific. For example, the prestige of the attack, rather than a reliance on ideas and practices of deliberate siegecraft, could encourage attempts to storm fortresses, but so could a need for speed, both in order to press on to achieve results and so as to deal with logistical problems.[65]

The notions of fitness for purpose, already raised when discussing Montalembert, were seen more generally. For example, James Glenie, a British military engineer, criticized the plan of Charles, 3rd Duke of Richmond, the master general of the ordnance, for fortifying the key British naval bases of Portsmouth and Plymouth. This measure was backed by the government of William Pitt the Younger, not least as a means to free the fleet for wartime offensive operations. Glenie, however, argued that the fortifications would cost too much and would limit the resources available for the navy, both reasonable points.[66] His *A Short Essay on the Modes of Defence Best Adapted to the Situation and Circumstances of This Island* (1785) contributed to the parliamentary defeat of the measure in 1786, largely on cost grounds. Glenie followed with *Observations on the Duke of Richmond's Extensive Plans of Fortification* (1786) and had to leave the army in 1787.[67]

Fitness for purpose was also a matter for siegecraft. Contemplating the invasion of Mysore, Charles, 2nd Earl Cornwallis, the British governor general and commander in chief in India, wrote to General Sir William Medows in 1791,

> We can only be said to be as nearly independent of contingencies, as can be expected in war, when we are possessed of a complete battering train, and can move it with the army; and whilst we carry a large stock of provisions with us, that ample magazines shall be lodged in strong places in our rear and at no great distance from the scene of our intended operations . . . I hope that by a systematic activity and vigour, we shall be able to obtain decided advantage over our enemy before the commencement of the ensuing rains.[68]

Fitness for purpose frequently referred to domestic control. The Bergenhus fortress in Bergen in Norway, which was completed in the late seventeenth century, was kept operational until the start of the nineteenth century in order to control the area on behalf of the Danish crown, a role that was encouraged by a local rising in 1765. In 1715, Joseph Clément, Prince-Bishop of Liège, claimed that "it is absolutely necessary that the citadel of Liège remains a fortress capable of holding the common people of Liège in awe. Without this restraint there will be no security for honest men, only murder and brigandage." He later wrote of the need "to prevent the evil schemes of the majority of the Liègois who would like to become a republic . . . only troops and fortresses can hold them to their obedience."[69]

WAR OF AMERICAN INDEPENDENCE

Forts indeed continued to play a major role in the last quarter of the century, both as defensive positions and as targets for attack. The War of American Independence (1775–83) is not generally seen in terms of fortifications, and many fortified positions fell rapidly. In the nineteenth century, British naval capability was to lead to a heavy emphasis in the United States on coastal fortifications in military doctrine, force structure, and expenditure. This, however, was not a viable solution during the War of Independence. The relevant forts were lacking at the strategic level. Operationally, garrisons in positions such as Fort Washington and Ticonderoga were unable to prevent British advances, as in the campaigns of 1776 and 1777. Instead, by fixing troops as garrisons and exposing them to attack, forts were actually a source of vulnerability, which the fall of Fort Washington in 1776 demonstrated. The British drove the Americans from their entrenchments in the Battle of Bunker Hill (1775) and rapidly captured Fort Washington (1776), the Delaware River defenses and the Hudson forts (1777), Savannah (1778), and, more particularly, despite its large garrison, Charleston (1780). The subsequent discussion of the war in the United States did not focus on fortifications or on sieges apart from the successful Franco-American siege of Yorktown in 1781, an effective siege of a force that had surrendered its mobility, a siege that overcame the resolution and resilience of the British war effort.

Nevertheless, fortifications were important at tactical, operational, and strategic levels. Much of the American strategy in the war was determined by their repeatedly proven inability to defend their own fortified positions and by their shifting ability to confront the British in a defended, fortified position. Fort Sullivan, on a sandspit that protected Charleston harbor, was attacked by British warships in 1776, but its thick earth walls, faced by palmetto logs, were not badly damaged by the British cannonballs, while the warships suffered heavily from the well-aimed cannon in the fort. The British failure was very important to the consolidation of the revolution in the South, although they were to be able to try again and to capture Charleston in 1780 after a brief siege of poorly commanded defenders. British artillery fire set houses alight, leading to a collapse of the defenders' morale. In turn, in 1781, Nathanael Greene pressed for the seizure of "all their little outposts":[70] the British positions that offered an appearance of control in the hinterlands of the well-fortified posts.

The Americans successfully used field fortifications, notably stone walls in New England in 1775 and breastworks and redoubts, against attacking British forces at the Battle of Saratoga (1777). Defeated there, Burgoyne argued that American entrenchments should be bombarded by artillery or outflanked by fast-moving light infantry units. He told the House of Commons in May 1779 that

> artillery was extremely formidable to raw troops; that in a country of posts, it was essentially necessary against the best troops; that it was yet more applicable to the enemy we were to combat; because the mode of defence they invariably adopted, and at which they were beyond all other nations expert, was that of entrenchment covered with strong abattis [felled trees with boughs pointing out] when to dislodge them by any other means, might be attended with continued and important losses . . . block-houses, a species of fortification unique to America.[71]

In contrast, the American inability, by both siege and storm, to take well-defended Quebec in the winter of 1775–76 was decisive in the failure of the attempt to conquer Canada. An attempt to storm Quebec in the early hours of December 31, 1775, under cover of snowfall, was betrayed by a deserter. However, in the darkness and the heavy snow, the defenders' confusion gave the outnumbered Americans a chance, only for the death of one commander and the wounding of another to rob them of the necessary decisiveness.

After this failure, the siege continued, but the Americans were affected by expiring enlistments; a shortage of provisions, powder, and money; and a lack of support from the local population. Making clear the reliance of siegecraft on a military infrastructure, an issue that regu-

larly confronted insurgent forces, an account from the American headquarters outside Quebec in March 1776 listed

> a catalogue of complaints. Indifferent physicians and surgeons . . . a
> few cannon without any quantity of powder or ball will never take a
> fortress if by a cannonade it is to be done. Three small mortars with a
> few shells will cut a despicable figure at a bomb battery and expose
> our weakness. Suppose you had a good train of ordnance with plenty
> of ammunition, we have not an artillery man to serve them . . . not an
> artificer . . . no engineer.[72]

A British relief force arrived in May when the ice melted on the St.
Lawrence River. The British, in turn, had abandoned Boston in March
1776 once American cannon threatened its anchorage, which demonstrated the reliance of fortified positions on their communications and
supplies, but the Americans failed to repeat this success against New
York, Savannah, or Charleston once they had been captured by the
British in 1776, 1778, and 1780 respectively. That was despite a Franco-
American siege of Savannah in 1779, a siege, however, that resolved
itself into a badly organized and unsuccessful assault. Thanks to a deserter, the British were forewarned, the attacking columns did not coor-
dinate their operations, and, despite the bravery of the South Carolina
Continentals and the French, they were repulsed with heavy losses.

At the operational level, Yorktown indicated the problems created
for defending forces in field fortifications if they were heavily outnumbered and, at the tactical level, the impact of artillery. The relief by sea
promised Cornwallis, the British commander, at Yorktown did not arrive because the French fleet was able to hold the entrance to the
Chesapeake against British naval attack on September 5. On land,
Cornwallis was outnumbered and unable to risk battle in the open field.
The American-French force took up positions around Yorktown in 1781
on the night of September 28 and on the 29th. Encouraged by the
promise of relief by sea, Cornwallis abandoned his outer works on the
night of the 29th in order to tighten his position in the face of the more
numerous besiegers. Washington's men occupied the outer works on
the 30th, although they had to cope with heavy fire from Cornwallis's
cannon until, on October 6, the besiegers' artillery arrived. They were
then able to begin conventional siegeworks against what was, by the
standards of the age, a weakly fortified position. On the night of the 6th,

the besiegers began to dig the first parallel, a trench parallel to the fortifications and a crucial part of normal siegeworks. They completed it on the 9th, and that afternoon they began the bombardment with a larger and heavier artillery force than that of Cornwallis, causing heavy casualties and damage and badly affecting the morale of the defenders. Cornwallis's headquarters were heavily damaged, forcing him to use a cave for staff meetings. On October 11, as his opponents dug a second and closer parallel, Cornwallis reported

> The enemy made their first parallel on the night of the 6th at the distance of 600 yards, and have perfected it, and constructed places of arms and batteries, with great regularity and caution. On the evening of the 9th their batteries opened and have since continued firing, without intermission, with about 40 pieces of cannon, mostly heavy, and 16 mortars. . . . Many of our works are considerably damaged; with such works on disadvantageous ground, against so powerful an attack we cannot hope to make a very long resistance.

On the 12th, he added a postscript: "Last night the enemy made their second parallel at the distance of 300 yards. We continue to lose men very fast."[73]

Many of Cornwallis's cannon had been silenced by the bombardment, while quite a few of his troops were wounded or ill. On the night of October 14, the besiegers bravely stormed the two redoubts that obstructed the path of the second parallel to the river. Cornwallis wrote the next day, "Experience has shown that our fresh earthen works do not resist their powerful artillery. . . . The safety of the place is therefore so precarious that I cannot recommend that the fleet and army should run great risk in endeavouring to save us."[74]

On the 16th, a sortie designed to spike the besiegers' guns had had only a limited and temporary effect. Cornwallis therefore decided to try to cross the York River that night, only to be thwarted by the weather. In Yorktown, under a ferocious bombardment that could not be countered, Cornwallis on the 17th proposed an armistice in order to settle terms for his surrender. As Cornwallis correctly pointed out, Yorktown, although entrenched, was an exposed camp. As was the case for the French at Dien Bien Phu in Vietnam in 1954, an inherently problematic position took on a disproportionate significance due to the ability it offered for an attack on weakly positioned forces.

As a result of Britain retaining New York and Charleston, the war ended with both sides obliged to negotiate terms. Equally, the strategic depth enjoyed by the Americans made their loss of individual positions less consequential. The situation was very different from 1778 when France intervened in the conflict, being followed by Spain (1779) and the Dutch (1780). This led to conflict in the colonial world, notably in the Caribbean, West Africa, and South Asia. The positions attacked lacked strategic depth. As a result, sieges were more significant but not necessarily successful. This was conspicuously demonstrated with the Spanish failure to capture Gibraltar.

EUROPE, 1780–1792

Fortresses and sieges remained significant in Europe in the 1780s. Austrian success in thwarting Prussia in the War of the Bavarian Succession (1778–79) owed much to the ability of Field Marshal Lacy to use massive concentrations of defensive forces in strong positions in the Bohemian hills in order to thwart Frederick the Great's bold plans for the conquest of Bohemia. Field fortifications played a significant role. Frederick II's move into northeast Bohemia was blocked by Austrian fieldworks along the western bank of the upper Elbe. He wanted to breach the Austrian positions near Jaromiersch but decided that their lines, composed of batteries, palisades, and *abates* (ramparts constructed of felled trees) supported by Field Marshal Lacy's one-hundred-thousand-strong Elbe army, were too strong. The Austrian reliance on the defensive denied Frederick the opportunity to catch advancing forces at a vulnerable moment.

The war was followed by a postwar Austrian fortification strategy designed to block possible Prussian invasion routes into Bohemia, particularly at Theresienstadt (later, in World War II, a German concentration camp) and Josephstadt, which were built to complement the prewar construction of Königgratz. Not all fortifications, however, were kept in good shape. In 1787, Major General Charles O'Hara complained from Gibraltar of "defenceless works, unserviceable artillery, exhausted stores, weak garrison etc etc all of which is most true to a scandalous degree."[75]

Sieges remained significant. The victorious Prussian intervention in the Dutch Crisis (or civil disorder) of 1787 ultimately rested on a successful and speedy siege of Amsterdam. At a very different scale, Russian victory over the Turks in the war of 1787–92 similarly rested on victorious sieges, notably, in 1788, of Ochakov, which became the center of an international crisis in 1791 as Britain and Prussia unsuccessfully pressed Russia to return it to the Turks as part of a peace settlement.

Instead of billeting troops with civilians and in taverns, barracks became more important in Austria, France, Prussia, Russia, and many other states in the second half of the century. This meant that there were more military positions to protect.

CONCLUSIONS

The eighteenth century is commonly presented by military historians in terms of a move from a somewhat static, limited warfare of positional operations under the ancien régime to a more vigorous style of campaigning under revolutionaries who pursued total warfare. The latter is presented as a goal, means, and style identified with the French Revolution, but often seen as prefigured in part with the American Revolution. Sieges are generally located in terms of supposedly limited, ancien régime warfare, and they suffer, accordingly, from the pejorative assumptions of indecisiveness and anachronism that are frequently asserted. So also with the argument that the means of conducting siege warfare became less bloody and ruinous.[76]

As part of a more generally misleading account of the nature, purposes, and timing of the character and changes in European warfare, this approach is seriously flawed. It does not capture the energy, determination, and, often, savagery involved in much siege warfare, for example the successful assaults on the Schellenberg height above Donauwörth (1704), Bergen-op-Zoom (1747), and Ochakov (1788) by the British, French, and Russians respectively. Jean-Martin de la Colonie, a French defender, recalled of the storming of the Schellenberg height in 1704, a storming in which the successful Anglo-Dutch force lost about 1,500 dead and 4,000 wounded:

> We were all fighting hand to hand, hurling them back as they clutched at the parapet; men were slaying, or tearing at the muzzles of guns and the bayonets which pierced their entrails; crushing under their feet their own wounded comrades, and even gouging out their opponents' eyes with their nails, when the grip was so close that neither could use their weapons.[77]

In 1714, Barcelona was defended with popular fervor against an overwhelming Franco-Spanish attack. A worker militia manned the walls, while popular enthusiasm was sustained by religious commitment, including the use of sacred relics.[78] There was similar activity when Genoa resisted Austrian attack in 1747, including women working on the fortifications.

Nor does the account of limited warfare capture the decisive strategic and political consequences that might stem from success or failure in sieges. Thus, success at Schellenberg was followed by the laying waste of much of Bavaria in an unsuccessful attempt to force Max Emmanuel, the Elector of Bavaria, to abandon his alliance with France. Both of these episodes tend to be ignored in general accounts, which focus instead on Marlborough's victory over a Franco-Bavarian army later in the year at Blenheim. The narrative and analysis of change mentioned in the first paragraph of this chapter's conclusions also has little meaning for non-Western societies.

Thus, as with other periods, rather than locating and minimizing the role of fortifications in a flawed general theory of military developments, it is more appropriate to note their continued military significance and the degree to which this was readily apparent to contemporaries. This role of fortifications, both fixed and field, was an aspect of the degree to which, although improvements in firepower might appear to give an advantage to the defense, the situation was more complex. Attackers could focus on artillery, but frontal attacks could still be successful, both in the field against entrenched units and against fixed fortifications. Moreover, maneuver warfare remained an alternative to siegecraft. This situation looked forward to that in the nineteenth century.

6

THE NINETEENTH CENTURY

The nineteenth century is not noted for its fortifications. There is no name to match that of Vauban, and there are few dramatic remains to stand alongside those of earlier centuries. Although there are exceptions, for example the Indian Mutiny (1857–59), the majority of the most famous clashes, certainly in Europe, Africa, and the Americas, are those of battles not sieges, and there is a sense of armies on a scale that prevailed over the obstacle posed by mere fortifications. Moreover, the increased range, artillery, mobility, and lethality of what was then modern artillery, both on land and at sea, made fortifications appear far more vulnerable. Each of these elements indeed had much significance, but they do not capture the continuing importance of fortifications.

EUROPE, 1792–1815

The situation during the French Revolutionary and Napoleonic Wars, from 1792 to 1815, is instructive. Battles were generally more important than sieges, in part because the doctrines and practice of the offensive, of mass formations, and of the destruction of the other side's forces could encourage the bypassing of fortresses. For example, after their advance on Paris was checked at Valmy in 1792 by a large French army drawn up in defensive positions and relying on superiority in manpower and cannon, the Prussians under the Duke of Brunswick retreated.

They ended the siege of Thionville and abandoned the major fortified positions of Longwy and Verdun they had captured. Attacked by the Austrians in 1792, Lille could not be completely besieged as they lacked sufficient troops. Instead, they tried to bombard the city into submission, destroying about six hundred houses. However, this did not lead to surrender, and the Austrians then retreated as the balance of advantage in the war moved toward the French. French victory at Jemappes on November 6, 1792, was followed, within a month, by the capture of all the Austrian positions in Belgium.

The folly of a focus on sieges was seen in Belgium in 1793. At Neerwinden, on March 18, the counterattacking Austrians defeated the French. However, the victorious commander, Prince Josias of Saxe-Coburg, did not march on Paris but, rather, sought the apparently surer capture of a major fortress that could also serve as a base. The campaign was frittered away in a series of sieges and, late in 1793, energetic French leaders, benefiting from the largely uncoordinated nature of their spread-out opponents, drove the invaders back by battles in which they achieved local concentrations of strength. Battle very much preempted siege in this case.

Nevertheless, the career of Napoleon showed, most clearly at Toulon (1793), Mantua (1796–97), and Acre (1799), that sieges could still be as important as battles. Success in capturing Toulon from a British-backed Royalist opposition made his name. Mantua demonstrated that sieges could lead to relief attempts that caused important battles: in Napoleon's case repeated victories over the Austrians that left France as the clearly dominant regional force. The inability to capture Acre led to the failure of his Palestine campaign. Acre was well fortified and ably defended, with the defense supported by the British navy. Napoleon's field artillery was short of ammunition. Earlier in 1799, Napoleon had captured El Arish from Ottoman (Turkish) forces on February 19 after a heavy bombardment by twelve-pounders, and mortars brought to an end a siege that had begun on February 11. Jaffa had fallen to direct assault by the French.

Much depended on the particular theater of operations, notably its geopolitics, environment, existing fortifications, and logistical circumstances. Fortified positions, such as Almeida, Badajoz, Burgos, Cadiz, Ciudad Rodrigo, Pamplona, San Sebastian, and Saragossa, and the sieges of them, were very important in the Peninsular War in Portugal and Spain (1808–14).[1] The creation, by Arthur, 1st Duke of Wellington, of the Lines of Torres Vedras, in order to protect both Lisbon and his army, led to the establishment of a large-scale entrenched position, its ends resting on major water lines, that thwarted the French advance in 1810–11 and then exposed the French to the problems of inadequate supplies. Exacerbating the impact of disease, this caused heavy French casualties. In the end, the French under Marshal Massena fell back. What in effect had been a large-scale siege of Lisbon by land had failed.

The French also failed in their long-standing siege from February 1810 to August 1812 of Cadiz, the capital of Spanish resistance, during the Peninsular War. Cadiz also challenged French control of Andalusia. In this siege, the Spaniards benefited greatly from the provision of support by the British navy, which prevented the French from starving the city into surrender. A key point in defending both the Lines of Terres Vedras and Cadiz was to deny ports to the French, which was a vital strategic requirement. Had Napoleon acquired these Atlantic naval bases, he would have been able to mount a far more effective challenge to British maritime commerce, on which the war effort depended. In contrast, held by Spanish forces, inland Saragossa fell after a bitter siege in 1808–09, with repeated French assaults finally successful.

Although spectacular and heroic, British siege warfare in the interior of Iberia was less significant. In 1812, Wellington stormed by night the two key French-held Spanish border fortresses of Ciudad Rodrigo and Badajoz, which controlled major routes between Portugal and Spain. These well-defended positions fell when costly attacks on breaches created by artillery fire were supported by subsidiary attacks at other points. Visiting the positions today makes clear the difficulties faced by the British. An attempt to storm Burgos later that year failed. Wellington's siegecraft suffered from the absence of an effective engineering branch. Nevertheless, more generally, victory in the field provided opportunities to capture undefended cities and to press on with sieges, that at Salamanca (1812) leading to the fall of Madrid and the unsuccessful attack on Burgos, while that at Vitoria (1813) enabled Wellington to besiege and capture San Sebastian and Pamplona, both formidable positions. The former fell only after a difficult siege in which the attackers lost heavily in two assaults.[2]

Fortresses in bulk, however, could have a value of their own. Explaining the weakness of his position on Spain's Mediterranean coast in

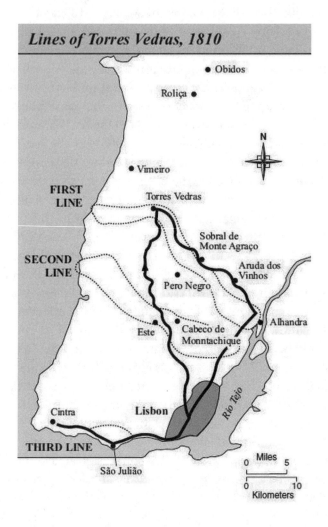

Figure 6.1. Lines of Torres Vedras

1813, Lieutenant General John Murray wrote, "The French General [Suchet] possessed in every direction fortresses around me to cover his army if defeated, to furnish his supplies, or to retire to if he wished to avoid an action for the purposes of bringing up more troops."[3]

Moreover, attacks on fortified positions faced many problems. The French had succeeded in storming Dutch-held Bergen-op-Zoom in the Netherlands in 1747, but a British attempt, in 1814, to storm the fortress, then French-held, failed. The British fought their way into the town, but the fighting then turned against them, the columns that were in the town received insufficient support and instead were ordered to retreat, and they were driven out with three thousand casualties. The British had been similarly unsuccessful inside Buenos Aires in 1807, with its barricaded streets and numerous garrisons actively supported by the population, and this failure led to the surrender of the British force.

The similar outcomes of the two operations indicated that formal fortifications were not necessarily the crucial element. Buenos Aires lacked the defenses of Bergen-op-Zoom but was still a formidable challenge, notably logistically. More generally, the ability of commanders on the two sides in sieges was usually a key factor.[4]

The British thought it worthwhile to invest in fortifications to protect against invasion. When in 1797 a French expedition had approached Fishguard Harbor, the garrison in the fort there had only three rounds of ammunition. However, in the 1800s, the British built numerous Martello towers along the south coast. Napoleon also built fortifications, as in Piedmont where he overhauled fortresses and also built smaller forts to protect bridges he had strengthened.

As with the sixteenth to eighteenth centuries, sieges generally played a smaller role in conflict in central and eastern Europe. However, even there they could be important, as with the successful French siege of Prussian-held Danzig (Gdánsk) in 1807, a siege that completed the military collapse of Prussia. In 1813–14, fortresses played a major role in strategy and operations in central Europe. Napoleon used Dresden as a key point d'appui in 1813 for the campaigning that finally failed when he was defeated at Leipzig. The fighting there had aspects of the urban fortress, although it was largely settled in open country. Colonel Hudson Lowe wrote of the attack on the French in Leipzig on October 19:

> Under cover of a most formidable fire from about fifty pieces of artillery, [the infantry] made their attack, the foremost battalions dispersing in small parties, and pushing the enemy at every point where the ground best admitted . . . the enemy firing from the houses (and streets which had been barricaded and filled with obstructions of every kind) and making at every corner and at every house a most obstinate resistance . . . the dead and the dying absolutely obstructed the passage in the gates and streets.[5]

Furthermore, on a pattern that was to be followed by Hitler in 1944–45, Napoleon insisted on trying to hold on to fortresses in East Prussia, Silesia, Poland, and eastern Spain, an insistence that reflected their determination not to concede defeat. In both cases, the fortresses did not prevent an advance on the center of power—Paris in 1814 and Berlin in 1945—a process also seen with the French advance on Madrid in 1808 and that of the Germans on Paris in 1870. The capture of the capital city was a major goal.

Forts played an even more significant role in transoceanic warfare between European powers, not least because the crucial harbors that were central positions in the wider European world were protected by fortifications. The techniques employed to capture forts varied greatly. The impact of disease and other problems of campaigning in the Tropics ensured that the British preferred to avoid sieges. Thus, Forts Leyden and Frederica in Dutch Guiana (Surinam) were taken in 1804 by bayonet attacks in the face of defensive grapeshot and musket fire: there was no preliminary bombardment. In contrast, Martinique fell in 1809, after the principal French position, the well-fortified and naturally strong Fort Desaix, was captured following an extremely heavy artillery bombardment. One of the shells detonated the principal magazine on February 24, leading to the surrender of the fortress later that day. Thomas Henry Browne recorded these events:

> February 20th. Our batteries began their fire, which was truly tremendous, they threw 500 shells, besides quantities of round shot, in the course of the evening. . . . 25th . . . The inside of the work presented a shocking spectacle of ruins, and blood, and half-buried bodies, and was literally ploughed up, by the shells we had thrown into it.[6]

During the French Revolutionary and Napoleonic Wars, there was considerable destruction of fortifications, not only in conflict but also as occupying forces sought to affect future options. It was common to destroy or damage fortifications when retreating, as the French did at Burgos. There was also destruction when advancing, as in 1810 when British forces moved forward from Gibraltar in order to destroy the facing Spanish fortifications, the Linea de Contravalacion, and thus prevent the French from using them in a future siege.

As in earlier centuries, and looking toward the twentieth century, sieges could be part of battles at the tactical level, notably at Waterloo in 1815. This battle in part involved the lengthy French sieges of two hastily fortified farmsteads, Hougoumont and La Haie Sainte, which, respectively, anchored the British right and protected its center. Soaking up a greatly disproportionate number of French troops, the first held out, despite repeated attacks, while the second, also despite much pressure, only fell late in the battle, and then in part because, in a major command failure, the garrison was not kept supplied with ammunition. Captain James Shaw Kennedy was scathing about the failure to prepare La Haie Sainte, a situation that contrasted with the preparations at Hougoumont:

> The garrison was insufficient, the workmen were taken away [to Hougoumont] . . . and nothing whatever was done during the night towards its defence; in place of which, the works of scaffolding, loopholing, building up gates and doors, partial unroofing, throwing out the hay and securing a supply of ammunition, should have been in progress all the night and during the morning.[7]

Its fall exposed the Allied center to damaging French firepower, and it would have been much more serious had it occurred earlier in the battle as it should have done had the French brought up artillery in support. In practice, the French repeatedly showed a serious lack of tactical integration at Waterloo.

The battle also involved hard, close-quarter fighting between the French and Prussians over the village of Plancenoit on the French right. The village was not walled, but many of the individual buildings became impromptu fortifications. Aside from their inherent significance, they were also important as providing firing positions from which advances along the thoroughfares could be contested. The fighting at Plancenoit would have been hard had it taken place in the open field, as each side, over several hours, fed in reserves in a struggle to determine the integrity of the French right and the security of the French route of retreat. However, the fighting was particularly difficult due to its taking place in a village. This setting not only provided fortifications but also disrupted the standard patterns of formation maneuver. Once the fighting was within villages, such as Plancenoit, attackers benefited from the cover they enjoyed thanks to the buildings. Bullet holes can still be seen on some of the buildings.

Victory at Waterloo permitted the British and Prussians to invade northeast France. Most French positions readily surrendered, for example St. Quentin. Those few that resisted did not delay the attack. On June 24, 1815, the British attacked both Peronne and Cambrai. At Peronne, a key defensive hornwork was stormed in the face of light resistance, and the garrison promptly surrendered. At Cambrai, as there was neither the time nor the artillery for a siege, the British attacked by escalade, the columns, covered by cannon, advancing under fire to scale the town's walls, succeeding with light casualties. The citadel held out but surrendered the next day. However, the British and Prussian commanders had agreed that they must focus on Paris and ignore both the border fortresses and the French army, a repetition of the successful Allied strategy in 1814. As in 1814, Paris did not serve as a fortified city. Instead, defeat in the field at Waterloo led to the speedy fall of the city.

EUROPE, 1815–1871

The sieges of recent campaigns were kept alive by illustration and by publications, such as Captain James MacCarthy's *Recollections of the Storming of the Castle of Badajos* (1836). In Spain, the resolute but eventually unsuccessful defense of Saragossa against French attack in 1808–09 became a potent symbol of national resolve.

More immediately, the Napoleonic Wars were followed with fresh fortification projects, not least as states sought to protect their positions without the large armies deployed in the Napoleonic Wars. Indeed, the equations of force moved due both to peace and to the particular factors of the postwar politics. In France, conscription, the practice under the French Revolutionaries and Napoleon, was seen as a political threat to the restored Bourbons, and there was a decision instead for a professional army of regulars. Alongside force availability, there were new possessions and boundaries to defend. For example, granted Belgium under the post-Napoleonic peace settlement agreed in 1814–15 by the Congress of Vienna, the Dutch refortified it against likely French invasion. As part of this new defensive system, Prussia had expanded to hold another portion of the frontier with France, that on the middle Rhine. Piedmont had gained Genoa.

The conflicts of the period saw a significant role for fortresses, although as part of military situations in which campaigning in the field was often the key element. In 1820–21, Austrian advances and successes in battle doomed opposition in Italy, opposition that had initially owed much to garrison risings in Alessandria and Turin against the government of Piedmont.

With fortresses on the coast, it was particularly important to cut them off from supply by sea. The availability of British supply had ensured that the French siege of Cadiz failed during the Peninsular War. In contrast, in 1823, when France intervened in a Spanish civil war and the British remained neutral, Cadiz, again the capital of resistance, this time of liberal opposition to the French-backed king, could be blockaded by sea as well as besieged by land, and it fell.

A very different type of fortress was shown in Brussels in 1830, when a Dutch attempt to reimpose control of Belgium was thwarted. The rebels focused on street fighting, employing the cover of barricades as well as fire from windows and housetops. The Dutch regulars fell back, the dynamism of their advance, and thus campaign, lost. This episode served as a reminder of the significance of fortifications that were scarcely at the cutting edge of military science. The Dutch retreated to Antwerp where, holding the powerful citadel, they bombarded the city, which had been captured by the insurgents. This bombardment was both reality and symbol of the established role of fortresses in overawing urban populations. In 1832, supported by a British naval blockade, a French army successfully besieged Antwerp.

In Spain, during the First and Second Carlist Wars of 1833–40 and 1873–76, fortifications not at the cutting edge also played a key role. The cities, such as Bilbao, tended to back the liberals. In Spain, there were the usual legacy fortresses dotted around large towns and key roads, which sometimes saw action whenever they found themselves in the path of Carlist invasions. Otherwise, the main fortification effort was in the Basque-Navarre-Rioja region along the river Ebro where, from 1834 onward, the Cristinos constructed a series of blockhouses in a manner similar to the French in Aragon during the Peninsular War. The Carlists responded in kind, and soon there were front lines etched by forts across wooded hillsides. Bilbao was besieged twice by the Carlists, in 1835 and 1836, and while defending Cristinos fortified outlying buildings on the hillsides, the Carlists did the same with trenches and small forts.[8] In the Portuguese Civil War, the Miguelist (conservatives) failure to storm the major cities, Lisbon and Oporto, in 1833 was very important to the course of the conflict. However, battles were important in both countries. In 1848, over ten thousand insurgents were killed in Paris when troops fought their way through the barricades.

In northern Italy, the Austrians benefited from controlling impressive fortresses, notably the so-called Quadrilateral: Legnano, Mantua, Peschiera, and Verona. In 1848, the Austrian commander, Josef Radetzky, responded to the crisis caused by rebellions in Milan and Venice, both Austrian cities, and the hostile intervention of Piedmontese troops by retreating from Milan into the Quadrilateral. These fortresses not only provided a refuge but also served as a base from which Radetzky advanced to defeat the Piedmontese forces and suppress the rebellions. Venice was besieged by the Austrians, and with cholera hitting hard, the city surrendered.

In the first half of the century, increased interest was devoted to the idea of detached forts as an aspect of defensive operations. Initially, these were a form of entrenched camp that was designed to provide defensive cover for field forces. Instead, they developed as a ring of detached forts in order to provide defense in depth for a fortress or fortified city, not least by increasing the line of investment that the besiegers had to man while, at the same time, providing cover and strength for a field force, thus acting as a large entrenched camp. This dual purpose or result serves as a reminder of the problems inherent in searching for a single explanation. The Prussians developed the idea and, in the 1830s and early 1840s, France followed suit, notably at Paris,[9] then at Belfort, Besançon, and Grenoble, and later at Metz, which again was near the eastern frontier. The emphasis on detached fortresses meant that less attention needed to be devoted to the main defensive position. This was seen with the major works at Antwerp begun by the Belgians in 1859, works designed to protect the city itself from bombardment by keeping opponents at a distance.[10] Thus, the main position was one protected at a distance, a pattern that major increases in the volume, range, and lethality of firepower had encouraged.

Russia's major Black Sea naval base, well-defended Sevastopol, was a serious challenge to besieging Anglo-French forces during the Crimean War of 1854–56. Providing defense against a distance, the Russian army was strongly entrenched outside the town, making able use of earth rather than masonry defenses, designed by Eduard Todleben, and was supported by over a thousand cannon. The Allies fired over 1,350,000 rounds of artillery. In a long-established pattern, the besiegers were in part besieged as major Russian forces sought to cut the supply route between the besieging army and the coastal anchorages from which they were supplied. This led to the battles of Balaclava and Inkerman. In the end, Sevastopol fell in 1855 after the French had, with a surprise attack, successfully assaulted the Malakoff redoubt, a key position in the defenses. However, the defense had caused major delays for the attackers, and this helped to narrow their strategic possibilities during the war.

Detached positions proved their value in the successful defense of Belfort against German siege in 1871, a defense that also proved very important for French morale as well as in the subsequent territorial settlement. Germany gained all the rest of Alsace, but the French retention of Belfort denied the Germans the opportunity to advance at the southern end of the Vosges Mountains. This meant that, in any future war, the Germans would not be able to advance through the Belfort Gap into southern Lorraine and Franche-Comté.

The French were less successful elsewhere during the war. Once isolated by advancing German forces and besieged, major fortified positions and their substantial garrisons surrendered, notably Metz and Strasbourg. Defeated in the field in August 1870, the French Army of the Rhine under Marshal Achille Bazaine had fallen back on Metz, surrendering both mobility and opportunities to block the Prussians and to prevent their own envelopment. In September 1870, the Germans, meanwhile, besieged Paris. There was no attempt to storm the city. The Germans initially relied on starvation, but the length of the siege posed major logistical problems for the Germans, which encouraged them to bombard Paris from January 5, 1871. The failure of relief attempts, Paris running out of food, casualties and damage caused by the shelling, and war weariness led to an armistice signed on January 28, 1871.

WAR OF 1812

Fortifications were seen as playing a significant role in any conflict between Britain and the United States. In particular, they were regarded as necessary in order to defend the British position in Canada from American attack and to defend American coastal cities from British naval assault. In 1812, a British veteran emphasized to Henry, Viscount Sidmouth, a prominent minister, that it was impossible to protect Canada from invasion, "but if we take care to retain possession of Quebec," then the Americans would be unable to consolidate their position and the British would be in a position to drive them from Canada, as they had done in 1776 after successfully holding Quebec.[11]

In turn, British operations against the coast were affected by American fortresses to a much greater degree than in the War of Independence. In 1793, concerned about the security of Baltimore, the Maryland House of Delegates authorized the construction of a fort at Whetstone Point, where Fort McHenry was to be established. In 1794, Congress passed an act to fortify America's major seaports. The landing on the river Patuxent in August 1814 was designed to avoid exposing the main force that advanced on Washington to fire from the Potomac forts.

The following month, the strength of Baltimore's defenses, including Fort McHenry, led to the abandonment of the attack on the city around which the Americans, since 1813, "had constructed a chain of palisaded redoubts connected by a small breastwork."[12] Rocket attacks and very heavy shelling did not inflict serious damage, while a nighttime amphibious attack lost its way in the fog. The resolute resistance ensured that the fort came to have a major part in the American public myth. This was captured in the poem "The Star Spangled Banner" by Francis Scott Key, which in 1931 became the national anthem, while there were also many and much-reproduced paintings, including John Bower's *A View of the Bombardment of Fort McHenry* (1816) and Alfred Jacob Miller's *Bombardment of Fort McHenry* (c. 1837).

Whereas American fortifications stood up well, unfortified and undefended Washington fell to British attack, and its public buildings were burned down. American field fortifications were crucial to the defeat of the British advance on New Orleans on January 8, 1815, providing the necessary cover for effective defensive fire.

In the interior, fortresses, and their sieges, were important to campaigning and to the politics of influencing the views of Native Americans. Thus, the failure of the British siege of newly constructed Fort Meigs in 1813, the biggest wooden fort built in North America, hit hard Britain's alliance with Native Americans in the Detroit region.[13] In turn, farther south, Creek positions proved vulnerable to American attack.

Native Americans were unwilling to mount frontal assaults on forts, and there were generally too few British regulars for the task, while the British and, especially, the Native Americans also lacked the heavy guns necessary to overcome fortifications. In 1812, the Native Americans tried to make two cannon out of hollow logs when they unsuccessfully attacked Fort Wayne. Neither these, nor the fire arrows (which the Americans countered using buckets of water to keep the defenses wet), led the defenders to surrender the fort, and the Native Americans did not mount a frontal attack.

Operations in the interior were affected by a lack of operational dynamic that in part reflected the poor state of transport. The movement of cannon and supplies was seen as crucial by President Madison in September 1812 when he argued that there was no point in attacking Detroit and invading nearby Canada unless they were available and that troops without such support were of scant value. James Monroe, the secretary of state, commented that month,

> 6 24 pounders, 10 18s, 10 12s, 6 6 pounders, and 14 8-inch howitzers are ordered to Fort Pitt [Pittsburgh]. They are necessary to batter and take Detroit and [Fort] Malden [Amherstburg], and although they may not be got there this year, they will be ready for the spring.[14]

The British attempt in 1814 to recapture Fort Erie on the Niagara front reflected the number of factors bound up with the success of operations. A night attack on August 15 led to the capture of one of the bastions, but the British could not exploit this success as the entrance into the fort itself was well covered. The powder magazine under the bastion blew up, with heavy British casualties, and the British then withdrew. They turned to a persistent artillery bombardment, only for the Americans, in a night sortie on September 17, to capture two of the three British batteries and spike many of the cannon. Pointless without artillery superiority, the siege was lifted. However, on November 5, with their garrison affected by sickness and desertion, the Americans evacuated the position, destroying the fortress. [15] Where the emphasis is placed in this account ensures that very different impressions can be created.

NORTH AMERICA

After the War of 1812, fortifications remained significant. The British eventually located the Canadian capital at Ottawa as a defensive measure to overcome the vulnerability of Kingston, Montreal, and Toronto. Concern about the British led to a program of coastal fortification in the United States, with New York harbor strengthened with Fort Hamilton from 1825 and Fort Wadsworth from 1847. This program served to give the Corps of Engineers, the Ordnance Department, and the artillery particular roles. As a result, they actively lobbied for it, especially in the early 1850s in the face of political opposition and concern about its military value given developments in naval artillery. The defense budget of the United States was dominated by the construction of coastal fortresses, including on the Great Lakes, although the cost meant that of the two hundred fortresses proposed, only forty-two were ever begun, while most were never finished. In comparison, the defenses against Native Americans were inexpensive, and transient works were suitable for a dynamic frontier. The best American army engineers worked on the Atlantic coast. The main use of Montalembert's system was in American coastal fortresses, where the firepower required to stop (by deterrence or action) attacking ships entering ports was far more important than the defensive strength of a low earthwork battery. [16]

Across the continent, fortifications remained particularly significant as an expression and means of control as an imperial presence was established and power was extended. Thus, on the Pacific seaboard of North America, expanding south from their positions in Alaska, the Russians founded a base in California at Fort Ross, north of San Francisco, in 1812. The Pomos, who lived nearby, reacted violently, but disease and Russian firepower cut their numbers. Fort Ross, 100 meters by 150 meters, was modeled on the Siberian *ostrog* (fortified place), with frequently spaced guard towers. An *ostrog* and its stockaded American counterparts were never intended to resist cannon fire. Nevertheless, California was too far for the Russians effectively to deploy their power: Fort Ross did not serve as the basis for fresh expansion, and it was abandoned in 1841.

In the extensive Oregon Territory between Alaska and California, the British-owned Hudson's Bay Company established many bases below the 49th parallel, including Forts Boise, Colville, Flathead, George, Nez Percés, Nisqually, Okanagan, Umpqua, and Vancouver, several on or south of the Columbia River, and this presence posed a challenge to American territorial pretensions and expansionism. However, a British report in the winter of 1845–46 on the company's forts categorized them as "capable of making a good defence against irregular or Indian forces," "incapable of making any defence," or "capable of resisting a sudden attack from Indians or an irregular force without field guns." The vulnerability of these forts to artillery was apparent.

On a long-standing pattern, the Americans built forts when they advanced westward, for example Fort Madison in Iowa in 1808 and Fort Harrison (Terre Haute) in 1811, and to stabilize the situation after defeats, for example Forts Meigs (Maumee) and Stephenson (Fremont) in 1813. Native American "prophets," such as those influencing the Creeks in 1813–14, might claim that they could make Native American villages impregnable, turn hills over the settlements of opponents, and bring down lightning on American forts. That, however, was not to be, as the Creeks discovered at Horseshoe Bend in 1814 when their fort was stormed by Andrew Jackson, who benefited in this major success from the support of some Cherokees and Creeks.[17]

In the difficult Second Seminole War in Florida (1835–42), a system of forts, and the roads that linked them, provided an infrastructure for the American forces. These forts could not prevent the Seminole from moving between them, but they offered security against Seminole attack. Similarly, in the Java War of 1825–30, the Dutch developed a network of fortified bases from which they sent out mobile columns.

After the War of 1812, American fort building included a chain from Lake Michigan to the upper Mississippi River, as well as forts farther south, for example Fort Smith in Arkansas in 1817. Environmental factors were important. Moving into the Great Plains and developing mounted forces for operations there permitted a lower density in fortifications than would otherwise have been necessary when the reliance had been on infantry columns, with forts such as Fort Scott in eastern Kansas established in 1842. This lower density was also related to the scale of the area that had to be covered, while there was not the clear pattern of routes to be protected provided by river valleys and passes through wooded regions and uplands farther east. While forts on the Great Plains could be bypassed by Native raiders, they were difficult for them to take.

The annexation of Texas and then the Mexican-American War (1846–48) were followed by a major extension of the fortification imprint. This was not a matter of random building. Instead, the forts reflected a series of politico-strategic objectives, objectives that cast much light on the purposes for which fitness had to be judged. The establishment of garrisons in forts met the needs of settlers for reassurance, needs vociferously reflected in the political process. In contrast, the War Department preferred to see troops concentrated in large forces, which was regarded as the best way to maintain discipline and training and also to intimidate opponents. In practice, the American forts were protected mustering points for the concentration of small forces for expeditions.

Border fortifications, which served to define the border and to mark a federal presence there, included Camp Ringgold at Rio Grande City (1848), Fort Bliss at El Paso (1848), Fort Duncan near Eagle Pass (1849), and Fort Drum at Zapata (1852). Forts were also built along the edge of a settlement in order to protect it from Native attack, which remained both a threat and a reality. Thus, the war was followed in Texas by the establishment of Fort Martin Scott (1848), Fort Worth (1849), Fort Graham (1849), Fort Gates (1849), Fort Croghan (1849), Fort Lincoln (1849), and Fort Inge (1849).

Westward moves of the line of settlement, and thereby of townships that needed to be protected, led to new forts and to the closure of many earlier ones. Thus, in Texas in the early 1850s, new forts included Merrill (1850), Belknap (1851), Chadbourne (1852), McKavett (1852), Terrett (1852), Ewell (1852), and Clark (1852). There were also camps such as Joseph E. Johnston (1852) and Elizabeth (1853). A double line of forts was seen as the best way to deter Native raids. However, rather than putting the emphasis on the defense, strategic thinking developed in favor of using forts as a base for offensive campaigns against Native homelands. The general desire to control the Native Americans led to the construction of forts in west Texas, for example Davis (1854), Lancaster (1855), Quitman (1858), and Stockton (1859).

American forts were also built farther north. The Santa Fe Trail was guarded by Forts Atkinson (1850) and Union (1851). In Minnesota, Fort Snelling, the first American fort there, built in 1819, was followed in 1848 by Fort Marcy, which was designed to keep the Winnebago tribe peaceful. The onward movement of the frontier of concern led to the foundation in 1853 of Fort Ridgely on the Sioux reservation on the upper Minnesota River and, in 1856, to an expedition to the Red River Valley in Minnesota and the establishment of Fort Abercrombie. Fort Ripley was evacuated in 1857, although that led the Chippewa to an outbreak of violence, which caused the reoccupation of the post. The effort and cost involved in supplying these distant posts were heavy, and fortification reflected the increasing wealth of the United States. In 1862, in the Minnesota rising, the Eastern Sioux failed to capture the forts. In 1877, Fort Missoula was built in Montana as a protection against the Nez Percé.

There was no equivalent enlargement of the American army to reflect the lands gained, but instead a transfer of forces from east of the Mississippi and, by 1860, the end of most garrisons on the Canadian border, on the Atlantic coast, in Florida (where the Seminole were under control), and in the Mississippi valley. This reflected the extent to which, from the 1840s, Americans were no longer interested in pushing the Natives back and instead now sought total control of the whole of America. This redistribution of garrisons was also a product of greatly eased relations with Britain in the 1850s. For example, Fort Scott was abandoned by the army in 1855. The British withdrew most of their forces from Canada after the settlement of Anglo-American differences by the Treaty of Washington (1871), with the exception of the well-fortified Atlantic naval base at Halifax and the Pacific naval base at Esquimalt. In turn, the American military presence in the Great Lakes and Puget Sound was reduced, with Fort Wilkins closed in 1870 and Fort Gratiot in 1879. Decrepit frontier bastions became national parks.

The process could also be seen elsewhere. Buying Alaska from Russia in 1867, the United States rapidly established forts in order to assert control there. The coastal location of these forts, which included Fort Tongass facing British territory in Canada, Fort Kodiak, Fort Wrangel on an island at the mouth of the Stikine River, and Fort Kenay near the head of Cook Inlet, reflected the distribution of population, the possibilities for trade, and the extent to which any attack by other powers would come by sea. This, in practice, would mean an attack from Britain, but fear of this declined from 1871.

THE AMERICAN CIVIL WAR

The American Civil War (1861–65) largely occurred in parts of the country where there were few fortifications other than those, such as Fort Sumter in Charleston harbor, designed to offer protection for coastal positions against British naval attack. In Charleston in 1863 and Mobile in 1864, Confederate coastal positions resisted Union naval attacks. In contrast, there was no system of fortifications in inland Virginia or Maryland. As a result, those forts that were present in the field of operations were important.

Moreover, there was a process of rapid entrenchment and fort construction in order to provide protection. Camps were provided with defensive facilities. The emphasis was on rapidly built, temporary works intended for use on a short-term basis and constructed by the troops with the materials at hand. An example was presented by the earthworks at what was called Fort Edward Johnson on the crest of Shenandoah Mountain constructed by the Confederacy on the western periphery of the Shenandoah Valley in 1862 in order to prevent Union access to the valley and the military depot at Staunton. Artillery batteries there were placed on platforms to provide overlapping fields of fire. Access to a constant supply of water was a key element in location.[18] Exposed to Confederate attack, Washington ended up perhaps the most fortified place in the world, with an elaborate system of mostly earthen forts, redans, batteries, and other works that formed a ring thirty miles around the city.

Artillery was not yet available in the quantity seen to be necessary in World War I (1914–18). Besieging the major Confederate fortress of Vicksburg, a key position on the Mississippi, the Union batteries mounted only 220 guns over twelve miles of siege line in June 1863.[19]

The construction of forts was not the sole issue. In addition, field fortifications were important. Taking forward the European experience

Figure 6.2.   Vicksburg from Fort Castle

during the Revolutions of 1848, railway lines provided improvised field fortifications, notably the embankments. Breastworks and trenches were designed to protect troops on battlefields, particularly against infantry attacks and against nonplunging cannon shot. Breastworks proved important aids to defenders, although, as with trenches, against those who focused on frontal advances rather than maneuver.[20] In 1864–65, the trenches dug during the drawn-out Union siege of Petersburg were deeper and the trench systems more complex than earlier. Edward Porter Alexander, a Confederate artillery general, recorded of the Union trenches near Petersburg,

> The enemy promptly built a strong line of rifle pits, all along the edge of the dead space with elaborate loop holes and head logs to protect their sharpshooters, and they maintained from it a close and accurate fire on all parts of our line near them. . . . We soon got our lines at most places in such space that we did not fear any assaults,

but meanwhile this mortar firing had commenced and that added immensely to the work in the trenches. Every man needed a little bombproof to sleep in at night, and to dodge into in the day when the mortar shells were coming.[21]

Trench warfare did not originate at Petersburg. For example, the Anglo-French forces that besieged Russian-held Sevastopol in 1854–55, during the Crimean War, had to face a type of trench warfare that was different from earlier sieges in terms of the intensity of artillery fire. Nevertheless, the trenches near Sevastopol can be seen as an aspect of a traditional siege rather than as a development of field entrenchments, as in Virginia in 1864–65. The entrenchments there, as at the lengthy Battle of Spotsylvania in 1864, looked toward those in World War I, although the more fluid nature of operations ensured that they were less developed. Barbed wire was in use in the conflict from 1863. In Petersburg, as in Sevastopol and also in Rome in 1849, the defenders were not entirely encircled.

There were parallels between trench warfare in 1864–65 and in World War I, for example defensive firepower, the limited value of cavalry, and sappers planning and planting siege batteries, parallels, saps, and wire entanglements and laying mines. Those on both sides called their moves "siege operations," and maps were titled "Siege of Petersburg."

The great difference, at least insofar as the Western Front in 1914–18 was concerned, was that in America there was no equivalent to the English Channel and neutral Switzerland to anchor the trenches at each end. Robert E. Lee, the Confederate commander, had to maneuver on a narrow front to defend the key logistical base of Richmond, a situation that has been described as a strategic siege, and the Confederate trenches could be outflanked, as Ulysses S. Grant, the Union commander, did with Lee in 1865. Lee could not put trenches all the way around Richmond, or he would have been starved out, and to the west the land went on all the way to the Pacific. In addition, it was not necessary to resist lengthy bombardments by heavy guns firing plunging shots, as in World War I, nor was there reinforced concrete with which to protect positions.[22]

LATIN AMERICA

Battles played the major role in the Latin American wars of independence, but fortresses were also important. In 1816, the batteries of the Real Felipe fortress at Callao in Peru repulsed an attempt by blockading ships to bombard the port, and in 1819 an attack on the fortress. It was successfully besieged in 1819–21, recaptured by the Spaniards, and then surrendered by them in 1826. In 1866, the fortress was bombarded by Spanish warships.

Newly independent states created new strategic issues and had to adapt to new technologies. Fortifications could be part of the response. For example, in Argentina and the Plate estuary in the independence period, the main fortress built was on Martin Garcia Island, in the river Plate, controlling access to the Paraná and Uruguay Rivers. Due to the lack of suitable rocks in the region, the fortress was quite modest, built with bricks, mainly in order to protect artillery intended to act against warships. There were some other emplacements on Argentina's Patagonian coast. These served to protect naval stations as well as to establish the Argentine presence in a recently occupied region. Gun emplacements were built at La Vuelta de Obligardo during the Anglo-French blockade in 1845. Finally, a coastal artillery emplacement complex was built at the end of the century. Better known as Baterias, it was a set of facilities built with the aim of serving as the defense of the Puerto Belgrano Naval Base, guarding its access channel. This was built of rock, as there was a mountain chain nearby.

Fortresses were also built in other states, notably those built by Paraguay for the Triple Alliance War (1864–70) against Argentina, Brazil, and Uruguay. The fortress of Humaitá (1854–68), known as the Gibraltar of South America, proved the key to Paraguay and the upper rivers. The site was a sharp horseshoe bend in the Paraguay River. Practically all vessels wishing to enter the republic of Paraguay, and indeed to steam upward to the Brazilian province of Mato Grosso, were forced to navigate it. The bend was commanded by a six-thousand-foot line of artillery batteries, at the end of which was a chain boom, which when raised detained the shipping under the guns. The fortress was protected from attack on its landward side by impassable swamps and earthworks stretching for eight miles. Blockaded for two years, the for-

tress surrendered in 1868, and the Triple Alliance insisted on its demolition. Field fortifications were also extensively used in that conflict.

In wars, the usual pattern was not a lengthy operation, as against
Humaitá, but a bombardment followed by a storming, as when in 1847
the Americans captured Chapultepec Castle, a hilltop position important for the defense of Mexico City.

Strategic needs drove fortification programs, including the decision
not to build. At the beginning of the twentieth century, Argentina and
Chile reached an agreement to resolve their border disputes peacefully,
which affected the need for fortifications. In Argentina, the Baterias
were still under construction, but part of the program was suspended.

THE GLOBAL DIMENSION

While the Americans built forts in the West, the Russians, in turn,
continued their establishment of fortified lines to anchor and cover
their advances. To the east of the Caspian Sea, the annexation in 1822
of the lands of the Middle Kazakh Horde both introduced administrative dominance based on forts and used fortified lines to bring much of
the best pastureland under control. In the 1830s and 1840s, the advance of Russian forts and settlers in Kazakhstan continued. In the
1860s and 1870s, Russian forces conquered southern Central Asia and,
along the way, took fortified cities such as Bukhara, Khiva, and Samarqand.

In the Senegal valley, under General Louis Faidherbe, the governor
of Senegal from 1854 to 1865, French expansion into the interior was
anchored by the development of an effective chain of riverine forts
linked by steamships. Forts such as Archambault were also used as the
bases for advances, in this case for the successful French campaign in
Chad in 1899.

In the late nineteenth century, as they conquered Angola and Mozambique, the Portuguese erected a number of forts in all their main
towns and seaports as well as in some rural areas. These were usually
built of stone along traditional lines: they were square in shape with
corner turrets and sometimes with strengthened bastions for mounting
artillery. In the Zambesi valley in Mozambique, the Portuguese took
over the strongholds of warlords they defeated and in some cases occu-

pied them with garrisons. The fortified post, sometimes called a presidio or *posto military*, was the nucleus for a rudimentary administration. For the most part, the soldiers who garrisoned them were "cipais," African soldiers fighting for Portugal.

On the North-West Frontier of India (now of Pakistan), forts were the focus of attacks, as in 1895 and 1897, and their relief was the crucial aspect of British campaigning, as in 1897 when a relief column ended the siege of the fort at Shabkadr. In the Sino-French War of 1884–85, the French succeeded, in March 1885, in relieving the besieged garrison at Tuyen-Qang, northwest of Hanoi. At Makale, an Italian garrison held off the Ethiopians for six weeks in the winter of 1895–96, while in confronting risings in Africa, the Germans had to defend positions, such as Mahenge in German East Africa in 1905.

Western forces built both forts and also entrenched camps. The latter were a variation on tactical defensive positions, but there were differences. In the Anglo-Zulu war in 1879, the British laagers at Gingindlovu and Kambula were prepared positions, unlike the British square that advanced on the Zulu kraal at Ulundi. All three successfully defeated Zulu attacks. Also in southern Africa, artillery and machine guns helped a British camp to defeat Matabele attackers at the Shangani in 1893.

The fortifications of non-Western powers could resist Western forces that lacked appropriate artillery, as with the four unsuccessful British attempts to storm Bharatpur in India in 1805 and the repeated difficulties the British faced attacking Gurkha hill forts and stockades in Nepal in 1814–15. At Bharatpur, General Gerard Lake had only four eighteen-pounders and insufficient ammunition and was unable both to neutralize the defensive fire and to blow the gates in. He also misjudged the depth of the ditch and the height of the walls, and his operations were affected by Maratha countermining.

Moreover, much fortification and siegecraft entailed conflict between non-Western forces. This was the case with one of the largest wars of the period, the Taiping Rising in China. It was also the case, for example, with Egyptian expansion in the early nineteenth century. In 1816, Egyptian forces advanced into the deserts of Arabia, seizing the Wahhabi strongholds, culminating in the capture of their capital, Dar'iyya, in 1818 after a six-month siege. The jihad launched in northern Nigeria in 1804 saw the isolation of the powerful fortified positions of the Hausa and by the end of 1808 their fall to irregular insurgents.[23]

Non-Western fortifications proved increasingly vulnerable to Western firepower, even if many of the attacks were driven home by storming, as with that on Constantine in Algeria by the conquering French in 1837, on the Central Asian city of Khoqand by Russian forces in 1866, and on the Abyssinian fortress of Magdala by the British in 1868. In the war of 1806–12, the extensive fortifications in the Turkish defensive system on the Danube delayed the Russians, but in 1809–10 they took them. In the next war with Turkey, the Russians were able to start farther south due to the territorial gains from Turkey in the peace treaties of 1774, 1792, and 1812 and from Poland in the First Partition of 1772. The Russians advanced into Bulgaria, capturing Rushchuk (1828) and Varna (1828) in a siege personally directed by Tsar Nicholas I. They went on to take Adrianople (Edirne) in 1829, which put great pressure on the Turks.

Storming was important in the British captures of the Mysore capital Seringapatam in 1799, the Maratha fortresses of Alegarh and Gawilgarh in 1803, and the sultan of Yogyakarta's *kraton* (royal residence) in the East Indies in 1812. Pangeran Arya Panular, a Sumatran whose diary covered the assault, was impressed by the combination of British discipline, bravery, and determination against what was a far larger garrison backed by numerous cannon.[24]

Surrenders were best, as assaults could be costly, and for both sides. At Khoqand, despite being assisted by a heavy bombardment, the Russians took heavy losses scaling the two lines of walls, as a result of which scaling they were able to throw open the gates from within. Their subsequent advance into the city was resisted from behind barricades and by snipers.[25]

In New Zealand, nevertheless, the Maori responded ably to British artillery, digging well-sited trench and *pa* (fort) systems that were difficult to bombard or storm and adopting layouts in order to increase the potential for their own muskets. The Maori inflicted serious checks on the British in the 1860s. As also later with Pathan defenses on the North-West Frontier of India, the British had to learn to adapt to Maori systems. Yet, as a reminder of the need to put the strengths and weaknesses of fortifications in a broader context, the availability of British, colonial, and allied Maori units, and the process of extending control

that included road and fort construction, ensured an eventual settlement on British terms.

The overall situation was less favorable for the British in Afghanistan. There, although they could make use of fortified positions such as
the city of Kandahar in 1880, where they resisted Afghan attack until
relieved by a force advancing from Kabul, they also faced the successful
Afghan use of relatively simple fortification techniques. Thus, that year,
Alfred Cane noted of a sortie against the village of Deh Khoja,

> We began by shelling the place. There was no reply so 800 of our
> infantry advanced to the attack when at once a galling fire was
> opened on them from loopholes around the village. Our men rushed
> on and entered the village on the south side but only to find it filled
> with armed men firing from the windows, doors and roofs. It was a
> hopeless task . . . had to return in hot haste under the same heavy
> fire.[26]

In 1885, General Frederick Roberts, who had relieved Kandahar in
1880, stressed the unsuitability of light guns: "In Afghanistan, from the
absence of roads, it is seldom that artillery can move faster than infantry, and no field gun that we now possess can make any impression on
the thick mud walls of which all forts and houses in that country are
built."

Speed and firepower were also significant elsewhere. In Senegal and
Algeria, the French employed artillery to breach the gates of positions
and then stormed them. Artillery, especially 95 mm siege guns using
powerful explosives, played a crucial role in the conquest of the Tukulor
forts by the French in 1890–91, and the walls of Kano in Nigeria were
breached within an hour by British cannon in 1903. In West Africa in
1898, it took French artillery two weeks to destroy the walls of Sikasso,
which had resisted a yearlong siege by Samory Touré, a local ruler, in
1887–88. Artillery was, more generally, important to European columns
as they advanced against non-European opponents. It provided a key
point-of-contact advantage.

As earlier in India, the fortifications the Europeans encountered in
Africa had not been developed to cope with them but, rather, with local
opponents. This was seen with those in western Kenya. Aside from their
defenses being designed accordingly, their location reflected the dy-
namics of local warfare, notably defensive locations, such as hilltops and

the confluence of rivers, as well as the availability of water. Confluences limited the options for attackers and provided defensive features. The mud walls of the fortifications in western Kenya, about three meters high, were surrounded by ditches, about two meters wide.[27]

The absence of resources and logistical infrastructure for lengthy sieges, as well as of siege artillery, encouraged the use of storming elsewhere. This was notably so in Latin America. In 1880, during the War of the Pacific, the strongly fortified Peruvian port of Arica resisted a Chilean naval bombardment and subsequently a land one before falling to a nighttime storming. Disease and climate were also factors. Major General Rufus Shafter, the commander of the successful American siege of the Spanish-held Cuban port of Santiago, noted that "whatever we did at that season had to be done very quickly."

Sieges, moreover, proved significant occasions. This was the case whether they were successful or not. Examples of the former included the heavy bombardment by Confederate forces of beleaguered Fort Sumter in Charleston Harbor in 1861 (over three thousand shells and shot were fired). So also with the fall of Sudan's capital, Khartoum, to Mahdist attack in 1885, with the garrison commander, Major General Charles Gordon, being killed, although this was an attack in which artillery was not an important element. This success demonstrated divine backing to the Mahdists and was seen as a Christian martyrdom by Gordon's enthusiastic British supporters. The relief expedition had not arrived in time.

The sieges of the Indian Mutiny also proved key episodes for British opinion, notably with mutineers massacring women, children, civilians, and prisoners at Cawnpore in 1857. In contrast, Colin Campbell's ability to lead a column to the relief of Lucknow in 1857 became an iconic occasion of soldiering.[28] In 1857, the British stormed Delhi and cleared the city in bitter street fighting.

Heroic literature focused on sieges in which small forces held out, as in the popular G. A. Henty adventure stories for children, including *With Clive in India* (1884). So also in France with forts in Algeria and in the United States with forts in the West. The image of small numbers of Europeans and Americans bravely repelling attacks by large forces of "savage peoples," while relief columns fought their way through, formed a potent image that encoded civilizational myths and racist assumptions. These views could then be extrapolated onto other conflicts, notably that of the British with the Afrikaner Boers in South Africa. Religious images were significant. In "Hold the Fort," his highly successful 1870 hymn, the American hymnist Philip Bliss (1838–76) had the refrain "'Hold the Fort, for I am coming,' Jesus signals still."

Examples of unsuccessful sieges included the Boer sieges of British garrisons at Kimberley, Ladysmith, and Mafeking in South Africa in 1899–1900 and the Boxer siege of the foreign legations in Beijing in 1900; all these inland positions were relieved in both South Africa and China. Subsequently in the Boer War of 1899–1902, the British used a blockhouse system supported by barbed-wire fences in order to extend fortified control and to thwart Boer raids. This was an instance of the long-term rivalry between cavalry and fortifications, one seen across a range of technologies.

CHANGING CONTEXTS

As in previous centuries, fortification policies were framed in the context of varied strategic cultures and contrasting goals, and with reference to significantly different resource levels. Thus, General Sir John Burgoyne, inspector general of fortifications, a figure of great experience, noted in 1856 that Britain needed to rely for its defense on its navy and fortifications because

> the peace establishment of its land forces is insignificant as compared with those by which it may be assailed; and we may assume that the feelings of the country, its policy, and perhaps its real interests, render it impossible to vie, in its standing military establishments, with the Continental powers.[29]

In 1860, Burgoyne proposed a defensive ring around London of twenty-eight forts and batteries, mounting 1,050 guns and to be manned by a permanent garrison of seventeen thousand troops. Colonel Sir Shafto Aclair followed in 1862 with a more extensive proposal for 71, 2,192, and 25,600 respectively.[30] Neither proposal was implemented. Britain instead relied on the Royal Navy.

Improved long-range firepower was a serious threat to existing fortifications, notably to masonry exposed to artillery fire. As a result, there was both obsolescence and much investment in improving some defensive positions. The obsolescence of existing fortifications encouraged the dismantling of city walls. This was a process fostered by the popular view that the age of towns as fortresses had passed, an assumption that was well founded as a response to current artillery, but not one that paid much attention to the situation if towns themselves became a battlefield. In 1857, Emperor Franz Joseph decided to raze Vienna's defensive walls, which made land around the new Ringstrasse available for development. Similarly, Copenhagen, formerly essentially a defensive citadel as a whole, with moats, ramparts, and gates protecting the city, was transformed, with the moats changed into parks, although the fortress remained as a separate citadel on the edge of the city, as it still does. Its easy capture with no casualties was an important step in the rapid German seizure of the city in 1940. Demolitions began in Turin from the late 1850s, with the citadel finally dismantled except for the keep, which now houses the National Historic Museum of Artillery. In France, many town walls were demolished in the 1880s, although the city walls of Paris, built between 1841 and 1844, were only demolished in 1919–29.

The American Civil War of 1861–65 and the Franco-German War of 1870–71 had shown the weakness of fortified positions. In the former case, European observers were deeply impressed by the failure of masonry before modern guns. In France, Strasbourg was successfully shelled into surrender, while the shelling of Paris in 1871, a response to the German unwillingness to risk the casualties a storming would entail, inflicted much damage and also led to surrender.

COASTAL PROTECTION

In 1806, John Gillespie unsuccessfully tried to interest the British government in a scheme for coastal defense against Napoleonic France. Impregnable batteries, each with one cannon firing balls of 150 pounds, were to be constructed. He claimed that 160 of them would suffice to defend Britain. This was one among[31] a number of ideas proposed, each of which answered to concerns about defensibility. Burgoyne suggested in 1856,

> The progress in the state of gunnery and steam navigation renders it necessary to reconsider from time to time the principles of attack and defence of coasts and harbours. Whatever improvements may be made in land batteries, their entire adequacy for the purpose of defence cannot be certain against the rapidity of steamers, and the facility of their manoeuvring power . . . but they may be powerful in combination with . . . the floating batteries with their sides coated with thick iron plates.[32]

In other words, a combination defense, of mobile and fixed fortifications, was seen as crucial. In attack, when a British fleet had bombarded Egyptian-held Acre in 1840, steamers had showed their ability to operate inshore, while a shell caused the explosion of the fortress's main magazine. However, the Anglo-French naval bombardments of the Russian ports of Odessa and Sevastopol in 1854 also underlined the vulnerability of wooden warships to effective fire.

The attack on Sevastopol, like those on Cadiz (1596), Louisbourg (1745, 1758), Havana (1762), Copenhagen (1807), Flushing (1809), and Antwerp (1809), was a product of the British tradition of attacking fortified naval positions.[33] Indeed, the Royal Engineers' syllabus in the nineteenth century was dominated by the attack and destruction of such positions. When Sevastopol fell, the engineers spent three months destroying the Russian dockyard, much as they had the dockyard at Flushing in 1809. This was a core feature of the "British way in warfare."

Results were mixed. Flushing fell to long-range bombardment without a breach in the fortifications. This reflected the superiority of British artillery, although they also used Congreve rockets, which caused extensive fires and panic. Bad weather, poor planning, and weak leadership, however, combined to lose time in 1809, with the delay in taking Flushing allowing the French to strengthen Antwerp. As a result, the British decided not to attack, while many troops died of diseases to which the weather and unsanitary conditions contributed. The expedition underlined the logistical issues involved in launching amphibious attacks on coastal fortifications.[34]

The vulnerability of fortifications to naval and amphibious attack was shown at Alexandria in 1882 and Weihaiwei in 1895, at the hands of the British and Japanese respectively. In 1882, fourteen British warships with powerful guns, including HMS *Inflexible*, which had four sixteen-inch guns, inflicted great damage, with few British casualties. However, the nature of the defense greatly magnified the British ability to inflict damage: the shore batteries were not particularly well handled by the Egyptians, and the British warships did not have to face mines or torpedoes.

Concern about the impact of steam power on naval capability, following the Royal Commission on the Defences of the United Kingdom (1859), led to an acceleration of fort building by the British, notably near the naval bases of Plymouth and Portsmouth, which had both seaward and landward defenses. Detached forts in a polygonal form employing bombproof barrel-vaulted casemates covered with concrete were built far enough out to keep enemy artillery out of range from the ports.[35]

EUROPE, 1871–1913

After defeat by Germany in 1870–71, the French launched a rapid rearmament. This policy led to a focus on land and a shift of resources from the navy, and in particular to the creation of an extensive defensive belt to prevent further German advances in the event of another war. Still outnumbered in troops, the French, if attacked by the Germans, now, as a result of territorial losses in Alsace and Lorraine in that war and the resulting peace settlement, had less space in which to maneuver. As a consequence, major French military bases, such as Belfort and Verdun, were surrounded with fortified positions. They were to be significant in the strategy and operational history of World War I.[36] Well defended, such fortified complexes could impose a heavy cost on the attacker, a cost in terms of time, manpower, and casualties.

Moreover, French defenses in the Alps were designed to prevent Germany's ally Italy from mounting an attack, and indeed served to deter the Italians from planning one. In the event of Italy attacking, these defenses were intended to lessen the need for manpower and thus to further the strategic goal of concentrating the army on the German threat. Italy, in turn, built forts in the Alps. That atop Monte Chaberton facing the French fort at Briançon was, at 10,430 feet, the highest in Europe.

Meanwhile, fortifications and sieges were important in Russia's wars with the Turks. In 1877, the Russians both successfully stormed Turkish-held Kars and unsuccessfully stormed the major fortified city of Erzurum. On the main axis of advance, invading Russian forces found Turkish-held Plevna and its redoubts a major obstacle in Bulgaria in 1877. In the defense, begun in July, the entrenched Turks, ably commanded by Osman Pasha and using American-manufactured Peabody rifles (the Russians were armed with American-designed Berdan rifles), inflicted heavy casualties on Russian frontal attacks, which suffered from inadequate preparation and planning. In the second assault, Russian casualties amounted to 23 percent of their rank and file. The successive attempts to storm Plevna prefigured many aspects of World War I, including the difficulties of destroying trenches by artillery fire, the employment of machine guns, and the heavy use of munitions. Plevna eventually fell after the defenders, their food stores nearly exhausted, mounted a sortie on December 9. It was defeated, and Osman Pasha then surrendered. Like Sevastopol in 1855, Plevna had fallen, but, again like Sevastopol, the strategic options for the attackers, both military and political, had been limited as a result of the commitments of manpower and time involved. The British were able to prepare to take action in support of the Turkish position in the Balkans, and the threat of this action affected the eventual peace settlement. In 1878, the Austrians bombarded and stormed Turkish-held Sarajevo.

The effectiveness of fortifications continued to be challenged by advances in explosives and artillery in the late nineteenth century—especially the development of rifled steel breechloaders, delayed-action fuses, and improved pneumatic recoil mechanisms that obviated the need for re-siting artillery before firing anew. These advances ensured that it was necessary to put more effort into strengthening fortifications and building detached fortresses at a greater distance from the main position. Vulnerability to artillery attack meant that there was considerable controversy over how best to respond, comparable to that over the best response to battleships, the controversy being linked to budgetary conflicts.

Stronger fortifications, in the shape of steel turrets and disappearing cupolas, was one remedy, one that sounded the death knell to the fortification designs initiated by the Italians during the Renaissance. This remedy was contested by commentators who emphasized a need for the location of guns in concealed positions and for moving them between such positions. The French experiments at Fort Malmaison in 1886 appeared to demonstrate the obsolescence of fortifications in the face of high explosive shells using a combination of melinite (a new high explosive), steel shells, and delayed-action fuses. Stone in particular was now very vulnerable.

These experiments led to the strengthening of revetments, notably through the use of armor-plated turrets and cupolas alongside concrete roofs. These defenses were to protect new-style quick-firing cannon and machine guns. Extensive fortress complexes, offering defense in depth and the mutual protection of the forts, were seen in a number of countries, including Romania, where the capital, Bucharest, was thus protected against Russian attack, and Belgium around the cities of Liège, Namur, and Antwerp, complexes designed by Henry Brialmont, the "Belgian Vauban," a significant point of reference. In France, several of the forts protecting Verdun, including Douaumont and Vauxhall, were reinforced between 1888 and 1913 by removing all the earth on top and then creating two layers above: 1.5 meters of sand and 2–2.5 meters of reinforced concrete. Concrete, a composite of cement, sand, and gravel, could be strengthened by higher cement content and by reinforcing it with steel sheets. Armor plating was first iron and then steel, eventually case-hardened steel, which is less fragile. In turn, the artillery developed cylindro-ogival shells with more powerful charges.

In fortifying Hong Kong, Britain in the 1880s responded to the growing strength of warship firepower, notably with rifled breechloaders, by building more shore batteries. These were particularly intended against the naval threat from Russia. This threat to British colonies troubled planners, especially after the Russians developed a Pacific naval base at Vladivostok, which they had acquired from China in 1860. As most of the British navy was in Home, Atlantic, or Mediterranean waters, there was a greater reliance on coastal fortifications. As part of the process of supporting them, the British backed the development of the new navy of Japan with which a treaty was signed in 1902.

FIELD FORTIFICATIONS

While the extent of defensive systems was altered by the range of modern artillery, the enhanced quality of defensive firepower also offered new possibilities for defending fortifications. These took the form of the development of practices and systems of field fortification, taking forward the trenches dug for the siege of Vicksburg in 1863[37] and even more those used in the last stage of the American Civil War in 1864–65, notably around Petersburg in Virginia, and the prepared positions used by the British when defeating Zulu attacks at the battles of Gingindlovu and Khambula in 1879. The latter positions are currently being absorbed by the vegetation. A letter signed "Colonel" and entitled "The Boer War—Attacks of positions," published in the [London] *Times* on December 27, 1899, noted, with reason,

> The modern method of fortifications, introduced with the breech-loading rifle, is based upon the practical indestructibility by modern artillery fire of properly designed earthworks, and the improbability of an attacking force being able to rush a properly prepared position defended by a sufficient number of troops armed with the breech-loading rifle. This improbability became impossibility, now that the magazine rifle is substituted for the breech-loader, until the defences shall have been seriously injured by artillery fire.

Although there were as yet no field-grade steam shovels, this situation looked toward the hybrid fortification systems of World War I: the strengths of fortified field entrenchments that came to define much of the conflict. In large part, these entrenchments demonstrated, in the face of improved field artillery, what was to be known as the "empty battlefield." That, however, was not the case during the nineteenth century. Instead, the emphasis across much of the world was still on the use of established means of fortification. Permanent fortification remained important in military planning, both for attack and defense. Choices repeatedly had to be made. It was necessary to consider where best to construct and maintain fortresses and what plan to use. It was also necessary to decide how strong the garrisons should be.[38]

In Cuba in 1868–78, and again in 1895–98, Spain successfully used *trochas* against revolutionaries. These were two fortified zones, each about 150 to 200 yards wide and entrenched on both sides, with a broad belt of wire obstacles, chevaux-de-frise, *punji* sticks, and mines. At about half-mile intervals, there were forts or blockhouses, between which were smaller fortified posts. The larger installations were connected by telegraph. Down the middle ran a single-track railway to facilitate the rapid movement of troops. Although the insurgents could occasionally infiltrate small groups of troops through the *trocha*, they were never able to break through in force, which permitted Spain to crush them piecemeal. Had the United States not entered the second war, which had been a political objective of the Cubans in both wars, Spain would have won.

The situation in the years running up to World War I can be variously assessed. Unable to appreciate the defensive potential of trenches and the value of mobility, powers, especially Russia, arguably spent too much on fortresses and fortress artillery, which were essentially static, as at Brest-Litovsk, Ivano-Georgievsk, and Kovno (Kaunas) in Russian Poland. In contrast, Russia did not spend enough on field artillery. The latter was mobile, while trenches themselves could be readily dug and were therefore far more flexible and dynamic than fortresses as a defensive system. At the same time, rather than thinking of a simple contrast, field fortifications were increasingly inserted as part of the system of fixed fortifications, and particularly so as the area to be covered by the latter increased and gaps were filled between positions.[39] This was another aspect of hybrid defenses.

In the years before World War I, fortified field entrenchments became most notably significant with the Russo-Japanese War of 1904–05. This conflict between two major powers included many elements that were to be seen in the world war, including trench warfare with barbed wire and machine guns, indirect artillery fire, artillery firing from concealed positions, a conflict that did not cease at nightfall, and a war waged with continuous front lines. Forward observers were linked by telephone to gunners, who were therefore able to fire on targets beyond visual range.

Advocates of the offensive argued that the Russians stood on the defensive and lost, while the more numerous Japanese took the initiative, launched frontal assaults on entrenched forces strengthened by machine guns and quick-firing artillery, as at Mukden in 1905, and eventually prevailed, despite horrific casualties. Field fortifications could, it appeared, be overcome by adequate numbers and willpower.

As a result, the likely result in what became World War I (wrongly) appeared apparent. So also with the Japanese capture of the fortress of Port Arthur, although it mounted a long and stout defense. The Japanese employed trenches in the assault on Port Arthur in 1904, an assault that took the Japanese five months due to the strength of Russian defensive firepower. The Japanese eleven-inch siege howitzers were unable to suppress the defenses, although they did eventually sink most of the Russian Port Arthur Squadron at anchor.

However, in 1912, in the First Balkan War, the Turks used a line of fortifications and natural features at Çatalca (Chataldzha), a line fortified from 1878, to halt a Bulgarian advance on Constantinople (Istanbul). The Bulgarian artillery had failed to destroy its Turkish counterpart, and the latter blunted the Bulgarian infantry assault, causing about twelve thousand casualties. The power of entrenched positions supported by artillery when neither had been suppressed by superior offensive artillery was fully shown. So also with the ability of the surrounded Turkish fortress of Adrianople (Edirne) to hold out for several months against Bulgarian attacks before surrendering in 1913.[40]

The Turks also mounted strong defenses of Scutari and Ioannina before they fell. Besieged by Montenegro with Serbian assistance from October 1912 to April 1913, several costly attacks, which led to the death of close to ten thousand Montenegrin troops, were required before Scutari surrendered. The surrender was facilitated by the payment of £10,000 to the commander Essad Pasha, who wanted to become king of Albania with Montenegrin support. He had had Riza Pasha, his predecessor who wanted to go on fighting, murdered.

Ioannina, the largest city in Epirus, was well defended, with a fortress area supported by concrete artillery emplacements, trenches, and about 102 guns. The system had been designed with German advice. In March 1913, in the Battle of Bizani, a fort that covered the approaches to the city, the Greeks, with heavy artillery support, defeated the Turks in large part thanks to a well-planned and implemented attack advancing on separate axes. Earlier attacks in December 1912 and January 1913 had failed with heavy casualties.[41]

But there was a general reluctance across the West to take this lesson of defensive power on board because of a conviction of the value of the offensive, a conviction that reflected cultural factors, notably ideas of heroism, but also the wish for a quick war. Concern about the obsolescence or vulnerability of fortifications could contribute to the same end, as in France. Moreover, in the Balkan Wars, aside from the capture of fortresses, there had been a successful storming of positions, including Greek frontal attacks at the Sarantaporos Pass in 1912, which opened the way into Macedonia.

BARRICADES

Alongside the cutting-edge developments in fixed and field fortifications came the frequency of barricades, an inner-city form of fortification. As with other forms of fortification, barricades had both functional and cultural values. In the West, the latter were seen with the linkage of barricades to nationalist and also progressive, later left-wing, causes. The nationalist linkage owed much to the "Year of Revolution," 1848, when barricades were constructed in many European cities, including Budapest and Prague, in both cases against Habsburg rule. In 1849, French regulars overthrew the newly established Roman republic after a siege, which showed the utility but also vulnerability of essentially "obsolete" defenses held by more or less amateur forces.

The military emphasis and image in other progressive causes owed much to the barricades constructed in Paris in 1830; Berlin, Naples, Paris, and Vienna in 1848; and the 1871 Paris Commune.[42]

The Paris Commune proved particularly influential as a symbol and, therefore, model. The Communards were able to seize control of Paris in 1871 but, despite major efforts, failed to hold it against the attack by Republican forces that May. This looked toward the more general vulnerability of irregular forces when holding cities against attack by regulars, especially if the latter were well supplied with artillery. Barricades played a key role for the Communards. An opponent, Jules Favre, wrote,

> Our soldiers were advancing only slowly, hindered at every step by barricades which they had to outflank by making their way through the houses. The barricade in the Place de la Concorde was formidably high, protected by a deep trench, bristling with guns. General Douay captured it, in spite of the desperate efforts of its defenders.

Jules Pau noted, "One of the most impressive barricades, as far as the defence was concerned, was the one in the Rue Royale. Equipped with cannon and *mitrailleuses* [machine guns]."[43] After extensive street fighting in which about ten thousand Parisians were killed, about the same number of Communards who had been captured were promptly shot. In part, holding a city compromised the opportunities for asymmetrical warfare, and this disadvantage could not be readily overcome by revolutionary enthusiasm. This looked toward an important aspect of fortification and siegecraft in the modern world.

7

WORLD WARS

WORLD WAR I

In many respects, World War I (1914–18) was about fortifications far more than any other major conflict of the previous century, for the large-scale trench systems that were constructed at the end of 1914 marked an effective form of fortification and one that was new on this scale. Moreover, tactically effective, this form was also operationally and, thereby, strategically appropriate. Large-scale trench systems were not only designed to repel frontal attack but also, by their length, to prevent outflanking and a campaign of encirclement. Furthermore, the speed with which a new trench line could be dug meant that a breakthrough by opponents, or their creation of a new axis of operations, could be thwarted, as Anglo-French forces discovered when they landed at Gallipoli in 1915 and Salonika in 1916, and would probably also have done had they landed elsewhere.

Initially, however, the war appeared to demonstrate the lack of viability of fortresses. The Belgian fortress complexes all fell in 1914 after bombardment by Austrian 305 mm and German 420 mm heavy howitzers, designed before the war specifically for this purpose. The latter fired 2,052-pound high-explosive shells able to penetrate ten feet of concrete, and this could be devastating.

Nevertheless, Liège took far longer to fall than the Germans had anticipated and planned: eleven days instead of two. This failure of the schedule of conquest hit the carefully planned, sequential character of the German advance, in particular because Liège was a major crossing point over the river Meuse and an important rail junction. As a result, the defense of Liège delayed the provision of an adequate supply system to support the German advance across Belgium. The initial attacks on Liège were driven back on August 5, but the fortification system depended on a powerful force to fill the gaps between the twelve armored forts. In its absence, the Germans were able to move through these gaps, although the forts continued to resist, some until August 16. The Germans thus gained mobility and were not subsequently held up in their advance on Paris by fortifications. Namur and Antwerp also fell—the first, another Meuse crossing point, after only four days bombardment—and the Germans were able to advance into France without worrying much about fortresses, although Maubeuge put up a good resistance.

Compared to the time taken to capture these fortresses on earlier occasions, the speed in 1914 indicated a greater potential against prepared defenses. Conversely, there had also been speedy captures earlier. One difference in 1914 was that of the extent of a fortress and, therefore, the scale of the effort potentially required in order to capture it, notably the deployment of huge masses of artillery, including really big guns and their heavy shells.

More conventional defenses, including old Ottoman fortifications and blockhouses as well as trenches, were successfully shelled when the Germans crossed the Sava and Danube Rivers to invade Serbia in October 1915.[1] Moreover, in the conflict outside Europe, there continued to be conventional-style sieges, albeit often with outcomes different from similar earlier occasions. In 1915–16, the successful Turkish siege of a British force in Kut-al-Amara proved a major blow to the British attempt to conquer Mesopotamia. The failure of the relief force and the fighting that involved was a classic element of the conflict.[2] In contrast, the fighting around Gaza in 1917, between Turkish defenders and British attackers, very much involved trench warfare on the western European pattern.

TRENCH WARFARE

As in 1870 and 1940, fortresses did not prevent the German advance. However, checked in the field by French and British defenders in 1914 (unlike in 1940), notably in the Battle of the Marne and later in the First Battle of Ypres, the German war of maneuver failed. In the first case, the Germans underrated the potential use of fortifications as a base of maneuver. During their gaming for an invasion of France, they at times encountered arms in the "entrenched camps" at Paris or elsewhere. In almost every game, the German officers playing the French put up a stout defense but did not attack the forces moving past their positions apart from in a 1911 war game when the "French" player made some spoiling attacks from Paris. All senior German commanders appear to have been convinced that entrenched camps need only be bypassed after being screened, a task for which they made inadequate preparations. Their neglect of the ability of French troops to attack out of their defenses contributed to the German failure of 1914 when the French Sixth Army attacked out of Paris, initiating the Battle of the Marne.

The war of maneuver was replaced by the creation of trench systems in order to mark a front line, to protect troops from machine guns, to lessen their vulnerability to artillery, and thus to hold on to territory. Indeed, World War I fit into a continuum in which, as small arms and artillery became more powerful during the nineteenth century, the role of trenches for protection increased. Ian Hamilton, the inspector general of British overseas forces, had proposed wheeled shields for the infantry in the 1900s, but trenches were a more viable response, not least as soldiers did not have to hold a defensive weapon as well. Trenches had already figured in the siege of fortresses in order to protect the attackers, as at Sevastopol in 1854–55, and the role of the use of trenches in assaulting an entrenched enemy was highlighted in the Russo-Japanese War of 1904–05 at Port Arthur.

In World War I, trenches came into their own on a different scale, and more for the defense than for the attack. The strength of trench positions owed much to the weaponry available for their protection and which they could protect, especially quick-firing artillery and machine guns with their impressive range and rapidity of fire. Barbed wire and concrete fortifications enhanced the defensive positions that were rapidly constructed, while reserves provided defense in depth.

Aside from trenches, there were also particular fortresses, such as Austrian-held Przemsyl in southern Poland;[3] Metz in Lorraine, then part of the German empire; and Verdun. The last had great symbolic significance for the French, notably for politicians who resolutely linked national glory to their presentation of the self-sacrificing dedication of the troops. Verdun was also seen as important to the defense of Paris against attack from the east, although it had not prevented such attack earlier, for example in 1792. Heavily attacked by the Germans in 1916, including with the use of 420 mm guns, Verdun was protected by a series of detached forts, notably Douaumont and Vaux. Their concrete casements and steel cupolas were resistant to bombardment. Although field defenses played the key role in the protection of Verdun, the struggle over these forts was important to the progress of the campaign, not least the sense of success. Thus, a strategic offensive became a matter of tactical struggle, with the defenses eventually blocking the Germans, although not stopping them from inflicting damage on the French by attrition, which became the German goal. The Germans captured both Douaumont (February 25) and Vaux (June 7), but their impetus was lost as units were moved to oppose the British Somme and Russian Brusilov offensives, and the French were able to regain the forts, on October 24 and November 2 respectively. Moreover, the French had been able to maintain the movement of supplies into Verdun, with the *voie sacrée* from Bar-le-Duc becoming a route for trucks (lorries).[4]

In 1917, the Germans pulled back from the current front line, the location of which reflected the results of the fighting that had hitherto taken place, notably the 1916 British Somme offensive, which was an instance of the more general aspect of creating a fortified system on a front line. Instead, the Germans moved to a planned, new shorter line that was designed to offer a more rational line and a more effective defense. This Siegfried Line, known to the Allies as the Hindenburg Line, replaced the earlier system of deep dugouts and continuous trench lines packed with infantry with one of mutually supporting concrete bunkers surrounded by obstacle belts. This system provided a more potent and relevant fortification system that included a flexible defense in depth, a defense that challenged traditional notions of siegecraft. As with the British positioning their forces (although not digging defenses) under Wellington at Waterloo in 1815, reverse-slope positions were used to reduce vulnerability to artillery, while, with its three defense lines, the "line" was up to fifteen miles deep. This was an aspect of the degree to which nomenclature was, as ever, not without problems, indeed ambiguous. There were issues with what a line meant and indeed with the contemporary use of the term *siege*.

The strength of defensive positions did not mean that there was no progress in developing techniques for the attack. As with other siege systems, there was interest, at the strategic level, in the contradictory methods of breaking through, attacking elsewhere, and blockade and, at the tactical level, in both bombardment and storming. Indeed, while, as the Germans showed in 1917, fortifications were developed to deal with changing tactics of attack, each in practice grew out of the other, and to a degree that had not happened in any previous war, nor since. The evolution of artillery tactics made linear defensive lines unworkable

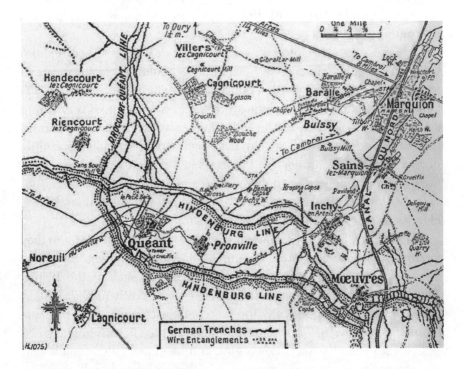

Figure 7.1. The Hindenburg Line

during the latter part of 1916 and into 1917, and this led to the globular defensive plans in which mutually supporting strongpoints with all-round defense interacted to make many square miles of territory dangerous to an attacker. When the Germans built the Siegfriedstellung, not only did they shorten the line, but they made the area between it and their old line into a vast killing zone. They cleared the civilian population and leveled villages and other obstacles in order to create clear fields of fire, and they utilized vast amounts of concertina wire in order to funnel an attacker into zones covered by machine guns, artillery, and mortars. By 1917, the Germans no longer manned "frontline" trenches, because such trenches no longer existed as such. Instead, the first line was a series of thinly manned outposts, because the Germans knew that in the event of an assault the front line would be hit hard. The British were in the process of constructing these sorts of defensive structures when the Germans launched their spring offensives in 1918, particularly in the Fifth Army area. Thus, from the autumn of 1914, defenses had evolved from a single trench line, often broken rather than continuous, to several lines by 1916 and to multiple lines many miles in depth by 1917, with the purpose of containing break-ins and preventing them from becoming breakthroughs.

The use of steel-reinforced concrete for defensive structures also developed, being employed at Verdun in particular. A big advantage of ferroconcrete was the speed of construction. The modern method was patented by François Hennebique in 1892. Ferroconcrete is very strong and tough, as it has high tensile and compressive strengths, unlike unreinforced concrete, which meant that high-explosive shells have little impact on it. While artillery and mortars found it difficult to penetrate the deep-dug defenses, such defenses were not invulnerable. In particular, Livens gas attacks on them were very effective because the gas cloud was so dense and could penetrate everywhere.

And once infantry got among the defenses, no matter how deep they were, they were vulnerable to demolition by sappers who had large charges ready for the purpose, made in facilities such as the British First Army Workshop. These charges were used mostly in raids. Infantry tactics, devised specifically for overcoming strongposts, were made more effective by 1917 by the development of the all-arms infantrymen skilled with rifle, bayonet, Lewis gun, and hand and rifle grenade and accustomed to working in cooperation with mortars and artillery. Thus, during the war, the evolution of infantry tactics and artillery tactics was instrumental in reducing the utility of fortifications.

The accuracy and strength of bombardment increased during the war, notably so in 1917 and, even more, in 1918. Aerial reconnaissance, which developed greatly during the war, played a key role in precise targeting, in understanding the battle space, and in registering progress. In addition, a degree of mobile bombardment at the tactical level was provided by tanks, notably in late 1918. To an extent, these acted as mobile battering rams, particularly in wrecking barbed-wire defenses.

Storming was seen with the use of "stormtrooper" techniques, as employed by the Germans in 1917 and 1918, although tried out earlier, especially in Romania in 1916. These techniques entailed well-equipped and trained infantry rush-advancing in small groups rather than in slow-moving lines, penetrating opposing positions, isolating strongpoints, and pressing on. These tactics proved particularly success-ful at the expense of the Italians in the Caporetto offensive of 1917, leading to a collapse of the Italian front line and an advance of eighty miles. The tactics were to be effectively used by the Germans on the Western Front in the Spring Offensive in 1918.

However, the key development was to be in bombardment and in the necessary coordination of artillery and infantry. The Allies used this repeatedly to break into, through, and beyond the German lines in the second half of 1918 in what became known as the "Hundred Days' Offensive." There were comparable breakthroughs against the Aus-trians, Bulgarians, and Turks.

There was, however, no equivalent overcoming of coastal fortifica-tions. These were significant in deterring the British from launching large-scale attacks on the German-occupied coastline of Belgium throughout the war. Nevertheless, the danger posed by exposure to a more rapid buildup of German forces in response to any landing was more significant. In that respect, the railways that enabled the Germans to move troops were a key element of any fortification system.

BREAKTHROUGH

The successful Allied assault on the Hindenburg Line near Cambrai on September 27, 1918, led the German generals to move rapidly toward an armistice. This assault reflected the development of appropriate artillery and infantry tactics, including "deep battle" in which targets beyond the front, such as headquarters, were being bombarded. Trench warfare had evolved into "deep battle," with important help from aerial reconnaissance, which provided guidance for the artillery. The Allies had also developed the mechanisms, notably greatly improved logistics, and deployed the resources, particularly large numbers of heavy guns, necessary to sustain their advance and offensive in the face of continual German resistance, and to do so across a broad front. Thomas Blamey, the chief of staff to the Australian Corps, noted that the campaign differed from earlier operations in that there was an emplacement of a large proportion of artillery within two thousand yards of the front line, which enabled the advance to be covered by an effective barrage to a depth of four thousand yards into enemy country.[5] The tactics for "deep battle" overcame the new-style German defenses.

The theory of artillery dominance over trench fortifications had been expressed in the report in the [London] *Times* on April 13, 1917, about the British attack on the Germans in the Battle of Arras on the Western Front and the value of knowledge gained from earlier offensives on that front:

> The chief lesson learnt is that against strong defensive positions the pace of a sustained attack is the pace of the heavy artillery. To attempt to force the pace is to neglect the searching preparation which alone can make assaults in force successful without overwhelming sacrifice of time. If time is given for the guns to get into position and to prepare the way for the infantry, then the strength of the defensive lines crumbles to chaos. . . . The role of the guns must be taken up again, and when they have played their part again, then the storming lines will go forward.

It is unclear what role fortifications would have played had the war continued into 1919, as was widely anticipated until shortly before it ended. There would have been new German trench lines to assault, but there would also have been fortresses. The latter would have been both those the Germans had already captured, notably Antwerp, Liège, and Namur, and prewar German fortresses, such as Metz. Had these been strongly defended, the Allies would have required more than just field artillery. It is unclear how much value they would have found from bombers given their limited capability, notably in accuracy and payload. Moreover, antiaircraft fire and interceptor fighters would have been an element in lessening any Allied capability advantage. Most probably, the Allies would have sought to act as the Germans had done in 1914, cutting off fortresses and then blockading them and bombarding them with heavy artillery. The key elements with fortification appeared to be those that could prevent, or at least affect, a would-be war of maneuver.

THE INTERWAR YEARS

The legacy of World War I for fortifications was complex. The heavy losses sustained in breaking into, and through, trench systems ensured that investment in fortifications appeared sensible, not least for states faced by opponents with more numerous forces. Conversely, the war had shown that defensive systems could be overcome and verdicts could be delivered, as with the knocking out of Russia in 1917 and of Germany in 1918, and nearly with Romania in 1916 and Italy in 1917. Responsibility for the success against Germany was variously explained at the tactical level, with, in particular, major contrasts between explanations focused on tanks and those centered on artillery. These differences had consequences for an understanding of the defensiveness of positions and of how best to design, maintain, defend, and attack them. Issues of strategy, doctrine, and funding were involved.

From another perspective, the conflicts that followed the war did not suggest that there would be much of a role for fortifications. This was true in particular of the Russian Civil War in 1918–20, the conflicts of the Chinese Warlord Era in the 1920s, and the war between Greece and Turkey in 1921–22. Each was a struggle in which mobile, rather than static, warfare was a key component. Sieges were not significant. If the Bolsheviks had to defend a central position in Russia, that comprising Moscow and St. Petersburg, against "White" attacks, this defense involved a war of maneuver rather than sieges. "White" forces did not reach St. Petersburg or Moscow. The rising by radical sailors in the Baltic island naval base at Konstadt in 1921 was crushed when Soviet forces successfully advanced across the ice, supported by air attack and covered by heavy artillery.

Fortifications nevertheless continued to play a significant role. In particular, this was true of colonial contexts where fortified bases anchored imperial control. In Morocco, during the 1924–26 Rif War, strong posts resupplied by air played a key role on the French side. Facing insurrection in Syria in 1926, French forces encircled Damascus with barbed wire and machine-gun posts. There was also considerable continuity in the use of pre-1914 forts in colonial policing. At the same time, there were new positions to protect, notably airfields.

Fortifications were also important in some civil conflicts. For example, in the Chinese Civil War of the 1930s between the Communists and the Nationalist (Kuomintang) government, the forces of the latter used blockhouses to try to seal the Communists into mountainous areas, notably in the 1933–34 campaign against Mao Zedong in the region of Jiangxi in which over ten thousand blockhouses were built by the Nationalists, along with roads and landing strips. In the Chaco War between Bolivia and Paraguay in 1932–35, the better-led Paraguayans, although outnumbered, knew how to fight a war of maneuver in the harsh, largely waterless scrub terrain of the Chaco region. Bolivian positions were encircled and their supply lines cut, the Paraguayans turning their tactical capability to operational and strategic effect. Paraguay conquered the Chaco, although an attempt to advance farther saw attacking forces defeated by strongly entrenched Bolivian machine gunners, which helped ensure a settlement.[6]

In the Spanish Civil War (1936–39), fortresses played a role, as in the Republican siege of the Nationalist-held alcazar (fortress) of Toledo in 1936. However, ad hoc fortresses, such as that the Republicans made of the city of Madrid in late 1936, were more significant and a harbinger of things to come. As a result of the resistance the Nationalists encountered there, Francisco Franco, their leader, chose to redirect the focus of his operations away from the capital and, instead, toward attacking secondary targets in what became a form of attritional war. The capture of ports reduced the possibility of the Republicans obtaining foreign supplies. Madrid did not fall until the close of the war.

The practice of fortification and therefore siegecraft was focused on trenches, but not on the scale or intensity of those of World War I. A critical J. F. C. Fuller, a retired general, sent a report to British military intelligence in 1937: "Though the nominal front is immense . . . its garrisons are minute." The following year, the British assistant military attaché in Paris commented after a visit, "Comparatively small forces are strung out on a vast length of front." He observed that, in general, tactics were "largely based on Great War principles," with creeping barrages and trenches, and that success owed much to an ability to concentrate field artillery.[7] Ad hoc fortresses were also established within towns, as by the anarchists in Barcelona in 1937, notably the telephone exchange. These positions were all stormed.[8]

Many of the military ideas of the period did not devote much attention to fortification. In part, this was a matter of the cult of the new in the form of the antiprofessionalism of Communist military concepts and the related focus on the "people under arms" and the offensive. In each case, this was a reprise for the views of the French Revolutionaries. Thus, the Soviet Union had relatively few mines in store in 1941 because an interest in mines was seen as a defeatist focus on the defense.

Very separately, there was the legacy of World War I in the shape of the influence of "artillery generals," commanders whose experience focused on the use of artillery, as did many British and French generals. The interest in a knockout blow delivered by air attack or tanks contributed to the same underplaying of the value of fortifications. So also did favor for the "indirect approach," the focus on wearing down opponents by engaging them in secondary theaters, and on the ability to open up campaigns by, and for, maneuver. This was the theme of military commentators, as, in Britain, with Basil Liddell Hart's *Decisive Wars of History* (1929) and *The Ghost of Napoleon* (1933).

Before World War II, however, there was much investment in systems of fortifications, notably with the French Maginot Line, but also the Finnish Mannerheim Line, the Dutch Water Line, the German West Wall, and the American fortifications to protect Manila Bay, particularly on the island of Corregidor, which was overoptimistically termed the "Gibraltar of the Pacific." The British fortified their new naval base at Singapore. Their record, and those of fortifications constructed during the war itself, were mixed. None of the fortification systems mentioned above prevented failure, but that does not exhaust the subject.

The lack of an appropriate, or at least (and differently) successful, plan was seen with the French Maginot Line, named after André Maginot, the minister of defense from 1928 to 1930. Begun in 1930 to offset

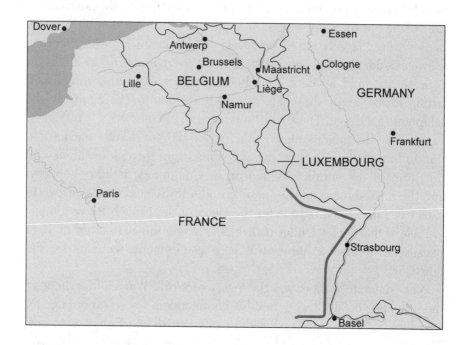

Figure 7.2. The Maginot Line

Germany's larger population and therefore capacity for a larger army, this was an economy-of-force measure and a means to create jobs. The fortifications covered the Franco-German frontier from Switzerland to Luxemburg, although they were denser in particular areas, and they were regarded by the French as an aspect of a force structure that could support an offensive or a defensive strategy. The fortifications were intended to constrain the options of any attacker,[9] as they indeed did in 1940. Early in the Cold War, before German rearmament, NATO commanders incorporated the Maginot Line into their plans, seeing it as a means to help channel a Soviet offensive.

In 1935, Sir Archibald Montgomery-Massingberd, the perceptive chief of the (British) Imperial General Staff, saw the Maginot Line as providing support for operational mobility, which is frequently an aspect of the strategic and operational value of fortifications. Referring back to World War I, he wrote,

> My recollections of our attacks against strong lines during the war, even with masses of heavy guns and tanks, is that this frontier, in

three or four years will be practically impregnable, always provided of course that the French keep up their present garrison and maintain everything at the standard they are doing at present. Here again the underlying idea of economy in men so as to set free as many troops as possible for the mobile army.

He also commented on the strength of the French fortifications facing Italy—"tunnelled as they are under 40 or 50 feet of rock, with embrasures for guns and machine guns covering every approach."[10] In turn, the Italians refurbished their Alpine fortresses, notably that on Monte Chaberton, although by 1940 it was vulnerable to long-range artillery. The French developed their coastal defenses in Provence to provide protection against Italian attack. The naval base of Toulon was particularly vulnerable. The coastal defenses were armed with battleship guns, an armament also used by the Americans. Similarly, in southern Tunisia, the French built the Mareth Line against invasion from the neighboring Italian colony of Libya. There were also fortifications on Corsica against possible Italian invasion.

Opposing the Maginot Line, the Germans constructed the three-hundred-mile long West Wall in 1936–40, and mostly from 1938. This was not designed to be as strong as the Maginot Line but, instead, to delay attackers so that reserves could be moved up, a facet of defensive systems that can be too easy to overlook. The focus was on mutually supporting pillboxes and concrete antitank defenses. In addition, in what is now western Poland, but was then eastern Germany, between the rivers Oder and Wartha, a fortified system, the Ostwall or Festungsfront im Oder-Warthe Bogen, was built to protect Germany's eastern border and thus also to create greater flexibility in the event of a German attack on Poland. The plans began under the Weimar Republic, but the project was realized by the Nazi government between 1934 and 1944. The line in part relied on lakes as an integral part of the system. However, in January 1945, the fortifications were relatively easily captured by Soviet forces.

Other states also invested heavily in fortifications. The Finnish Mannerheim Line was constructed across the Karelian Isthmus, the most vulnerable point to Soviet attack. Forty miles long, it comprised fieldworks strengthened by forty-four concrete bunkers, and the main line was backed by two rear lines of fieldworks. Poland began to build fortifications in the early 1920s. The priority was to provide protection against the Soviet Union, which had invaded in 1920. This remained the priority, but fortifications against Germany were also built from 1934. Most started too late to provide protection when Poland was invaded by both Germany and the Soviet Union in 1939. The lengthy nature of the Polish frontier created a major strategic problem, one that was accentuated when Germany took over Czechoslovakia in 1939. Similarly, in 1938, the viability of Czech defenses in the Sudetenland against German attack was in part compromised when, earlier in the year, the Germans took over Austria, making the Czechs vulnerable to invasion from the south. The Czech defenses were planned by French engineers on the same design as the Maginot Line.

Defenses could be indirect. At the top of the Gulf of Bothnia, Sweden, from 1900, constructed the Boden Fortress against the Finnish frontier, not in order to protect against invasion by Finland but so as to resist any Russian, later Soviet, invasion via Finland, which was a Russian possession until the collapse of the Romanov dynasty. The fortress, which was comparable in design to Belgian and French fortresses from the same period, was never completed according to plan, in part because of defense reductions in the 1920s and until 1936.

Separately, the operational level of fortification warfare was seen in the Japanese campaigns for Shanghai and Nanjing in 1937. The capture of these cities ultimately depended on overcoming what were in effect extensive outer defenses in the shape of Chinese units in the field.[11]

Alongside the strengthening of defenses in some areas, there was a failure to maintain cutting-edge capability in others, a problem accentuated by the rising completion and cost of such capability. This was seen for example in the British Empire, the largest in the world. The problem posed by air power made many defense systems appear inadequate, while also encouraging the idea that defensive and/or deterrent air power was the best possible protection against air and sea attack, as with the B-17 "Flying Fortresses" deployed by the Americans in the Philippines. In consequence, coastal defenses were run down, for example by the British on Ceylon (Sri Lanka) and at Bermuda. By 1939, only two guns were in operation in Bermuda, compared to the twenty-two in 1910.[12] The defenses of the British colony of Malta were vulnerable to Italian air attack.

Many states used old fortifications. The Italians used Palmanova, an *alla moderna* fortress built by Venice in 1593, extended by Napoleon and made use of by Austria during World War I. In Ireland, there was an even greater reliance on legacy sites. The Department of Finance, whose officials were former British civil servants, of the now independent country considered spending on defense to be a waste of money as the British could be relied upon to protect the country.

WORLD WAR II

It is instructive to review what happened to prewar fortifications. In the event, in 1940, despite, rather than because of, their major prewar investment in fortifications, the French proved unable to devise and implement an adequate plan for effective mobile warfare, not least due to the commitment of the mobile reserve to advancing toward the Netherlands. The Maginot Line, which contained about four hundred thousand troops, guided the direction of the German attack to the north of the line through Belgium. However, advancing to break through the French positions on the middle Meuse, the Germans brilliantly gained and retained the initiative in the area in which they advanced. The failure of the Maginot Line continues to be a much-cited instance of the failure of fortification and defensive strategies as a whole, as well, more particularly, of the French in 1940. This failure is often held up as the product of the drawbacks of resting on the defensive. The Maginot Line was penetrated in places on June 16, but, more seriously, the forces in it were cut off by German advances to their rear, while earlier they had not been able to intervene against the German offensive.

Farther north, the force and speed of the German attack, including by tanks and airborne forces, and the inadequate nature of the response ensured that the combination of Dutch geography, especially water features,[13] and defenses, notably the Ysel Line, rapidly failed. So also with the Belgian defenses. Rather differently, fortifications could be blasted through by artillery, as the Soviets did with the Mannerheim Line in February 1940. This triumph brought their 1939–40 Winter War with Finland to the successful conclusion that is generally neglected due to the usual focus on earlier Finnish successes. The breaking of the Mannerheim Line underlined the central problem of maintaining fortification integrity, that of the limited means of keeping opposing heavy artillery at bay. The lack of maneuverability of fortresses was thus a key defect.

Japanese air and artillery bombardment weakened the defenses of Singapore in 1942 and of American-held Corregidor in 1942, preparing the way for successful nighttime amphibious assaults and the rapid fall of the islands. The Mareth Line was ably used by the Italians in March 1943 to provide protection in a stage of the German-Italian retreat into Tunisia.[14] Nevertheless, it fell to advancing British forces.

There were also failures at a grander scale. In 1941, the German invasion of the Soviet Union had been delayed in its early stages by the strong defense of fortified positions, notably at Brest-Litovsk and Odessa, but they all had fallen to the attackers. The Soviets had had scant time to prepare the defenses of areas they had seized in 1939–40: Karelia (from Finland), Estonia, Latvia, Lithuania, eastern Poland, and Bessarabia (from Romania), and Stalin devoted relatively little energy to the task. However, the advance of the Germans late in 1941 was held up by firmly defended and rapidly established defenses near Leningrad and Moscow. Antitank guns proved particularly effective against tanks. The Germans were neither able to sustain mobile warfare nor to switch from it to offensive positional conflict.

The Atlantic Wall built from 1942 by the Germans to defend the French coast against Allied invasion showed in 1944 that ferroconcrete was very resistant to high explosives. A total of 17.3 million cubic tons of concrete were used on this part of Hitler's Festung Europa (Fortress Europe). However, the defenses were damaged or rapidly outflanked on June 6, "D-Day," in the Anglo-American-Canadian invasion of Normandy. The Atlantic Wall neither prevented the landings nor seriously impeded them, the very difficult American experience on Omaha Beach notwithstanding. Even there, the troops still managed to get ashore and press inland in a matter of hours, and losses, although grievous, were modest compared to the major tactical, operational, and strategic achievement.

In 1944 in Normandy, bunkers and other individual fortified positions were vulnerable and, once engaged, the occupants (as was commonly the case with fortifications) were trapped inside unless a counterattack hit the attackers when they were held up by the bunkers. All bunkers and casemates required apertures for guns, access for their crews, and ventilation. With the right tactics and weapons (demolition charges, flamethrowers, grenades, and tanks), most fortifications could be taken by attacking the occupants through these apertures, although it was time consuming and tiring. The tactics used in World War I had been relearned. In 1944, the Germans lacked sufficient mobile forces forward enough in Normandy to act in cooperation with the fixed coastal defenses attacked by the Allies on D-Day.[15] Major Anderson of the Special Observer Party landed on D+6 to assess the damage inflicted by Allied naval and air bombardments. His appraisal of the Mont Fleury site showed that although the casemate housing the battery's only operational gun had been hit by a five-hundred-pound bomb, the gun was undamaged. The British navy reported that even fifteen-inch naval shells had been unable to penetrate the steel-reinforced structures of the German defenses. The Second Tactical Air Force took to using Typhoons to fire semi-armor-piercing rockets into the embrasures of the big coastal gun casemates. The Germans then hung heavy steel chains over the embrasures to detonate the rockets, a form of spaced armor.

The subsequent use of such defenses to delay the Allies' capture of ports, notably Cherbourg, where the Germans employed demolition charges to destroy much of the harbor, was countered by the Allies' ability to supply their forces across the Normandy beaches. When the Americans attacked St. Malo following the Normandy breakout, they chose to make a frontal assault. The ferroconcrete defenses proved almost intractable, and the Americans had to use tank destroyers, artillery, bazookas, and flamethrowers to fire point-blank into the embrasures and take the bunkers one by one. The Americans did not repeat their St. Malo experience: St. Nazaire and Lorient, naval bases fortified by the Germans and held until the end of the war, were bypassed and blockaded by the Allies, mostly French and American. After 1945, the concrete blockhouses of the war proved difficult to remove, and many remain today.

In contrast, the Allies (mostly Americans) were far more successful in overcoming German defenses and fortifications when they invaded Southern France in August 1944. In part, this was because there were fewer defenders than in Normandy and their caliber was lower.[16] In addition, the Allies deployed formidable air and naval support, while the cohesion of the German position in France had been broken by the invasion of Normandy, which also soaked up German reserves.

Similarly, to put the role of fortifications in context, the American attack on the German frontier, the area of the West Wall, or Siegfried Line, protecting Germany's frontier, which the Germans had upgraded in 1944, largely failed later that year. In part, this was because of the fortifications, but also because the terrain and weather helped the defenders. Moreover, the recent rapid tempo of the American advance across France and Belgium had not prepared them for such fighting, not least due to major strains on American logistics. The Americans finally captured the German city of Aachen in October, but that fighting caused heavy casualties and considerable delay, as did that in the difficult terrain of the nearby Hürtgen Forest. The tactics used effectively in Normandy proved less effective because of the terrain, the trees, and the weather. The trees themselves became part of the defenses because of the way they splintered under artillery bombardment. The splinters were as deadly as shell fragments.

However, once the Allies had consolidated their forces and resumed their offensive in 1945, the defenses of the Siegfried Line proved vulnerable, in particular to concentrated and mobile firepower. Tank-infantry teams, supported by artillery fire and demolitions, had a major impact on individual positions. Aside from tanks, the Allies used self-propelled tank destroyers and motor gun carriages. The American 155 mm M-12 motor gun carriage could penetrate seven feet of reinforced concrete at two thousand yards. In addition, phosphorus rounds could blind defenders.[17] The defenses were overcome. The Germans had constructed additional lines of defense, as in the Reichswald forest southwest of Cleves. Clearing those defenses in February–March 1945 involved a heavy use of bombardment and proved much like the fighting of World War I, rather than the emphasis on tanks in an actual or would-be war of movement seen the previous year.

These varied campaigns indicated that, as with other weapon systems, fortifications, both fixed and field, proved most effective as part of a combined-arms force, while the combined dimension was also dependent on an appropriate plan. As across time and across the world, fortifications required a flexible supporting counterattack defense, as the Japanese, for example, had shown when resisting Mongol attacks in the thirteenth century. The Germans benefited in their blitzkrieg attacks from the lack of such defenses. On April 9, 1940, the German naval task force making its way from the North Sea up the Oslo Fjord toward

Oslo, the Norwegian capital, was engaged by the guns and torpedoes of the forts about twenty miles south of the city. Hit, the cruiser *Lützow* turned back, but the heavy cruiser *Blücher*, the most modern ship in the German navy, was sunk. However, the forts were on their own, and the Germans compensated for this failure by relying instead on airborne forces to seize Oslo.

With Singapore, which fell to the Japanese in February 1942 in what proved a major blow and humiliation for the British, an argument is frequently made that the British had prepared fortifications prewar with the naval guns pointing in the wrong direction. This criticism should be reassessed by noting that these defenses, essentially high-specification coastal defenses, were directed against the possibility of a Japanese naval attack, and reasonably so given the size and relative proximity of the Japanese navy and the vulnerability of Singapore to such attack. The guns could be swung around to face back into the jungles of Johore on surprisingly wide arcs.

In the event, the Japanese conquered all of Malaya before invading Singapore from the north. The failure in both Malaya and Singapore was not because of a lack of fixed defenses but rather due to the serious mishandling of the forces available and the underestimation of Japanese capability. The main defenses for Malaya were the chain of airfields built across the peninsula. There were plans to give the RAF a leading role in the defense of Malaya. The army built shoreline positions at coastal towns on the west coast, but not much more than that. During the campaign, the British lacked the necessary combined-arms capability because of the earlier destruction of British air and naval forces in the region.

There were also broader strategic issues. The British had been over-stretched prior to the war and were even more so during the conflict. Concerned about the war with Germany and Italy, the British mistakenly hoped that the defense of Malaya and Singapore would benefit from the strength of the American fleet in the western Pacific, while their ability to deploy sufficient forces to the region was affected by the war with Germany and Italy, which was particularly significant for the allocation of naval and air units.

During the war, individual fortresses were important to the course of the conflict, notably British-held Tobruk in North Africa. The need to capture it delayed the German advance on the Nile in 1942. Sevastopol in Crimea, which the Germans captured in 1942 and the Soviets in 1944, was also significant. The first campaign proved a major distraction to German operations in 1942, with positional warfare using up troops.

This was again to happen later that year when the Germans surrendered mobility and attacked Stalingrad, a city that became an improvised Soviet fortress, as Leningrad already had in late 1941. Taking Stalingrad assumed a great and increasing symbolic importance for Hitler, substituting a political goal for operational flexibility. On the pattern of the Germans attacking the French fortress of Verdun in 1916, Hitler also hoped that Stalin would commit his forces to hold the city and thus enable the Germans to destroy them. By forcing battle on the Soviets, Hitler hoped to achieve a result of strategic consequence and thus to avoid the need to wage comparable struggles against other cities.

Hitler, however, concentrated military assets on what, in large part due to German bombing, became a wrecked urban terrain. As a result, armor and air attack could achieve little, the Germans could not utilize their skill at mobile warfare, and much of the fighting was at very close range. As losses mounted, more and more German forces were sucked into the battle and expended in repeated attempts to seize individual complexes, especially the Tractor, Red October, and Barricades factories, each of which took on significance because of the intractable nature of the struggle. The increasing use of reinforced concrete for the construction of industrial plants and other installations proved an important factor in the defense of Stalingrad and other places.

The difficulties the Germans encountered at Stalingrad were exacerbated by poor command decisions, including a failure both to drive against the flanks of the Soviet position in the city, in an attempt to cut it off from the river, and to focus on the same targets throughout. Instead, the Germans attacked on a broad front and switched targets. Strategy had been swallowed first by operational considerations and then by tactics, or, looked at differently, there was an operationalization and tacticalization of strategy. This was linked to the tendency to follow particular courses because it was possible to do so or because one was good at it, a process that could defeat strategy. This is a persistent problem with siegecraft and one that explains why technical factors have to be approached from a broader perspective, a point more generally true of military history.

German concentration on the city itself, and a more general failure to give heed to Soviet capability, helped clear the way for a skillfully planned and prepared Soviet counterattack that drove in weakly held flanks and encircled the Germans in and near Stalingrad, inflicting a major defeat that had strategic consequences. The Germans proved unable to sustain a defense comparable to that mounted earlier by the Soviets, in large part because they were surrounded and deprived of supplies, as the Soviets had not been, and because aerial supply did not deliver the required amounts. Moreover, the Germans found it difficult to improvise the necessary defenses.

In addition to Leningrad and Stalingrad, Berlin, Brest, Budapest, Königsberg, Mandalay, Manila, Riga, and Sevastopol were among other cities that were in effect fortresses for ground fighting during the war. In these cities, the formal prewar fortified positions were but part of a broader wartime ad hoc fortress, although, as in Budapest and Mandalay in 1945, they could be particularly important parts. Budapest was designated as a fortress that must be held to the last man as the city was surrounded by the Soviets in December 1944. Indeed, Hitler was not interested in having his forces break out. The Germans fought very hard, with each street fought over. The battle for control took nearly two months, but the Soviets were successful, with the Germans losing about 150,000 troops. They had been fixed by the order to defend Budapest. Japanese-held Mandalay was captured by the British in operations that involved storming that was almost on the pattern of Wellington's campaigns in the peninsula.

Fighting in Warsaw proved particularly brutal, as there it opposed German forces who frequently acted in a murderous, even genocidal, fashion to civilians. This was seen first with the fighting in the Warsaw Ghetto in 1943. Underground bunkers were important positions in this resistance. In 1944, there was a second rising, this time by the Polish Home Army. It was larger in scale than that in 1943 but also only lightly armed. Again this became a house-to-house rising. The failure of the nearby Soviets to provide the Poles with anticipated support proved a key element in 1944 in the eventual success of the more heavily armed German forces who applied anti-societal methods. In turn, Warsaw fell to the Soviets the following winter.

Repeatedly when the Soviets attacked during the war, the Germans, under the influence of Hitler's focus on willpower, designated positions as fortresses that were to be held to the last man, for example Vitebsk, Orsha, Mogilev, and Bobruisk in Belarus in 1944 and Breslau (Wrocław) in Silesia in 1945. From the Soviets, the Germans, who had hitherto focused on the offensive, had borrowed the idea of "hedgehog" fortresses. However, this policy, which worked for the Germans to a considerable degree in limiting the impact of the Soviet winter offensive in 1941–42, failed in 1944–45 because of the dynamic and scale of the Soviet advance. In the latter case, positions were isolated and had scant influence on the campaigning. This had happened to the German forces in early 1943 in the part of Stalingrad they had captured.

Soviet operational art, notably as practiced in 1944 but already as clearly seen in 1943, overcame the Germans on the defensive, in part because Hitler's preference for holding positions was circumvented. Rather than seek encirclements, the Soviets deployed their forces along broad fronts, launching a number of frontal assaults designed to smash opposing forces and maintain continued pressure. The Soviets denied the Germans the ability to recover from attacks, reduced their ability to move units to badly threatened positions, and searched out the weakest points in their positions. This lessened the value of German defensive hedgehogs. While they had an operational importance on narrow-front campaigns, narrowing the advance and challenging its flanks and rear, these hedgehogs were less significant in resisting broad-front attacks, especially when they could not rely on air support or armored counter-offensives. The loss of air support also ensured that it would not be possible to reinforce encircled positions by air. Thus, the Germans could not respond as the British could, in the Admin Box battle and at Imphal and Kohima, to Japanese attacks on the Indian-Burma (Myanmar) frontier in 1944. Instead, the German positions were vulnerable, as British defensive "boxes" had been in North Africa to the Afrika Korps in 1941–42. The Germans adopted the designation of fortresses elsewhere, for example for Breskens in the Scheldt estuary against advancing Canadian forces in September 1944.

In contrast to individual fortresses, defensive lines could play a role, as with the German Gustav and Gothic lines in Italy and the German positions west of the Oder River in April 1945. These lines benefited from natural features, but in each case the lines were breached. The Gustav Line was the name by which the Bernhardt Line northwest of Naples came to be called. Originally it was a fallback for that line, which was strongly fortified in October 1943. This was then supplemented by the Hitler Line, constructed in November, but with its name changed to the Senger Line in January 1944 so that Hitler's prestige should not be compromised by its loss. The Gothic Line took advantage of the defensive strength offered by the Apennine Mountains, a difficult chain, but it was breached in September 1944. Elsewhere in Italy, the Germans benefited from other mountains and, in particular, from the extent to which the steeply indented river valleys that ran west and east from the Apennines to the sea provided opportunities for defenders and obstacles for attackers, a pattern later to be seen in the Korean War (1950–53). This was yet another instance of the environmental character of fortification. These valleys were made further valuable for the defense by the rivers being in spate after rainfall, in other words overflowing due to sudden floods. As in Korea, the topography in Italy worked against the use of tanks, while the peninsula nature of the battlefield meant that the search for an open flank was dependent on amphibious operations, as at Anzio (1944) and Inchon (1950). These factors all put a premium on infantry and artillery in both defense and attack, and the positional nature of the warfare contributed greatly to the ability of fortifications to enhance the defense.

Many lines, however, were breached with far greater ease. The fast-moving German offensive smashed through the Aliakmon and Metaxas Lines in the successful invasion of Greece in April 1941, one in which air support played a significant role. Some lines turned out, as far as campaign outcomes were concerned, to mean little more than additions to the map.

At the tactical level, minefields played a major part in defensive systems. For example, in late 1942, Irwin Rommel laid half a million antitank mines and also many antipersonnel mines in order to protect his position at El Alamein in Egypt against British attack. Alongside antitank guns, mines had become more significant due to the new emphasis on attacks by tanks, which could counter barbed wire and machine guns. Mines were responsible for between 20 and 30 percent of wartime tank casualties. Mine techniques and production developed rapidly during the war. Mine clearing therefore became an aspect of siegecraft, and this also saw developments, including the use of handheld electronic detectors and flail tanks. In turn, there were innovations with mines, notably in producing, from 1941, mines that were resistant to blast-clearance devices and, from 1943, nonmetallic mines to defeat mine detectors. Anti-lifting devices were also introduced.

Similar races for capability advantages could also be seen with anti-aircraft and antisubmarine defenses. These and other races, which were variously significant for attack and defense, saw a need for scientific advances, technological application, resource allocation, doctrinal revision, training, and tactical understanding as part of a combined-arms viability. To isolate simply one factor is mistaken.

Alongside the defenses developed in areas of conflict, there was much investment elsewhere in preparation to repel attacks that did not in the event occur. This was particularly the case with planned or apparently possible invasions, such as of England by the Germans, as indeed was planned in 1940, and of Norway, Sardinia, and the Pas-de-Calais by the Allies, as was suggested by Allied deception exercises that were intended, in large part, to cover the invasions of Sicily (1943) and Normandy (1944). Such deception underlined the major opportunity costs involved in defensive preparations, both in terms of the construction of fortifications and their manning. These were particularly serious for Germany in 1943–44 as it struggled in its strategic formulation and implementation to reconcile defensive commitments in the face of mounting Allied pressure. The dynamic between threats and preparations more generally captured the way both attacking and defending sides established parameters for the other.

Preparations were far flung. In southern England in 1940, there were defenses on the likely invasion beaches, particularly in Kent and Sussex, but also inland to contest possible landing zones for airborne forces. Concrete pillboxes were erected accordingly, many providing zones of fire across large fields that could be used by gliders and parachutists, as the Germans had done when attacking Denmark, Norway, the Netherlands, and Belgium earlier in the year.

In Britain as elsewhere, there was a degree of reuse of existing positions, a reuse that reflected the significance of the sites and the value of existing facilities. This was seen in particular at Dover, long a well-fortified stronghold, where there was extensive tunneling in order to enhance defensive facilities and provide strong command-and-control positions. So also at Gibraltar, where there was renewed tunneling within the Rock. Dartmouth Castle, where guns had been mounted during World War I, had two installed in 1940.

After American bases were agreed for parts of the British Empire in 1940, the Americans both built the first airfield in Bermuda and began coastal defense works against the possibility of German naval attack. These included the installation of railway guns left over from World War I.[18] Similarly, there were preparations to protect the defenses of the Atlantic naval base at Norfolk, Virginia, from German naval attack, including the installation of long-range artillery able to outrange the *Bismarck*, Germany's most powerful warship. It was sunk in the Atlantic by British naval forces in 1941, which, in protecting British convoy routes, thus acted as the forward defense for American coastal fortifications.

Japan's entry into the war in December 1941 spread this process, notably with American, Australian, and New Zealand coastal fortifications, as at San Pedro, California, which had sixteen-inch guns emplaced and Stony Batter at the eastern terminus of Waiheke, off Auckland, New Zealand. Concern about a possible amphibious invasion of Queensland led Australia to defense preparations. The Americans proved highly capable base builders, using resources, skills, and organizational capability to that end.

Neutral powers also included fortifications in their defense preparations. Thus, Sweden constructed coastal fortifications in the outer archipelago in order to protect Stockholm at its most vulnerable point.

Alongside changes in geographical concern, there was the need to defend against new threats. During World War II, antiaircraft protection became an important aspect of fortifications, as with German flak towers, of which many were built in response to the Anglo-American air offensive.[19] Antiaircraft defense towers were built in Berlin and Vienna. Protection led to an emphasis on strengthening buildings against attack from above in the shape of bombing. Concrete played a major role, as in German submarine pens, for example on France's Atlantic coast.[20] The use of underground facilities to provide protection against bombing was also important, as with German underground manufacturing. The risk of air attack affected the location, structure, and defense of fortifications.

There was also protection against airborne assaults by parachutists or gliders. The success of German airborne forces in 1940 in capturing the supposedly impregnable Belgian fortress of Eben Emael which guarded the Albert Canal bridges had made a significant impact. In practice, airborne forces, although important and successful in some instances, notably in the German invasion of Crete in 1941, in securing the flanks of the Allied invasion of Normandy in 1944, and in helping in the Allied assault across the Rhine in 1945, did not fulfill the hopes of many protagonists. As a consequence, defenses against their landing were often of no value. The range of threats helps to explain the variety of fortifications that emerged.[21]

In strategic terms, Roosevelt was correct to point out that the Festung Europa had no roof, although this was only because German air defenses were overcome. For Germany as for other powers, air defense involved ground positions, aircraft, and control systems. These were conceptualized in terms of fortification. Air defense was described with reference to boxes, zones, and lines, as defenses were organized in a spatial fashion, with the particular requirements of interception and control of units being made more dynamic by technological changes, notably in radar. Thus, the Germans developed in 1940 what was known as the Kammhuber Line after the general responsible. So also with air defenses in Britain. This nomenclature continued into the Cold War, as with early-warning systems to protect the United States against Soviet air attack.

Alongside fixed fortifications, there were their field counterparts. Improvised fortifications, and thus fortresses, were developed by the Allies as well as by their opponents. They were seen in particular in response to German advances, notably with the Ardennes offensive in 1944, the Battle of the Bulge. These positions greatly limited the German advance, especially at Bastogne, where American troops from the 101st Airborne Division bravely and successfully resisted that December despite being surrounded. So again on what became the shoulders of the Allied defense, shoulders that helped form the "Bulge," while around St. Vith a successful American defense delayed the German advance before being pulled back to avoid being cut off.

So also, earlier in 1944, with British defensive boxes on the Indian-Burma (Myanmar) border, particularly at Imphal and Kohima. These saw off Japanese attacks in large part because all-round defenses, and their concentric fire zones, meant that the Japanese ability to outflank positions was increasingly of limited consequence. This had already been seen with Japanese attacks on Australian forces in southeast New Guinea. The tactical capability gap between the two sides had ended, not least because the Japanese did not develop new tactical innovations in their attacks on fortified positions. In contrast, the Allies did so, notably the Americans in the Pacific.

A conspicuous instance of field fortifications occurred in 1943 in opposition to Operation Citadel, the German Kursk offensive. Forewarned by accurate intelligence information, the Soviets had prepared a dense defensive system of six belts, appropriately designed to resist tank attack, including extensive antitank defenses, field fortifications, and minefields. This provided a defense in depth and artillery-support system that inflicted heavy casualties when the Germans attacked. Without achieving its goals, the German offensive was called off.

Prominent instances of fortifications that were variously fixed and field included those constructed by the Japanese in the Pacific islands attacked by the Americans. These fortifications included the offshore defenses of mines and other obstacles but were largely onshore. Taking forward the long-established practice of using underground fortifications, a practice now encouraged by American air, sea, and land bombardment, the Japanese where possible used caves, as on Iwo Jima and Okinawa. Both islands were very heavily fortified. The Japanese discovered that attacking the invading forces was a mistake as it exposed them to American firepower. Instead, they increasingly waited for the Americans to advance into their fire zones.

The reefs, shores, and bluffs of Pacific islands act as a reminder that field fortifications, like their fixed counterparts, owed much of their strength and significance, as well as siting, to natural features, which are more significant on islands than on large continental masses. So also, though, on landmasses with the need to cross rivers, and thus the extent to which fortification could be an aspect of an opposed crossing. Each element was important, as with the British crossing of the Seine at Vernon in 1944, and with the difficulties and failure later in the year in the Netherlands.[22]

Military doctrine emphasized the importance of temporary positions in the field, such as foxholes and weapon emplacements.[23] These have been extensively affected by postwar degradation and are rarely preserved or documented. Woodland that has escaped intensive postwar management is the best environment for their preservation.[24]

CONCLUSIONS

World War II is usually discussed in terms of campaigns and battles of movement in open country and with reference to generals, such as General George Patton, who were prominent accordingly. Important as they were, this can lead to a downplaying of the extent of conflict that took place in cities. These proved a terrain that was intractable for armored warfare, as the German tanks discovered in attacking Warsaw in 1939 at the outset of the war in Europe. Linked to this was the frequency of sieges of towns and cities, which, by their importance and the relative ease of defending them, lent themselves to use as fortified positions. The long and unsuccessful German siege in 1941–43 of Leningrad, which the Soviets had never planned to become a fortress and which did not have surrounding forts, was the key event in the campaign in northern Russia, while sieges of Sevastopol were crucial to those in the Crimea,[25] and so on. Rommel felt it important to capture Tobruk before he advanced toward the Nile.

Such sieges can be viewed in two lights. It can be argued that, like the Napoleonic and Franco-Prussian Wars and World War I, the fate of fortified positions and unfortified cities was settled by the war of movement, for example the fall of Singapore to the Japanese in 1942 following that of Malaya; the two captures of Manila (1942, 1945) following successful landings in Luzon, by the Japanese and Americans respectively; and the Battle of Berlin in 1945 following the Soviet destruction of the German positions to the west of the Oder. At Tobruk in 1942, the British overreliance on defensive boxes enabled Rommel to direct the flow of the battle, and once heavily attacked, they could not be held.[26] Alternatively, it can be pointed out that fortified positions, such as Leningrad and Stalingrad, provided, or helped anchor, defenses that curtailed and could help determine campaigns of movement.

Some of the postwar discussion searched for historical parallels. This was most striking with the article "Armor and Counter Armor" in the May 1944 issue of the *Infantry Journal*, in which J. F. C. Fuller described all-round defense against tank attacks in terms of castles and wagon fortresses. In turn, World War II became a history that has remained highly significant, if not iconic, to the present for many of the leading societies of the world. Thus, the fortifications of the period are visited, depicted in films and electronic games, and discussed. This is particularly the case with the German defenses overlooking Omaha Beach in Normandy, defenses that have not been destroyed. A literature of prison escape focuses on the German use of Colditz Castle to detain high-ranking prisoners. This situation ensures that the post-1945 world of fortifications consists in part of the recovered and constructed memory of their use during World War II.

8

SINCE WORLD WAR II

GOALS AND TECHNOLOGY

Forts continued to be significant after World War II, although their role tends to be seriously downplayed. Indeed, this omission constitutes a flaw in some work on the history of fortifications, let alone that on warfare. Major fortifications were dismantled after the war, for example the sixteen-inch gun emplacements at Fort Tilden (1924) and Navesink Highlands (1943) that had served to protect New York Harbor and the comparable positions protecting the naval base of Norfolk, Virginia. The latter had been upgraded to protect against a German naval attack that appeared a serious prospect in 1940–41.

America's postwar strength as a naval power made attack by sea on America or its allies appear unlikely. So also with changes in the character of naval firepower. The age of the battleship passed, the last British one being broken up in 1960, and the Soviet Union, which had no battleships, focused its challenge to the United States on submarines and missile carriers. In turn, although the United States (eventually alone) retained battleships, its offensive capability at sea, at the subnuclear level, concentrated on aircraft carriers while, at the nuclear level, this capability at sea was provided by carriers and then submarines.

More generally, antiship artillery appeared redundant in an age of air power, as the latter became more effective in its specifications than had been the case during World War II. In 1956, coastal defense was declared obsolete throughout most of the British Empire, including

Bermuda. So also with the abandonment of the important fixed defenses at both ends of the Panama and Suez Canals.

During the 1930s, the United States began converting some coast artillery units to antiaircraft guns. After World War II, the Coast Artillery branch became the Air Defense Artillery, and many coast artillery installations converted from antiship artillery to antiaircraft missiles.

The equations of defense and deterrence meanwhile changed with new geopolitical relationships and weaponry, as with British plans to defend Hong Kong.[1] At the same time, the defense of all positions had to emphasize protection against air attack. For this defense, the use of natural features continued, as in the major Soviet submarine base in Crimea with its under-the-cliff character. There was a continuation of wartime patterns of defense against air attack, including fixed ground defenses, aircraft, and control systems.

More generally, mobility and firepower might, separately and in combination, appear to have put paid to the need for fortifications. However, the contrary has been the case, and in a way that is instructive for considering earlier changes, while admitting at the same time the difficulties posed by comparisons across time. Fortifications might provide a clear target for attack, but they also offer a base to protect firepower as well as to counter the impact of enemy mobility and to support that of one's own side.

In 1967, the Israeli forces attacking Egypt in the Six Days' War and benefiting from the rapid gain of air superiority showed greater operational and tactical flexibility, not least in successfully searching for vulnerable flanks and thus overcoming the strength of prepared Egyptian positions. After conquering the Sinai in 1967, Israel constructed the Bar-Lev Line to the east of the Suez Canal. It fell to Egyptian attack in 1973, in large part because the weakly held defenses were totally taken by surprise, while Israeli air cover was thwarted by effective Soviet-supplied Egyptian surface-to-air missiles, which provided what was at once a new type of bombardment and a new obstacle and deterrence to relieving forces. The Egyptian forces encountered far more problems when they advanced farther east into Sinai beyond the range of their missiles.

Another canal line was the Ichogil Canal Line on the India-Pakistan border in Punjab. India's aim was to use its conventional superiority to launch a massive tank attack along the Lahore-Kasur sector. In re-

Figure 8.1.   The Bar-Lev Line

sponse, Pakistan, in the early 1960s, constructed an in-depth bank-cum-ditch defense along the canal. The western bank of the canal was made higher by eight to ten feet, and machine guns, pillboxes, artillery, and antitank guns were deployed on the bank. The canal was ten to fifteen feet deep. Pakistan's plan was that, if the Indians attacked, their forces would reach the eastern bank, only to receive fire from the higher western bank. In addition, the Indian army lacked the tools required to cross the deep canal. Pakistan's defensive strategy succeeded in stopping the massive tank attack launched by India in this sector during the 1965 war.

The situation was affected by the increasing use of air attack, notably precision munitions, both missiles and guided bombs, against fortifications and other targets, as by the Americans and their allies in the 1991 Gulf War. The vulnerability of these fortifications was abruptly displayed by the use of cruise missiles and was caught on camera. The Iraqis who were heavily defeated in 1991 had faced a very different situation in the 1980–88 war with Iran. This was a conflict in which conventional trench warfare had played a significant role for both sides, helping to limit the mobility of each.

THE COLD WAR

The Cold War between the West and the Communist bloc from 1946 to 1989 saw a mass of fortification, and at very different scales. Military bases were protected, notably against air attack. For example, at Legnica in Poland, a Soviet army headquarters, shelters remain. Fortification was particularly apparent along the Iron Curtain in Europe and in Korea. The prospect of Soviet attack in northern Europe, notably advances through armor corridors—the Fulda Gap and the Hof Corridor—led, in NATO planning and preparation, to a measure of fortification. During the early years of NATO, before West German rearmament, the Maginot Line figured in NATO defense planning. There were calls to fortify the inter-German border, but the stress was on mobile defense and notably on air power. There were also fortifications at a more basic level. In Albania, the isolationist Hoxha regime constructed thousands of individual pillboxes as part of a simple surveillance and defense system. Meanwhile, the memory of wartime fortresses was kept alive, as in the Soviet Union, with the defense of Brest-Litovsk in 1941 leading to its being called a "hero fortress" in 1965.

States that were not part of the competing blocs also saw a changing use for fortifications. In Sweden, as a result of air power and mechanized warfare, Boden was no longer seen as a border fortress against the Soviet Union but rather as part of a delaying defense zone along roads toward the Norwegian coast and the Atlantic. The last fortifications were abandoned in 1997. During the 1950s, Sweden constructed subterranean nuclear-proof coastal fortifications, hangars, and naval facilities. Almost all of these were closed down at great cost after the Cold War. In 2016, Sweden reactivated its coastal defense antiship missile system, but it was based on mobile mission teams rather than fixed coastal defensive positions.

The actual use of fortifications in Cold War conflicts varied greatly. Within individual conflicts, the course and success of operations was the key element in setting the context for use. This was very much the case in the Chinese Civil War in 1946–49. The Communists did use fortifications when they chose to defend specific points, as in the Second Battle of Siping and in the blocking operations at Tashan and Heishan in the Liao-Shen campaign. However, in large part, the Communist forces preferred maneuver, tempting or forcing the Nationalists into motion and then fighting them, as when Nationalist positions were attacked in order to ensure that a relief column that could be destroyed was sent.

When the Communists began trying to seize cities, they were more concerned with the destruction of fortifications. Zhu Rui (Lin Biao's artillery chief) sought to establish how most effectively to use artillery to create breeches in the massive Ming and Manchu city walls that the Nationalist forces used in their defense of places like Yixian and Jinzhou, and also in Shandong. He established that the most effective approach was to aim at the middle of the wall, weakening it so that the upper parts would collapse and create a pile of rubble that the infantry could use as a ramp to climb up one side and over the other.[2] This was another instance of the manner in which Chinese armies had been dealing with ways to overcome city walls for many centuries, indeed several millennia, including the use of ladders, flooding, sapping, and explosives.[3]

COUNTERINSURGENCY WARFARE

The growing tendency from 1945 for insurrectionary warfare to become relatively more significant has meant that fortifications have become important for regular forces, both to protect them from irregulars, whether or not operating using conventional tactics, and also from terrorist attacks, for example protecting checkpoints.[4] This situation was seen in a range of conflicts, notably in defending colonial possessions, as with the French in Vietnam from 1946 to 1954. The Viet Minh were defeated in 1951–52 when they switched to mass attacks on French *hérissons*, fortified hedgehog positions, in the open areas of the Red River delta, for example at Vinh Yen and Mao Khé. In contrast, French strongpoints at Dien Bien Phu were outgunned in 1954 by mass infantry attacks combined with innovative tactics and engineering skill. The standard explanation in terms of artillery dominance by the Viet Minh has been challenged. Operating in bad weather and at considerable range, French air support proved inadequate.[5] This battle led to the French presence in Vietnam being associated with defeat and encouraged France to pull out of Vietnam later that year.

In the later Vietnam War, "firebases," from which operations could be mounted, were established and fortified by the Americans and their allies, for example the Australians. These bases were designed to provide all-round protection against attack. Cleared fire zones around the perimeter were a key element. In turn, the Viet Cong and North Vietnamese besieged and assaulted American-held bases that appeared vulnerable, such as Plei Me in 1965 and Khe Sanh in 1968, although these assaults provided a focus for American air attacks which, in effect, provided defensive, especially counterbattery, fire. The bases were supplied by air, ensuring that the ability to bring airstrips under artillery fire was an important aspect of siege operations. The Americans also supported the idea of strategic hamlets as a way to regain control over the land. This was a program organized and carried out by the South Vietnamese military.

The Vietnam War also saw a more conventional-type siege when the Americans attacked the Viet Cong in the old city of Hué in 1968 after the insurgents had readily captured it in the Tet Offensive that year. The massive use of air and artillery power during the recapture of Hué destroyed about half the city, which did not fall until after both difficult house-to-house struggles within its walls and an eventually successful cutting off of supply routes into the city. More typically, the Americans attacked or were attacked by forces concealed in jungle positions. The Americans found dug-in North Vietnamese and Viet Cong forces—operating from deep, camouflaged bunkers—difficult targets, as at Dak To in 1967. Again, there was an emphasis on operating from underground as a means to thwart surveillance, lessen the impact of hostile firepower, and provide a capacity for mounting ambushes, notably from tunnels.

More generally, fortification as a physical reality went through several overlapping stages from 1945, with differing emphases and varied perceptions. The protection of colonial control was the key theme from the late 1940s to the early 1970s. With Western colonial control largely ceasing after 1976, this need for protection was then supplanted by the response to a wave of violent opposition within states, notably in Central America. These conflicts were also an aspect of the Cold War.

As troops were major targets of insurgents, there were repeated attacks on barrack facilities. Fidel Castro launched his insurrection in Cuba with an attack on the barracks in Santiago in 1953. This proved a mismanaged fiasco. It was possible to get into the barracks but not subsequently to gain, let alone retain, control of the situation. Once he gained control of Cuba, Castro closed the barracks in 1960 and used it for a school, a museum, and a public space. In 1983, neither the Americans nor the French could prevent the destruction of their headquarters in Beirut by lorries full of high explosives driven by suicide drivers. The British, more attuned to terrorist moves thanks to their experience in Northern Ireland, blocked a comparable move. The losses and a more general sense of political impotence ensured the withdrawal in 1984 of the Western forces sent to bolster Lebanon's stability.

ANTITERRORISM

Terrorism became a greater concern after the end of colonial control and affected the pressure to protect. This was particularly seen with airports, which became a major target of terrorist activity. The hijacking of aircraft, prominent from the 1970s, encouraged another line of defense at airports, that against passengers bringing on material that might aid hijacking or an explosion. X-ray machines and other forms of detection became a key element in the resulting protection systems.

In the 2000s, concern about terrorism combined with interventionist and counterinsurgency warfare by American-led coalitions that fortified bases against attack. This was true of large positions, especially air bases such as Bagram near Kabul and that near Kandahar. Similarly, in

1987–88, the Angolan air base of Cuito Cuanavale was the site of a conventional defense and siege during the Angolan Civil War. Mine-fields, artillery, and air support were important to the successful de-fense in depth of this position.[6] In Afghanistan, as with other periods of fortification, it was the range in scale that was most apparent. Many bases were rapidly constructed on Afghanistan's open plateau by using local soil and sand to fill preprepared containers piled atop each other. These proved highly resistant to rocket-propelled grenades.

This was an aspect of the flexibility that makes a distinction between fixed and unfixed fortifications unhelpful. So also with the use of under-ground fortresses. The Taliban made extensive use of them in Afghani-stan, for example in the mountains at Tora-Bora, in order to lessen exposure to American air attack. More generally, the use of naturally occurring or man-made space underground in fortification has been widely underrated.[7]

The protection of troops against insurgent or terrorist attack, as by interventionist forces in Afghanistan, did, however, suffer from the drawback that the local population was not protected.

At a different scale, civil wars created the need for fortified posi-tions. In insurrections in "metropoles" (home countries, not colonies), there was an overlap between the protection of troops and that of the police. This was seen, for example, in Northern Ireland where the Pro-visional IRA, a radical Catholic separatist movement, sought, from the late 1960s to 1998, to overthrow the government and the link with Britain and to terrorize the Protestant majority. In the face of ambushes of ground transport, including the use of mines, there was an extensive use of helicopters to supply the fortified posts of the police and military, as again in Iraq and Afghanistan in the 2000s and 2010s. In Northern Ireland, the posts were made of prefabricated parts. In Northern Ire-land, British forces designed the new urban motorway in Belfast in order to provide a barrier between Catholic and Protestant zones. This was an important element of the construction of physical barriers, in-cluding walls, in order to reduce the risk of communal violence. Against car bombs, the British used concrete flower boxes at the side of roads.

Checkpoints were a major feature, in many states, in attempts to monitor and control the situation, but these checkpoints in turn became targets. Israel's concern about the situation posed by Palestinian terror-ism led, notably from the 1990s, to the construction and strengthening of defenses, including the use of walls as well. Separately, there was anxiety about the use of tunnels by terrorists seeking to get under the border, notably from the Gaza Strip, and about their deployment of rockets. The former led to extensive Israeli surveillance and intervention, and the latter in the 2000s to the establishment of an "Iron Dome" designed to provide antimissile defenses in the shape of interceptor missiles. Hamas made much use of tunnels to stage attacks during the 2014 Gaza war, and in 2017 Israel announced that it would spend $800 million on building an underground barrier along the forty miles of its frontier with the Gaza Strip. This was to be forty meters deep, much of it concrete latticed with iron bars and pipes carrying sensors. It was also planned to build a six-meter-high steel barrier above ground. Concrete factories were built to that end. The barrier is to extend into the Mediterranean to prevent Hamas frogmen from swimming ashore.

In response to Islamic terrorist attacks in Britain in 2017, three-foot-high concrete and metal barriers protecting pedestrians from terrorist attacks by cars and lorries were installed on London bridges. The profits of the company making these barriers rose. Earlier, fixed defenses, including barriers and a gate, had been put in place to protect Downing Street, the site of the prime minister's residence and office, from terrorist attacks. Similarly, in New York, the streets around the United Nations were restructured, and there have been more recent developments around the Freedom Tower. Bollards line particularly important sidewalks, numerous cameras have been installed, and trash receptacles (rubbish bins) have been removed.

The standard pattern of protective features, one of blast-proof features, narrow slit-type windows with toughened glass, barbed wire atop walls, outside obstacles in order to prevent any direct or close approach by vehicles, and protected compounds became commonplace across the world. They did so for a range of buildings, some more obvious than others, from the British Secret Intelligence Service (MI6) building, Vauxhall Cross, in London, as well as military bases and police stations, to embassies, court buildings, banks, and shopping centers. Cameras were seen everywhere. Alarm systems, including nighttime motion detectors, were an aspect of the defenses. Shields were also used by paramilitary forces confronted by rioters and proved particularly helpful against petrol bombs, which became the weapon of choice of rioters. Terrorism also made increased use of hacking and other computer attacks. As a result, computer firewalls and antiviral defenses became more important aspects of fortifications.

PRIVATE SECURITY

In areas with a high rate of instability and lawlessness, such fixed defenses were important for all nonreligious centers of authority (and often religious ones), and even for many households. The latter was also seen with internal protective rooms or "cages" in the event of housebreakers coming in, as in Johannesburg, South Africa, and other African cities. Such rooms may become more common in other countries. Thus, in London, the use of sledgehammers by burglars in the early twenty-first century in order to break into houses through the front doors encouraged the construction of iron gates and fences to protect access via the front garden.

The situation clearly paralleled that of the medieval period, with the need to fortify both public and private buildings. In one light, fortification was a key aspect of what can be seen as insurance, with the latter both public and private and offered by public and private bodies, although in a relationship that differs both geographically and across time. Indeed, the histories, both of fortification and of insurance, can be profitably considered in this light.

Protection was not only seen in unstable areas. Indeed, it has become a characteristic of modern living as a whole, particularly so in major cities: "We went up to a sixth floor walkway and looked out across the roofs to the steel and glass giants rising just across Nine Elms Lane and marvelled at their sheer size. 'Nine Elms is quite unlike any development London has ever seen; it is a totally cornered-off luxury fortress,' he said. 'It's so visually symbolic and obvious.'"[8]

Some gated communities are staffed by private security guards, notably present at the gates although also patrolling more widely. By the mid-1990s, about 2.5 million American families lived in such communities.[9] The numbers have grown greatly since, not only in new developments, but also with retrofitting. The social dimension has also spread. Initially there were private streets and fenced compounds for the affluent, notably on the East Coast and in Hollywood, but from the late 1960s, the practice spread, first to retirement developments, subsequently to resorts, and then to suburban tracts. Similar patterns were seen in other countries. Concern about "others," whether criminal or not, is the key issue. As such, gated communities were another aspect of rising gun ownership in the United States and, in practice, bear little relationship to actual crime rates. Moreover, gun ownership leads to a marked rise in suicide rates for men and women. Fear of crime "encodes other social concerns including class, race, and ethnic exclusivity as well as gender."[10] The extent to which such security considerations have been mentioned in advertisements for house sales (and also for renting) in the United States is notable and has become more prominent and normative with time.

There has been less scholarly work on the situation outside the United States, but it is clear that such communities are increasingly a norm for the urban affluent, including in Latin America, Africa, and parts of Asia. They are also found in Europe, particularly in retirement and leisure enclaves, as in southern Spain, for example at Marbella, and in major cities. A major surprise to see in Britain outside London in the 2000s, in places like Birmingham and Exeter, these communities have since become more normal. So also, far more commonly, with refer-

Figure 8.2. A gated community

ence to security in house details. This is a matter both with the specifications of a property and with its location, although the mention in advertisements in the latter case may be subliminal. Indeed, there can be an element of shadowboxing in discussions about sales and rentals.

There have also become more specific concerns. Anxiety about the safety of children became a particularly marked feature in parts of the Western world and, less vocally, elsewhere. Many schools became sites delimited by iron fencing and gates and to which access was less easy as a prominent part of a process in which children's life and play were more supervised and common spaces were less readily or easily used. Access to children's play areas has become more regulated, notably so in the United States and Britain.

The idea of fortification as protection extended to the physical and mental defenses of the body. It was particularly employed with reference to cancer, but not only that. Fortification is a term used in the context of migraines. Sufferers often experience a "fortification spectrum" or "fortification illusion" at the start of an attack. This is a zigzag or battlement-like visual disturbance that spreads across the visual field for about fifteen minutes before the headache begins. In psychiatry, there is the phrase "Freudian defenses," while Bruno Bettelheim's *The Empty Fortress: Infantile Autism and the Birth of the Self* (1967) proved influential in lay understanding of autism, notably the theory of "emotional refrigeration." Grayson Perry's etching *Map of Days* (2013) presented a metaphorical self-portrait which took the form of a map of a walled city.[11]

Fortifications continued to play a prominent role in popular culture, notably in films and video games. *Starship Troopers*, a 1998 film of black humor by the Dutch filmmaker Paul Verhoeven, presented a siege of fortifications by evil bugs, including a "bug" wave attack on the fortress. The locust-like bug was a primitive warrior without any resemblance to "civilization," an approach with echoes of nineteenth-century Western public opinion. In the film, the bugs use a testudo-like approach to scale the walls and gain height. The villains also have cockroach-like allies with flamethrower power. There have been similar themes in films set either in Antiquity or in the future.

The nature of fortifications in the post-1945 world will not leave much in the form of the architectural record. In large part, as earlier with wooden palisades, this is due to the construction techniques employed, techniques that permitted the rapid establishment of fortified bases, as in South Vietnam and Afghanistan. The character of the protection envisaged is significant. That required in order to thwart ground attacks by irregulars is different from that necessary against air attack, and increasingly so. Indeed, in the first case, the clearance of fields of fire is a crucial element of the fortifications, but not one that leaves anything positive in the shape of the built environment. Protection against air attack is very different, as seen in hardened aircraft hangers. These were notable with the inland Syrian air base attacked by American sea-launched cruise missiles in 2017.

In addition, it is unlikely that these fortifications will be judged to have architectural merit or aesthetic appeal. Indeed, as of 2018, the extent of surviving fortifications from the post-1945 period is surprisingly poor. In part, this situation arises from the location of so many in tropical areas, such as Vietnam, where the jungle swiftly restored its presence. The situation also reflects the deliberate dismantling of works, as when the Israelis withdrew from the Gaza Strip in 2005 and also by the British in Northern Ireland. In Germany, where Cold War bunkers are decaying, they are not accessible, and this is part of the more general neglect there of the conflict.

Public interest in fortifications focused on the medieval and early modern periods. The preservation of medieval castles extends to rebuilding as in Japan. Thus, Iwakuni Castle (1608) was rebuilt in 1962, while Gifu was also rebuilt. Destroyed by bombing in World War II, Nagoya Castle was rebuilt. Castles were shown in Japanese films, as with *Ran* (1985) by Akira Kurosawa, which used Himejī Castle. The focus in Western and Chinese films was also on fortifications that were centuries old, at once dramatic physical presences and obvious. So also with electronic games.

In Britain, the 1955–58 issue of high-value commemorative stamps was devoted to four castles: Carrickfergus, Caernarfon, Edinburgh, and Windsor. New issues, again showing these castles, appeared in 1988 and 1992. The 1966 Landscapes series depicted Harlech Castle for its stamp devoted to Wales. The investiture of the Prince of Wales in 1969 led to five stamps, three devoted to Caernarfon. Two of the four stamps in the 1978 British Architecture: Historic Buildings series were devoted to castles—the Tower of London and Caernarfon—and the other two,

Holyroodhouse and Hampton Court Palace, were shown with castle features.

It is not only post-1945 works that are at issue, because the sites of the "recent past" going long back are often threatened by a greater range of active destructive processes than those that affect Ancient sites.[12] In particular, on a long-standing pattern, forts became handy sources of building materials[13] and of development. Others became museums, as with the Swedish fortress of Boden and with fortresses in Argentina where the emphasis had been on air defense.

As so often, the focus on defenses is on "public" and, even more, military works, and not on those for "private" defense. The consequences of the latter for architectural features will not always be apparent, and with gates, fences, alarm systems, and toughened glass, it is unclear how long these additional features will last.

PROBING THE FUTURE

The likely future nature of fortification will probably be affected by the increased opportunities for attackers created by missiles, drones (which are rapidly becoming more effective), and, very differently, cyberattacks. The opportunities for missiles and drone attack will be enhanced by the aerial reconnaissance readily gained from drones and satellites. Indeed, because of these threats, fortifications will take on some of the characteristics of units in the field. They will have to offer an active defense that aims to destroy attacking platforms, weapons, and projectiles at a distance. In this respect, individual units will bring together the fixed fortification and field units of the past. The same points will also be valid for other sites and defenses. Jails are now mindful of the threat from drones, while households are aware of new and developing challenges from aerial surveillance.

At the same time, fortification, albeit of a very different type, is also pursued by the opponents of authority, notably in trying to mobilize civilian support and turn neighborhoods into what they term "no-go zones." This process was symbolized, in the nineteenth century, by the building of barricades. This process remains a particular facet of urban rebellion and resistance, as in Paris in 1968 and in Belfast and Londonderry in the early stage of the IRA activities in Northern Ireland, before the British army overcame these positions in Operation Motorman in 1972. In 2017, in Caracas, demonstrators against the forces of the Maduro government in Venezuela employed streetcars as impromptu barricades.

In turn, there were responses. All these defenses were suppressed, in part because they provided a concentrated target. Moreover, in Bucharest in 1989, the Securitate, the Romanian Secret Police, used tanks to smash through barricades hastily erected by demonstrators. Only the intervention of the army led to the overthrow of the Romanian regime. However, in Russia in 1991, the military failed to gain control of the situation when it tried to stage a coup in Moscow. Trolleybuses and street-cleaning machines were used to construct antitank barricades.

Urban positions could be exposed to heavy firepower, as with Grozny, the capital of the rebellious region of Chechnya, which fell to the Russians in 1995 after a lengthy siege in which they employed devastating artillery and airstrikes. So also with the fall of Aleppo to Syrian government forces in 2017. In Mosul the same year, American and Iraqi forces faced ISIS defenders using tunnels in order to move around the city and ambush attackers. In turn, the attackers employed precision munitions.

There were rural counterparts with the fortification of individual buildings and villages and of natural features such as caves.[14] In 1937, J. F. C. Fuller, a retired British major general, visited Spain during its 1936–39 civil war, reporting to British Military Intelligence, "The front is totally unlike the fronts in the World War . . . in no way continuous. . . . The villages normally are natural fortresses, generally walled all round, and whichever side holds them 'holds' the intervening gaps as well."[15] A reporter in Normandy in 1944 referred to "every farmhouse" as "an armed farmhouse."[16] In 1999, when the Russians threatened the breakaway republic of Chechnya in the Caucasus, President Maskhadov of Chechnya called on all men to mobilize themselves and declared that "every village must be turned into a fortress." In parts of Africa, where forts were abandoned during the colonial period, they were frequently replaced by measures to prevent intruders, notably cattle rustlers, including fencing villages with proper guarded gates.[17] These devices continue to the present.

These examples underline the degree to which fortification remains a key means and objective in military matters, and indeed in the use of power and force by a variety of agencies, both of the state and of its opponents. Moreover, the reuse of fortifications maintains this process. Thus, in northern Iraq, the military bases of Saddam Hussein's forces frequently made use of Ottoman fortresses, and in turn the bases were taken over by militias.

There is no sign that this situation will change, and technologically focused discussion of the future of war needs to devote more attention to the subject. The technological focus, as in discussion, particularly in the United States, in the 1990s of a supposed Revolution in Military Affairs and in the 2000s of a Transformation, however, is very different in its concerns due to the general emphasis on the attack and, in particular, its effectiveness. Thus, the tank and the aircraft dominate attention as the key platforms in network-centric operations. Discussions of the future highlight how they will be replaced and not, instead, analyses and narratives of warfare that center on fortifications. This is the case for instance with manuals of military doctrine and also with accounts of the future of war, both factual and fictional, analytical and impressionistic. In practice, the fortress of the future may itself be a communications stronghold able to rely on its own sensors and information in order to operate.

9

CONCLUSIONS

"The natives of New England . . . are a cowardly set that will not fight, but when fenced by trees, houses or trenches." Alexander Campbell, a Scot who served as a volunteer in the British army at Bunker Hill (1775), left his father in no doubt that American field entrenchments did not seem honorable to him.[1] Such psychological and cultural responses to fortifications are always significant, but professionals, who were scarcely immune from them, had to respond to the world as it was. Thus, the new American forces had to work out how best to confront the professionals of the British army. General Earl Percy referred to the Americans near New York City in November 1776 as "entrenched up to the eyes in three rows of lines."[2] In June 1779, Charles, 3rd Duke of Richmond, a leading opposition politician who subsequently became master general of the ordnance and a keen advocate of enhancing fortifications at Britain's naval bases, urged the House of Lords to "learn from America" in considering how to defend Britain from a possible invasion by France and Spain:

> Let the ministers consider to what it was that the long continuance of the war across the Atlantic was ascribable—to their entrenchments. Every Gazette account, from the affair at Bunker Hill to the very last action, told us that the Americans had been uncommonly active in their works of this kind; that they were entrenched up to their teeth; that as soon as one work was demolished, another at a little distance presented itself, and another after that; in short, that the industry displayed in this kind of defensive operation was astonishing.[3]

The British constructed defense lines near Philadelphia in 1777–78 after they captured it. Entrenchments were not the only defenses at issue during the American War of Independence (1775–83). There were also town walls and forts. To separate these out in a typology, however, is misleading, as it is the common characteristics that are more significant. The fortifications were designed to enhance defensive firepower, both providing a cover for the troops involved and an obstacle—tactical, operational, and strategic—to attackers.

As such, there was a continuing process in which different technologies posed issues, but primarily those of adaptation. Moreover, as the American War of Independence indicated, the similarities between fixed and field fortifications were more significant than the differences. Particularly (but not only) in the case of rebellions and other civil wars, the likely routes of military operations for both sides were unclear, and it was necessary therefore to respond speedily to developments. This situation encouraged the rapid construction of defenses, and thereby their ad hoc character, rather than putting an emphasis on long-standing fixed fortifications. The ad hoc character of many fortifications, and of their use—a related but separate issue—tends to be underplayed. It is a factor that varies as specifications alter, but in much of the world, the adaptation and use of existing buildings, whether military or not, was and is the key element.

Fortifications were frequently the most costly aspect of military infrastructure and the aspect that took the longest to construct/deploy, although there are major problems in assembling and analyzing figures, such that no data set exists at the global level or at a long-term chronological one. This cost and time encouraged caution in constructing new fortifications and difficulties in maintaining them. The cost led to the frequent reuse of earlier structures but could also give a stopgap character to fortification policy. Both aspects tend to be underplayed due to a focus on impressive, purpose-built sites. Nowadays, fortifications are far from the most costly aspect. Instead, missile systems and aircraft take that position. They can be defensive in their intention, but the offensive capability of missiles and aircraft offers a defensive consequence by providing a deterrent. That, however, is not the case against insurgents and terrorists. Instead, it is necessary to fortify potential targets in order to protect them.

Field fortifications entailed far lower costs in money and time than their fixed counterparts. They were fundamentally to protect troops on campaign rather than sites, with the latter the goal of fixed fortifications. Again, however, differences should not be pushed to the point of contrasts, as many fixed fortifications also existed to protect troops. This could be seen, for example, with the Roman forts on Hadrian's Wall, but also more generally with frontier fortifications, where it was the presence of troops that defined and sustained the frontier rather than the exact location of their fortified bases.

In each case, fortifications were most effective if they were an aspect of a sophisticated strategy of defense, one that understood how the environment could be an ally, indeed a crucial one. Examples included the repeatedly successful defense of the Spanish American empire against British maritime attacks,[4] and also the use of fortifications, settlement colonies, and native allies in the defense of China against steppe attacks.[5] Environmental factors helped ensure a seasonality in attack and defense, with specific periods being of particular vulnerability, these usually linked to disease and climate, but including the impact of the growing season on supplies, notably of forage. The related understanding of possibilities and constraints was a key element in the situational awareness and intelligence that was important to the planned understanding of what fortifications could mean. In turn, the environmental dimension, like that of geopolitics, contributed to the different strategic cultures of particular states. These ensured distinct goals, force structures, doctrines, and, as part of this, approaches to fortification and indeed to artillery provision.[6]

Different goals emerge at present and can also be seen in the past. For example, in the seventeenth and eighteenth centuries, the Russians had different goals and means in terms of controlling territory and basing forces on their frontiers with Sweden, Poland, and Turkey, on the one hand, and, on the other, in Siberia. There, the Russians were primarily anchoring tributary-taking spots and trade passageways with the peoples of southern Siberia, Central Asia, and China.

The relationship between forces and defenses has been long standing. Defenses rely on forces, but forces need to be defended, and the very presence of the military entails bases that have defensive characteristics. Each element is significant, but neither is static. For example, the availability of manpower was greatly affected in many societies by the introduction or abolition of conscription. Indeed, the end of conscription in many countries, including the United States, Russia, Britain, and Germany, over the last sixty years, and more particularly the last quarter century, can be regarded as one of the most significant factors affecting fortification. There are far fewer troops to man fortifications and, from another direction, far fewer military facilities that require protection. The opportunity costs of using troops for particular purposes have risen, while there is also more concern to give troops rewarding tasks. These changing equations are readily apparent from considering the military estate internationally, and also in noting the changes in military infrastructure that stem from technological change. The significance of conscription in the recent history of fortification serves as a reminder of the importance of the state and of society to this history as a whole, and, linked to this, of the need to put "military factors" in a broader context of causes.

In part, the implications of the end of conscription require qualification in terms of a privatization of defense, with protection tasks accordingly taken by the police, other government agencies, and private security, with the relationship varying by state. An instance of these other agencies is provided by border control agencies that seek to control migration and trade. The political sensitivity of migration has made fortification of a country's space against illegal immigration a key element for many states from the twentieth century. This is an important instance of the degree to which the conventional discussion of military matters, including, in this case, fortifications, is mistaken because it emphasizes war as opposed to a range of relevant concerns and criteria.

The razor wire and other measures taken at Spain's North African enclaves of Ceuta and Melilla are apt demonstrations of such fortifications, as is President Donald Trump's talk in 2016–18 of a wall against immigration from Mexico into the United States. Illustrations of proposals for this wall reflect the range of factors that play a role, both functional and cultural. There is an expectation that a wall should look like a wall. In terms of practicality, there were questions of cost and effectiveness, with issues of length and height being important in the latter. At the same time, there were attempts to make the wall more attractive both by decorative features and by adding benefits, as with Trump's endorsement in 2017 of the idea that the wall include solar panels. The defenses of the Channel Tunnel near Calais became the scene of clashes with would-be migrants to Britain, notably, but not only, in 2016, and were strengthened accordingly. This strengthening was in part a matter of the deployment of more French police, but also of stronger and more extensive physical defenses, notably fencing, and of more surveillance equipment. Against a military threat, Tunisia, in the mid-2010s, built a two-hundred-kilometer (125 mile) earth wall along its border with Libya to protect it from Islamic State jihadists.

The controversy in 2016–18 over the American-Mexican wall is a reminder of the emblematic as well as practical significance of fortifications. More generally, mapping the fortress into the visual and cultural context of war and peace is significant. The flare-up in Britain in 2017 in response to Spanish claims about Gibraltar reminds us that fortresses can still occupy a very powerful place in the popular imagination. "As Strong as the Rock of Gibraltar" became a British standard of power in the nineteenth century, replacing Dover Castle as the ultimate icon of a newly expanded and powerful nation. This iconography had a long history. J. M. W. Turner painted Dover Castle more than any other subject, as the gateway to England and the front line against Napoleon. Gibraltar provided a more imperial account of British fortifications.

Figure 9.1. Border fence separating Mexico and the United States

Fortresses have exercised an enduring fascination since the dawn of recorded history, whether as strongholds, battlefields, or ruins. This fascination is reflected in the visual arts, as in the recent American television series *The High Castle*, as well as in imaginative fiction. Thus, Horace Walpole's *The Castle of Otranto* (1764) was the first of the gothic novels, with the castle serving as a setting and symbol for suspense, gloom, and the occult. So, more recently, with Mervyn Peake's *Gormenghast* trilogy—*Titus Groan* (1946), *Gormenghast* (1950), and *Titus Alone* (1959)—and with J. R. R. Tolkien's *The Lord of the Rings* (1954–55), with one of the trilogy titled *The Two Towers*, and J. R. R. Martin's *Game of Thrones*, at once an immensely popular book series and a successful television one.

The qualification of an apparent recent decline in state-manned fortifications in terms of the privatization of defense underlines the need to think of defense and fortification in the broadest of terms, including of definitions. Allowing for this factor, it is nevertheless the case that there has been a decline in the public provision of fortification. In large part, this was due, first, to the end of conscription in most countries and, second, to the emphasis on mobility in military operations, notably from the 1980s, especially with the development of the concept of the operational level of war. The respective weight of these factors varies by state and period.

So also with the issues posed by competing cost and manpower commitments in the defense field. The rising cost of weapons systems has left scant money for those that appear of lesser significance. Moreover, the "military-industrial complex" has no stake in fortifications. In America, "base closure" is an issue in state politics, but the issue is usually considered with reference to employment and is not generally discussed in terms of the value of fortifications.

At the same time, there is, at least in part, an issue of reconceptualization. The private provision of security has increased greatly in recent years, is continuing to increase, and is likely to go on doing so. Whether or not there is a need for such increases, the impression created is that there is a need and a responsibility for individuals, companies, and institutions to provide protection. This situation is encouraged not only by real levels of criminality and disorder, but also by perception, anxiety, media presentation, insurance issues, and legal concerns. These factors will each continue to ensure pressure for fortification against fear.

Both private space and shared space has to be protected space. Such is the pressure from assumptions, but also that stemming from legal liabilities and institutional accountability to customers, staff, and others. Terrorism greatly exacerbates this situation, particularly the use of suicide bombers, as the element of deterrence by punishment no longer plays a role. These bombers became more prominent from the 2000s.

Many of the points that arose in the early periods discussed in the first few chapters remain germane today. This may appear counterintuitive, as the emphasis in so much military history is on technology and, therefore, on technological change. Hopes from technology have frequently been directed against fortifications and at the strategic and operational levels, as well as the tactical one. The idea of a magic bullet was particularly seen with air-power enthusiasts in the 1920s and thereafter, who presented bombing as a way to fly over and make redundant strategies of land advance and defense, the related operations focused on trench warfare, and the possibilities of fortified defensive systems.

Earlier examples came with gunpowder and related possibilities and have affected discussions of the impact of cannon, both at the time and by later commentators. There were even bolder hopes. In February 1776, William Gosforth, a New York artisan who had become a radical politician and military commander, wrote to Benjamin Franklin, a prominent American revolutionary also noted for his experiments with electricity,

> I understand you are a great man, that you can turn the common course of nature, that you have power with the Gods, and can rob the clouds of their tremendous thunder. Rouse once more my old Trojan, collect the heavy thunders of the united colonies, and convey them to the regions of the north, and enable us to shake Quebec's walls or on the other hand inform us how to extract the electric fire from the center. Then perhaps we may be able to draw a vein athwart their magazine and send them upwards cloathed as Elijah was with a suit of fire.[7]

Today, the impact for both public and private of the capacity for attack (or only surveillance) posed by drones attracts attention, and notably what this will mean for defenses. Ideas for blocking drones focus on electronic jamming, although there is also the need for physical defenses.

The alternative stress, that on war and society, also puts the focus on change. The end of conscription is an important element in recent decades, but so are changing patterns in gun ownership. At a crude level, fixed household defenses can be a substitute for gun ownership, with greater reliance in the United States on the latter and in Britain on burglar alarms.

Yet, without discounting changes in technology, as well as in war and society—which are key factors in the military equation, indeed axes in the relative analytical matrix—it is important to note that these factors do not exhaust the analysis. It is not so much that the matrix exists in three (or more) dimensions, but rather that there are a range of situations and variables and, crucially, that reductionist explanatory accounts, however plausible, do not work. There is in practice uncertainty over how the subject should be covered, and notably so if it is considered, as it should be, at the global level.

Restricting oneself at this point to technology and society, each, or rather what is bound up in each, affects the objective and subjective aspects of understandings of fortification and defensiveness. Moreover, the resources that are acceptable to use for fortification, and the means and methods that can be employed for attacking fortifications, are also in part social and cultural "constructions." This is notably the case with the treatment of civilians by both sides, but it also reflects modern environmental sensitivities. Thus, in 2017 there was controversy over the use of white phosphorous (to produce smoke) by Iraqi and American forces attacking ISIS elements in Mosul.

Again, however, principles and practices occur across time, rather than simply being specific to a particular period. These variations do not leave the methods of inquiry clear. This ensures that there is not only room for much research but also space for offering new analytical accounts.

So with a basic point about community protection. It is a social and cultural "construction" as well as a physical reality. Turning to the latter, although not so important today, and notably not in the West, defense was a key element of the layout and social organization of communities, whether towns, villages, or households. The last two tend to be neglected. However, each type of defense throws light on others, not least due to "the interpretive value of comparative analysis of the gross spatial patterns of many site types,"[8] and the relevance of all types for assessing the cultural context of those patterns. Prestige could be an important factor for large fortifications.[9]

In each case, it is necessary to widen the historical gaze on the issue, not only by comparing eras, needs, and responses, but also by placing supposedly post-fortification military thinking into the context of fortification analysis. Slit trenches, observation posts, CIWS (close-in weapon system) naval defense systems, computer firewalls, and gated communities are all aspects of fortification. Thus, it is important to examine seemingly disparate ideas and practices within the same context.

War-torn regions in recent or current history, such as Syria in the 2010s, scarcely suggest that the relative neglect of fortification is appropriate. The physical appearance of fortifications and fortresses, whether fixed or not, may continue to change, as it has done across time, but the underlying reality of their significance remains the same.

Aside from changing contexts, technological, military, and political, goals have to be assessed when discussing the value of fortifications. Were they primarily designed to deter attack, delay advances, or to make them costly, and which criterion proved most appropriate and which most successful? These points are valid if fortification is extended to include defenses against cyberattacks, an increasingly important issue that yet again provides evidence of the difficulties of defining the subject. Moreover, the overlaps between such attacks and criminality, political gesturing, international pressure, and individual anger reflect the difficulties of defining war and of then moving forward from this definition to assess fortification and much else.

These points are to the fore at present because of renewed interest in the efficacy of security barriers, notably against terrorism, migration, and crime. Whether considering walls to manage and stem the flow of people, airport security, or cybersecurity, all sorts of barriers are designed to prevent the disruptive entry of adversaries. These and related issues are much discussed in the news and in strategic studies. A history of fortifications is an appropriate approach to considering these issues and responses in the present day. The central issue in fortification relates to the protection of assets and systems that are considered important. In part, therefore, the changing nature of society and of the character of war become key elements in understanding the context of defenses, a context that needs to be played back into the past when considering definitions of fortification and the way in which fortifications are understood. The character, context, and implications of fortification change, but fortification nevertheless remains crucial to conflict.

NOTES

PREFACE

1. Adam Smith, *An Inquiry into the Nature and Causes of the Wealth of Nations*, Roy Campbell, Andrew Skinner, and William Todd, eds. (Oxford: Clarendon Press, 1976 [1776]), 689–91; see also, William Robertson, *The History of the Reign of the Emperor Charles V: With a View of the Progress of Society in Europe*, vol. I (London: W. Strahan and T. Cadell, 1782 [1769]), 5–6; Edward Gibbon, *The History of the Decline and Fall of the Roman Empire (1776–88)*, John Bury, ed., 7 vols. (London: Methuen, 1897–1901), I:93, V:358–59, VII:2.

2. Smith, *An Inquiry*, 708.

3. David Bachrach and Bernard Bachrach, "Bruno of Merseburg's *Saxon War: A Study in Eleventh-Century German Military History*," *JMH* 81 (2017): 365–67.

4. Plutarch, *Lives*, Bernadette Perrin, trans., vol. VII (London: William Heinemann, 1919), xxv.

5. Julius Caesar, "The Spanish War" in A. G. Way, trans., *Caesar, Alexandrian, African and Spanish Wars, with an English Translation* (London: William Heinemann, 1955), 32.

6. Graham Dominy, *Last Outpost on the Zulu Frontiers: Fort Napier and the British Imperial Garrison* (Champaign: University of Illinois Press, 2016).

7. Amy Holmes, *Social Unrest and American Military Bases in Turkey and Germany since 1945* (Cambridge: Cambridge University Press, 2014).

8. Burcu Özgüven, "*Palanka* Forts and Construction Activity in the Late Ottoman Balkans," in Andrew C. S. Peacock, ed., *The Frontiers of the Ottoman World* (Oxford: Oxford University Press, 2009), 171.

9. Uzi Baram and Lynda Carroll, eds., *A Historical Archaeology of the Ottoman Empire: Breaking New Ground* (New York: Kluwer Academic, 2000); Andrew C. S. Peacock, ed., *The Frontiers of the Ottoman World* (Oxford: Oxford University Press, 2009).

10. Hamid Omrani Rekavadi, et al., "The Enigma of the 'Red Snake': Revealing One of the World's Greatest Frontier Walls," *Current World Archaeology* 27 (February/March 2004): 12–22.

11. Brendan Simms, *The Longest Afternoon: The 400 Men Who Decided the Battle of Waterloo* (New York: Basic Books, 2015).

12. David Kilcullen, *Out of the Mountains: The Coming Age of the Urban Guerrilla* (Oxford: Oxford University Press, 2013).

13. Daniel Egan, "Gramsci's War of Position as Siege Warfare: Some Lessons from History," *Critique* 44 (2016): 435–50.

14. Paul Malmassari, *Armoured Trains: An Illustrated Encyclopaedia 1825–2016* (Barnsley: Seaforth Publishing, 2017).

15. Steven Zaloga, *Defence of the Third Reich 1941–45* (Oxford: Osprey, 2012).

16. Jeremy Black, *Combined Operations* (Lanham, MD: Rowman and Littlefield, 2017).

I. ORIGINS

1. James Tracy, ed., *City Walls: The Urban Enceinte in Global Perspective* (Cambridge: Cambridge University Press, 2000); Lawrence Keeley, Marisa Fontana, and Russell Quick, "Baffles and Bastions: The Universal Features of Fortifications," *Journal of Archaeological Research* 15 (2007): 55–95; Richard Eaton and Philip Wagoner, "Warfare on the Deccan Plateau, 1450–1600: A Military Revolution in Early Modern India?," *Journal of World History* 25 (2014): 5–50.

2. Julie Field, "Explaining Fortifications in Indo-Pacific Prehistory," *Archaeology in Oceania* 43 (2008): notes 3–4; Roger Green, "Interpretations of Samoan Fortifications," *Archaeology in New Zealand* 45 (2002): 309–24.

3. Siegfried Dobat, "Danevirke Revisited: An Investigation into Military and Socio-political Organisation in South Scandinavia (c. AD 700 to 1100)," *Medieval Archaeology* 52 (2008).

4. Jim Storr, *King Arthur's Wars: The Anglo-Saxon Conquest of England* (Solihull, UK: Helion, 2006).

5. Michael J. Rowlands, "Defence: A Factor in the Organization of Settlements," in Peter Ucko, Ruth Tringham, and Geoffrey Dimbleby, eds., *Man, Settlement, and Urbanism* (London: Duckworth, 1972), 447–62.

6. Israel Finkelstein, "Middle Bronze Age 'Fortifications': A Reflection of Social Organisation and Political Formations," *Tel Aviv* 19 (1990): 201–20.

7. Elizabeth Arkush and Mark Allen, eds., *The Archaeology of Warfare: Prehistories of Raiding and Conquest* (Gainesville: University Press of Florida, 2006).

8. Avraham Faust, "The Negev 'Fortresses' in Context: Reexamining the 'Fortress' Phenomenon in Light of General Settlement Processes of the Eleventh–Tenth Centuries BCE," *Journal of the American Oriental Society* 126, no. 2 (2006): 135–60, quote on 153.

9. Julius Caesar, *Caesar, Alexandrian, African and Spanish Wars, with an English Translation*, A. G. Way, trans. (London: William Heinemann, 1955), 72.

10. Gideon Shelach, Kate Raphael, and Yitzhak Jaffe, "Sanzuodian: The Structure, Function and Social Significance of the Earliest Stone Fortified Sites in China," *Antiquity* 85 (2011): 11–26.

11. Barry Cunliffe, *Europe between the Oceans* (New Haven, CT: Yale University Press, 2008).

12. Vicente Lull, Rafael Micó, Cristina Rihuete-Herrada, and Roberto Risch, "The La Bastida Fortification: New Light and New Questions on Early Bronze Age Societies in the Western Mediterranean," *Antiquity* 88 (2014): 395–410.

13. Edgar Peltenburg and Tony J. Wilkinson, "Jerablus and the Land of Carchemish: Excavation and Survey in Syria," *Current World Archaeology* 27 (February/March 2008): 23–32.

14. William Hamblin, *Warfare in the Ancient Near East to 1600 BC: Holy Warriors at the Dawn of History* (New York: Routledge, 2006).

15. Julius Caesar, "The Spanish War," in A. G. Way, trans., *Caesar, Alexandrian, African and Spanish Wars, with an English Translation* (London: William Heinemann, 1955), 8.

16. Paul Collins, *Assyrian Palace Sculptures* (London: British Museum Press, 2008); Paul Kern, *Ancient Siege Warfare* (Bloomington: Indiana University Press, 1999).

17. Frederick Winter, *Greek Fortifications* (Toronto: University of Toronto Press, 1971); Arnold Walter Lawrence, *Greek Aims in Fortification* (Oxford: Oxford University Press, 1979); Jean-Pierre Adam, *L'architecture militaire grecque* (Paris: Picard, 1982); Frederick Cooper, "The Fortifications of *Epaminondas* and the Rise of the Monumental Greek City," in James Tracy, ed., *City Walls: The Urban Enceinte in Global Perspective* (Cambridge: Cambridge University Press, 2000), 155–91.

18. Thucydides, *Peloponnesian War*, Charles Forster Smith, trans., vol. VI (London: William Heinemann, 1921), 32.

19. Plutarch, *Lives*, vol. VII, Bernadette Perrin, ed. (London: William Heinemann, 1919), xvii.

20. Konstantin Nossov, *Greek Fortifications of Asia Minor, 500–130 BC* (Oxford: Osprey, 2009).

21. Way, *The Spanish War*, 41.

22. Polybius, *The Histories*, vol. I, William Roger Paton, trans., revised by Frank Walbank and Christian Habicht (Cambridge, MA: Harvard University Press, 2010), 24, 38.4.

23. Julius Caesar, "The African War" and "The Spanish War," in A. G. Way, trans., *Caesar, Alexandrian, African and Spanish Wars, with an English Translation* (London: William Heinemann, 1955), 5, 13, 23, 38, 56.

24. Lucan, *The Civil War*, book I, James D. Duff, trans. (London: William Heinemann, 1928), 143–53.

25. Sextus Julius Frontinus, "Strategemata," in Mary McElwain, ed., *The Stratagems and Aqueducts of Rome* (London: William Heinemann, 1925), 4.7.3; David Whitehead, ed., *Aeneas Tacticus: How to Survive under Siege*, 2nd ed. (Bristol: Bristol Classical Press, 2002). For a valuable contextualization, see Alessandro Roncaglia, "Corbulone e la politica romana in Germania," *Rivista di Studi Militari* 6 (2017): 7–32.

26. Ian A. Richmond, "The Roman Siege-works of Masàda, Israel," *Journal of Roman Studies* 52 (1962): 142–55.

27. Xu Pingfang, "The Archaeology of the Great Wall of the Qin and Han Dynasties," *Journal of East Asian Archaeology* 3 (2002): 259–81; Hans Schönberger, "The Roman Frontier in Germany: An Archaeological Survey," *Journal of Roman Studies* 59 (1969): 144–97.

28. Nicola Di Cosmo, *Ancient China and Its Enemies: The Rise of Nomadic Power in East Asian History* (New York: Cambridge University Press, 2002), 155–58.

29. Richard J. Brewer, ed., *Roman Fortresses and Their Legions: Papers in Honour of George C. Boon* (London and Cardiff: Society of Antiquaries of London/National Museums & Galleries of Wales, 2000).

30. Hugh Elton, *The Frontiers of the Roman Empire* (Bloomington: Indiana University Press, 1996).

31. Simon James, "Stratagems, Combat, and 'Chemical Warfare' in the Siege Mines of Dura-Europos," *American Journal of Archaeology* 115 (2011): 69–101; Anthony McNichol and Nicholas Peter Milner, eds., *Hellenistic Fortifications from the Aegean to the Euphrates* (Oxford: Clarendon Press, 1997).

32. Bernard Bachrach, "The Fortification of Gaul and the Economy of the Third and Fourth Centuries," *Journal of Late Antiquity* 2 (2010): 38–64.

33. James Dyer, *Hillforts of England and Wales* (London: Shire Publications, 1992).

34. Francis Griffith and Henrietta Quinnell, "Settlement c. 2500 BC to c. AD 600," in Roger Kain and William Ravenhill, eds., *Historical Atlas of South-West England* (Exeter: University of Exeter Press, 1999), 64.

35. Anne Johnson, *Roman Forts of the 1st and 2nd Centuries AD in Britain and the German Provinces* (London: A. and C. Black, 1983), 92.

36. John Maloney and Brian Hobley, eds., *Roman Urban Defences in the West* (London: Council for British Archaeology, 1983).

37. Stephen Johnson, *The Roman Forts of the Saxon Shore* (New York: St. Martin's, 1976).

38. Bernard Bachrach, "Imperial Walled Cities in the West and Their Early Medieval Nachleben," in James Tracy, ed., *City Walls: Form, Function, and Meaning* (Cambridge: Cambridge University Press, 2000), 192–218, and "Fifth-Century Metz: Later Roman Christian *Urbs* or Ghost Town?," *Antiquité Tardive* 10 (2002): 363–81; Bernard Bachrach and David Bachrach, "Early Saxon Frontier Warfare: Henry I, Otto I, and Carolingian Military Institutions," *Journal of Medieval Military History* 10 (2012): 17–60.

39. Simon Coupland, "The Fortified Bridges of Charles the Bald," *Journal of Medieval History* 17 (1991): 1–12.

40. Martin Biddle and Birth Kjølbye-Biddle, "Repton and the 'Great Heathen Army,' 873–4," in James Graham-Campbell et al., eds., *Vikings and the Danelaw* (Oxford: Oxbow Books, 2001).

41. Peter Ettel, "The State of the Question Regarding Early Medieval Fortress Construction in Southern Germany," *History Compass* 12 (2014): 112–32.

42. Bernard Bachrach, "Medieval Siege Warfare: A Reconnaissance," *JMH* 58 (1994), and "On Roman Ramparts, 300–1300," in Geoffrey Parker, ed., *The Cambridge Illustrated History of Warfare* (Cambridge: Cambridge University Press, 1995), 64–91; David Bachrach, *Warfare in Tenth-Century Germany* (Woodbridge: Boydell and Brewer, 2012).

43. David Bachrach, "The Military Organization of Ottonian Germany, c. 900–1018: The Views of Bishop Thietmar of Merseburg," *JMH* 72 (2008): 1068–70.

44. Bernard Bachrach, "Charlemagne and Carolingian Military Administration," in Peter Crooks and Timothy Parsons, eds., *Empires and Bureaucracy in World History* (Cambridge: Cambridge University Press, 2016), 194.

45. Edward Schoenfeld, "Anglo-Saxon 'Burhs' and Continental 'Burgen': Early Medieval Fortifications in Constitutional Perspective," *Haskins Society Journal* 6 (1994): 49–66; Richard Abels, "English Logistics and Military Administration, 871–1066: The Impact of the Viking Wars," in Anne N. Jørgensen and Birthe L. Clausen, eds., *Military Aspects of Scandinavian Society in a*

European Perspective, AD 1–1300 (Copenhagen: Danish National Museum, 1997).

46. Stephen Bassett, "Divide and Rule: The Military Infrastructure of Eighth- and Ninth-Century Mercia," *Early Medieval Europe* 15 (2007): 53–85.

47. Martin Biddle and David Hill, "Late Saxon Planned Towns," *Antiquaries Journal* 51 (1971): 70–85.

48. Denis Sullivan, *Siegecraft: Two Tenth-Century Instructional Manuals by "Heron of Byzantium"* (Washington, DC: Dumbarton Oaks Research Library and Collection, 2000).

49. David Graff, *The Eurasian Way of War: Military Practice in Seventh-Century China and Byzantium* (New York: Routledge, 2016).

50. Herbert Franke, "The Siege and Defense of Towns in Medieval China," in Frank Kierman and John Fairbank, eds., *Chinese Ways in Warfare* (Cambridge, MA: Harvard University Press, 1974), 151–201; Joseph Needham and Robin Yates, *Science and Civilisation in China*, vol. V, *Military Technology: Missiles and Sieges* (Cambridge: Cambridge University Press, 1994), 241–485.

51. Benjamin Wallacker, "Studies in Medieval Chinese Siegecraft: The Siege of Yü-pi, AD 546," *Journal of Asian Studies* 28 (1969): 789–802.

52. Nicholas Tackett, "The Great Wall and Conceptualizations of the Border under the Northern Song," *Journal of Song-Yuan Studies* 38 (2008): 99–138.

53. Elizabeth Arkush and Mark Allen, eds., *The Archaeology of Warfare* (Gainesville: University Press of Florida, 2006).

54. Nadine Moeller, "Evidence for Urban Walling in the Third Millennium BC," *Cambridge Archaeological Journal* 14 (2004): 261–65.

55. Frontinus, *Stratagems*, Mary McElwain, ed., III, preface.

56. Polybius, *Histories*, I:24.

57. Emily Hammer, "Highland Fortress-Polities and Their Settlement Systems in the Southern Caucasus," *Antiquity* 88 (2014), accessed May 3, 2017.

58. David Graff, "Dou Jiande's Dilemma: Logistics, Strategy, and State Formation in Seventh-Century China," in Hans van de Ven, ed., *Warfare in Chinese History* (Leiden: Brill, 2000), 82–84.

59. Denis Twitchett, "Tibet in Tang's Grand Strategy," in van de Ven, ed., *Warfare in Chinese History*, 106–08.

2. THE MEDIEVAL CASTLE

1. Ivy Corfis and Michael Wolfe, eds., *The Medieval City under Siege* (Woodbridge: Boydell and Brewer, 1995).

2. John Pryor, "A Medieval Siege of Troy: The Fight to the Death at Acre, 1189–1191 or The Tears of Salah al-Din," in Gregory Halfond, ed., *The Medieval Way of War: Studies in Medieval Military History in Honor of Bernard S. Bachrach* (Farnham: Routledge, 2015), 97–115.

3. Ruth Dunnell, *Chinggis Khan* (New York: Longman, 2009), 64.

4. I have benefited from reading unpublished material by Tim May.

5. For a film showing the firing of a rebuilt trebuchet, see https://www.youtube.com/watch?v=hyEtC4GjNXg, accessed July 14, 2017.

6. Tim May, *The Mongol Art of War: Chinggis Khan and the Mongol Military System* (Yardley, PA: Westholme, 2007).

7. Huang K'uan-chung, "Mountain Fortress Defence: The Experience of the Southern Song and Korea in Resisting the Mongol Invasions," in Hans van de Ven, ed., *Warfare in Chinese History* (Leiden: Brill, 2000), 222–51.

8. Kate Raphael, "Mongol Siege Warfare on the Banks of the Euphrates and the Question of Gunpowder, 1260–1312," *Journal of the Royal Asiatic Society*, series 3, 19 (2009): 355–70, particularly 370.

9. Richard Eaton and Philip Wagoner, "Warfare on the Deccan Plateau, 1450–1600: A Military Revolution in Early Modern India?," *Journal of World History* 25 (2014): 8–12.

10. John Burton-Page, "A Study of Fortification in the Indian Subcontinent from the Thirteenth to the Eighteenth Century AD," *Bulletin of the School of Oriental and African Studies* 23 (1960): 508–22; Jean Deloche, *Studies on Fortification in India* (Paris: Ecole Française d'Extrème-Orient, 2007); Kaushik Roy, *Warfare in Pre-British India—1500 BCE to 1740 CE* (London: Routledge, 2015).

11. John France, "Crusading Warfare and Its Adaptation to Eastern Conditions in the Twelfth Century," *Mediterranean Historical Review* 15 (2000): 49–66.

12. Ronnie Ellenblum, *Crusader Castles and Modern Histories* (Cambridge: Cambridge University Press, 2007).

13. Anis Chaaya, "The Castle of Smar Jbeil: A Frankish Feudal Stronghold in Lebanon," *Journal of Eastern Mediterranean Archaeology and Heritage Studies* 4 (2016): 209–10.

14. Ibid., 237.

15. Thomas Edward Lawrence, *Crusader Castles* (Oxford: Oxford University Press, 1988 [1910]).

16. Jim Bradbury, *The Medieval Siege* (Woodbridge: Boydell and Brewer, 1992); Randall Rogers, *Latin Siege Warfare in the Twelfth Century* (Oxford: Clarendon Press, 1992).

17. Laurence Marvin, "'Men Famous in Combat and Battle . . .': Common Soldiers and the Siege of Bruges, 1127," *Journal of Medieval History* 24 (1998): 243–58.

18. Laurence Marvin, "War in the South: A First Look at Siege Warfare in the Albigensian Crusade, 1209–1218," *War in History* 8 (2001): 373–95, and *The Occitan War: A Military and Political History of the Albigensian Crusade, 1209–1218* (Cambridge: Cambridge University Press, 2008).

19. Nicholas Riasanovsky, *A History of Russia*, 6th ed. (Oxford: Oxford University Press, 2000), 70.

20. Andrew Lowerre, *Placing Castles in the Conquest: Landscape, Lordship and Local Politics in the South-Eastern Midlands, 1066–1100* (Oxford: John and Erica Hedges, 2005); "A GIS Analysis of the Location of Late-Eleventh-Century Castles in the Southeastern Midlands of England," in Jeffrey Clark and Emily Hagemeister, eds., *Digital Discovery: Exploring New Frontiers in Human Heritage. Proceedings of the 2006 (34th) Conference on Computer Applications and Quantitative Methods in Archaeology* (Budapest: Archaeolingua, 2007), 239–52; and "Why Here and Not There? The Location of Early Norman Castles in the South-East Midlands," in Christopher Lewis, ed., *Anglo-Norman Studies 29: Proceedings of the Battle Conference 2006* (Woodbridge: Boydell and Brewer, 2008), 121–44.

21. John Rickard, *The Castle Community: The Personnel of English and Welsh Castles, 1272–1422* (Woodbridge: Boydell and Brewer, 2002), 25.

22. David Cornell, "A Kingdom Cleared of Castles: The Role of the Castle in the Campaigns of Robert Bruce," *Scottish Historical Review* 87 (2008): 233–57.

23. Andrew Saunders, *Dartmouth Castle*, 4th ed. (London: English Heritage, 1995), 24.

24. Robert Higham, "Public and Private Defence in the Medieval South West: Town, Castle and Fort," in Higham, ed., *Security and Defence in South-West England before 1800* (Exeter: University of Exeter Press, 1987), 40–42.

25. Iqtidar Alam Khan, "Coming of Gunpowder to the Islamic World and North India: Spotlight on the Role of the Mongols," *Journal of Asian History* 30 (1996): 27–45.

26. Pierre Brun, "From Arrows to Bullets: The Fortifications of Abdullah Khan Kala (Merv, Turkmenistan)," *Antiquity* 79 (2005): 616–24.

27. Bert Hall, "The Corning of Gunpowder and the Development of Firearms in the Renaissance," in Brenda Buchanan, ed., *Gunpowder: The History of an International Technology* (Bath: Bath University Press, 1996), 93–94.

28. Robert Smith and Kelly DeVries, *The Artillery of the Dukes of Burgundy, 1363–1477* (Woodbridge: Boydell and Brewer, 2005).

29. Dan Spencer, "'The Scourge of the Stones': English Gunpowder Artillery at the Siege of Harfleur," *Journal of Medieval History* 43 (2017): 59–73, and "The Provision of Artillery for the 1428 Expedition to France," *Journal of Medieval Military History* 13 (2015): 179–92; Anne Curry, "Guns and Goddams: Was There a Military Revolution in Lancastrian Normandy, 1415–50?," *Journal of Medieval Military History* 8 (2010): 171–88; Joanna Bellis, ed., *John Page's "The Siege of Rouen": London, British Library, MS Egerton 1995* (Heidelberg: Universitätsverlag Winter, 2015).

30. Cliff Rogers, "The Medieval Legacy," in Geoff Mortimer, ed., *Early Modern Military History, 1450–1815* (Basingstoke: Palgrave, 2004), 6–24, especially 20–23.

31. Marios Philippides and Walter K. Hanak, *The Siege and the Fall of Constantinople in 1453* (Farnham: Ashgate, 2012); Theresa Vann and Donald Kagay, *Hospitaller Piety and Crusader Propaganda: Guillaume Caoursin's Description of the Ottoman Siege of Rhodes, 1480* (Farnham: Ashgate, 2015).

32. Ferenc Szakály, "The Hungarian-Croatian Border System and Its Collapse," in János Bak and Bék Király, eds., *From Hunyadi to Rákóczi: War and Society in Late Medieval and Early Modern Hungary* (New York: Brooklyn College, 1982), 141–58.

33. Weston Cook, "The Cannon Conquest of Nāsrid Spain and the End of the Reconquista," *Journal of Military History* 57 (1993): 43–70.

34. Kelly DeVries, "Facing the New Technology: Gunpowder Defenses in Military Architecture before the *Trace Italianne*, 1350–1500," in Brett Steele and Tamera Dorland, eds., *The Heirs of Archimedes: Science and the Art of War through the Age of Enlightenment* (Cambridge, MA: MIT Press, 2005), 37–71.

35. David Grummitt, "The Defence of Calais and the Development of Gunpowder Weaponry in England in the Late Fifteenth Century," *War in History* 7 (2000): 253–72.

36. Abdul Rahman Zaky, "Gunpowder and Arab Firearms in the Middle Ages," *Gladius* 6 (1967): 45–58.

37. Peter Purton, *A History of the Late Medieval Siege, 1200–1500* (Woodbridge: Boydell and Brewer, 2010), 405.

38. Francesco Guicciardini, *History of Florence*, John Hale, ed. (London: Washington Square Press, 1964), 20.

39. Simon Pepper, "Castles and Cannon in the Naples Campaign of 1494–95," in David Abulafia, ed., *The French Descent into Renaissance Italy, 1494–95: Antecedents and Effects* (Aldershot: Variorum, 1995), 263–93.

40. Kenneth Wiggins, *Anatomy of a Siege: King John's Castle, Limerick, 1642* (Woodbridge: Boydell and Brewer, 2001).

41. Stephen Turnbull, *The Hussite Wars, 1419–36* (Oxford: Osprey, 2004).

42. Arthur Demarest, et al., "Classic Mayan Defensive Systems and Warfare in the Petexbatun Region," *Ancient Mesoamerica* 8 (1997): 229–53.

43. William Ritchie and Robert Funk, *Aboriginal Settlement Patterns in the Northeast* (Albany: University of the State of New York, 1973).

44. Conrad Heidenreich, *Huronia: A History and Geography of the Huron Indians, 1600–1650* (Ottawa: McClelland and Stewart, 1971).

45. Warren Moorehead, ed., *Exploration of the Etowah Site in Georgia: The Etowah Papers* (Gainesville: University Press of Florida, 2000).

46. Charles Hudson, *Knights of Spain, Warriors of the Sun: Hernando de Soto and the South's Ancient Chiefdoms* (Athens: University of Georgia Press, 1997).

47. For methodology, Chris Green, et al., "Understanding the Spatial Patterning of English Archaeology: Modelling Mass Data, 1500 BC to AD 1086," *Archaeological Journal* 174 (2017): 244–80.

48. Peter Lape and Chao Chin-Yung, "Fortification as a Human Response to Late Holocene Climate Change in East Timor," *Archaeology in Oceania* 43 (2008): 11–21; Sue O'Connor, et al., "Examining the Origin of Fortifications in East Timor: Social and Environmental Factors," *Journal of Island and Coastal Archaeology* 7 (2012): 200–218.

49. Peter Mitchell, *The Archaeology of Southern Africa* (Cambridge: Cambridge University Press, 2002).

50. Lawrence Keeley, Marisa Fontana, and Russell Quick, "Baffles and Bastions: The Universal Features of Fortifications," *Journal of Archaeological Research* 15 (2007): 55–95.

51. Thegn Ladefoged and Richard Pearson, "Fortified Castles on Okinawa Island during the Gusuku Period, AD 1200–1600," *Antiquity* 74 (2000): 411.

52. Kritovoulos, *History of Mehmed the Conqueror*, Charles T. Riggs, trans. (Princeton, NJ: Princeton University Press, 1954), 154–55, 182.

3. THE SIXTEENTH CENTURY

1. Charles Maier, *Once within Borders: Territories of Power, Wealth, and Belonging since 1500* (Cambridge, MA: Harvard University Press, 2016), 63–64.

2. Simon Pepper and Nicholas Adams, *Firearms and Fortifications: Military Architecture and Siege Warfare in Sixteenth-Century Siena* (Chicago: University of Chicago Press, 1986).

3. Gaudenzio Claretta, *L'edificazione della Cittadella di Torino 1564–1573* (Turin: Paravia, 1890).

4. Thomas Arnold, "Fortifications and the Military Revolution: The Gonzaga Experience, 1530–1630," in Cliff Rogers, ed., *The Military Revolution Debate* (Boulder, CO: Westview Press, 1995), 201–26.

5. Michael Mallett, "Siegecraft in Late Fifteenth Century Italy," in Ivy Corfis and Michael Wolfe, eds., *The Medieval City under Siege* (Woodbridge: Boydell, 1995), 244–55.

6. Geoffrey Parker, *The Grand Strategy of Philip II* (New Haven, CT: Yale University Press, 1998), 115.

7. Lonnie Shelby, *John Rogers: Tudor Military Engineer* (Oxford: Clarendon Press, 1967).

8. Geoffrey Parker, *The Military Revolution*, 2nd ed. (Cambridge: Cambridge University Press, 1988).

9. John Lynn, "The *trace italienne* and the Growth of Armies: The French Case," *JMH* 55 (1991): 297–330; Mahinder Kingra, "The *trace italienne* and the Military Revolution during the Eighty Years' War, 1567–1648," *JMH* 57 (1993): 431–46.

10. John Hale, "Printing and Military Culture of Renaissance Venice," *Medievalia et Humanistica* 8 (1977): 21–62; Catherine Wilkinson, "Renaissance Treatises on Military Architecture and the Science of Mechanics," in Jean Guillaume, ed., *Les Traités d'architecture de la Renaissance: Actes du colloque tenu à Tours du 1er au 11 juillet 1981* (Paris: Picard, 1988), 467–76.

11. Niccolò Machiavelli, *The Prince*, George Bull, trans. (London: Penguin, 1999), 70–71.

12. Niccolò Machiavelli, *The Art of War*, Ellis Farneworth, trans. (Cambridge, MA: Da Capo Press, 2001), 183–201, quote on 183.

13. Kelly DeVries, "Facing the New Technology: Gunpowder Defenses in Military Architecture before the *Trace Italienne*, 1350–1500," in *The Heirs of Archimedes: Science and the Art of War through the Age of Enlightenment* (Cambridge, MA: MIT Press, 2005), 62.

14. Peter Brown, "Muscovite Arithmetic in Seventeenth-Century Russian Civilisation: Is It Not Time to Discard the 'Backwardness' Label," *Russian History* 39 (2012): 440.

15. Evgeniĭ M. Zhukov, ed., *Sovietskaia istoricheskaia entsiklopediia*, 16 vols. (Moscow: Sovietskaia Entsiklopediia, 1961–76), IV:706–7.

16. George Satterfield, *Princes, Posts and Partisans: The Army of Louis XIV and Partisan Warfare in the Netherlands, 1673–1678* (Leiden: Brill, 2003).

17. John Womack Wright, "Sieges and Customs of War at the Opening of the Eighteenth Century," *American Historical Review* 39 (1933–34): 629–44.

18. James Raymond, "Henry VIII and the English Military Establishment," *Archives* 28 (2003): 105–6.

19. Akdes Kurat, "The Turkish Expedition to Astrakhan in 1569 and the Problem of the Don-Volga Canal," *Slavonic and East European Review* 40 (1961): 7–23.

20. John Laband, *Bringers of War: The Portuguese in Africa during the Age of Gunpowder and Sail, from the Fifteenth to the Eighteenth Century* (Barnsley: Frontline Books, 2013).

21. Ray Broussard, "Bautista Antonelli: Architect of Caribbean Defense," *The Historian* 50 (August 1988): 507–20.

22. Gábor Ágoston, *Guns for the Sultan: Military Power and the Weapons Industry in the Ottoman Empire* (Cambridge: Cambridge University Press, 2005).

23. Stephen Spiteri, *Fortresses of the Cross: Hospitaller Military Architecture, 1136–1798* (Valetta: Heritage Interpretation Services, 1994).

24. Simon Phillips, "The Shining Virgin, Sappers and Silent Night Assaults: Comparisons with the Precursors to the 1565 Siege," in Maroma Camilleri, ed., *Besieged: Malta 1565*, 2 vols. (Valletta: Malta Libraries and Heritage Malta, 2015), I:109.

25. John Guilmartin, "The Siege of Malta and the Habsburg-Ottoman Struggle for Domination of the Mediterranean," in David Trim and Mark Fissel, eds., *Amphibious Warfare, 1000–1700: Commerce, State Formation, and European Expansion* (Leiden: Brill, 2006), 149–80.

26. Gianni Perbellini, *The Fortress of Nicosia: Prototype of European Military Architecture* (Nicosia: Anastasios G. Levantis Foundation, 1994).

27. Muhammad Adnan Bakhit, *The Ottoman Province of Damascus in the Sixteenth Century* (Beirut: Librairie du Liban, 1980), 94, 98, 225; Andrew C. S. Peacock, ed., *The Frontiers of the Ottoman World* (Oxford: Oxford University Press, 2009).

28. I would like to thank Faisal Husain for drawing this to my attention.

29. Gábor Ágoston, "Habsburgs and Ottomans: Defense, Military Change and Shifts in Power," *Turkish Studies Association Bulletin* 22 (1998): 126–41; Géza Pálffy, "The Origins and Development of the Border Defense System against the Ottoman Empire in Hungary (up to the Early Eighteenth Century)," in Géza Dávid and Pál Fodor, eds., *Ottomans, Hungarians, and Habsburgs in Central Europe: The Military Confines in the Era of Ottoman Conquest* (Leiden: Brill, 2000), 3–70.

30. Darran Fa and Clive Finlayson, *The Fortifications of Gibraltar, 1068–1945* (Oxford: Osprey, 2006), 17–22.

31. Jean Deloche, "Mysore Hill Forts (1400–1800)," in Latika Varadarajan, ed., *Indo-Portuguese Encounters: Journeys in Science, Technology and Culture* (New Delhi: Aryan Books, 2006), 796–817.

32. Jean Deloche, "Gunpowder Artillery and Military Architecture in South India [15–18th Century]," *Indian Journal of History of Science* 40, no. 4 (2005): 573–96.

33. Kaushik Roy, *Military Transition in Early Modern Asia: Cavalry, Guns, Governments and Ships* (London: Bloomsbury, 2014).

34. Jean Deloche, *Four Forts of the Deccan* (Pondicherry: École Française d'Extrême-Orient, 2009); Richard Eaton and Philip Wagoner, "Warfare on the Deccan Plateau, 1450–1600: A Military Revolution in Early Modern India?," *Journal of World History* 25 (2014): 26–33.

35. Jean Deloche, *Studies on Fortification in India* (Pondicherry: École Française d'Extrême-Orient, 2007), 153–86.

36. Kenneth Swope, "Clearing the Fields and Strengthening the Walls: Defending Small Cities in Late Ming China," in Kenneth R. Hall, ed., *Secondary Cities and Urban Networking in the Indian Ocean Realm* (Lanham, MD: Lexington Books, 2008), 123–54.

37. Herbert Franke, "Siege and Defense of Towns in Medieval China," in Frank Kierman and John Fairbank, eds., *Chinese Ways in Warfare* (Cambridge, MA: Harvard University Press, 1974), 151–201.

38. George W. Bernard, *Power and Politics in Tudor England* (Aldershot: Ashgate, 2000), 145–47.

39. Edward Harris, *Bermuda Forts, 1612–1957* (Bermuda: Bermuda Maritime Museum Press, 1997), 17–18.

40. Parker, *Grand Strategy*, 226.

41. Tessa Morrison, "Albrecht Dürer and the Ideal City," *Parergon* 31 (2014): 137–60.

42. Nicholas Rubinstein, "Fortified Enclosures in Italian Cities," in John Hale et al., eds., *War, Culture and Society in Renaissance Venice* (London: A& C Black, 1993), 1–8; Michael Wolfe, *Walled Towns and the Shaping of France: From the Medieval to the Early Modern Era* (Basingstoke: Palgrave, 2009).

4. THE SEVENTEENTH CENTURY

1. Martha Pollak, *Military Architecture, Cartography and the Representation of the Early Modern European City* (Chicago: University of Chicago Press, 1991), but also in other civilizations, including China.

2. Richard Blakemore and Elaine Murphy, *The British Civil Wars at Sea, 1638–1653* (Woodbridge: Boydell and Brewer, 2017).

3. Peter Harrington, "Siegefields: An Archaeological Assessment of 'Small' Sieges of the British Civil Wars," *Journal of Conflict Archaeology* 1 (2005): 93–113.

4. Glenn Foard, "The Civil War Defences of Northampton," *Northamptonshire Past and Present* 9 (1994–95): 4–44.

5. Ronald Hutton and Wylie Reeves, "Sieges and Fortifications," in John Kenyon and Jane Ohlmeyer, eds., *The Civil Wars* (Oxford: Oxford University Press, 1988), 195–233; Barbara Donagan, *War in England, 1642–1649* (Oxford: Oxford University Press, 2008); Stephen Bull, *The Furie of the Ordnance: Artillery in the English Civil War* (Woodbridge: Boydell and Brewer, 2008); David Lawrence, *The Complete Soldier: Military Books and Military Culture in Early Stuart England, 1603–1645* (Leiden: Brill, 2009).

6. Julianne Werlin, "Marvell and the Strategic Imagination: Fortification in *Upon Appleton House*," *Review of English Studies* 63 (2012): 370–87.

7. *Edo and Beijing: Cities and Urban Life in the 18th Century*, Edo-Tokyo Museum and Capital Museum of Beijing, Tokyo, Japan, 2017.

8. John Lynn, "Food, Funds, and Fortresses: Resource Mobilization and Positional Warfare in the Campaigns of Louis XIV," in John Lynn, ed., *Feeding Mars: Logistics in Western Warfare from the Middle Ages to the Present* (Boulder, CO: Westview Press, 1993), 137–60.

9. Mark Stein, *Guarding the Frontier: Ottoman Border Forts and Garrisons in Europe* (London: Tauris, 2007), but see review by Gábor Ágostan in *Journal of the Economic and Social History of the Orient* 52 (2009): 159–63.

10. Alfred Rébelliau, *Vauban* (Paris: Editions Fayard, 1962); Michel Parent and Jacques Verroust, *Vauban* (Paris: Editions Jacques Freal, 1971); Bernard Pujo, *Vauban* (Paris: Albin Michel, 1991); Christopher Duffy, *The Fortress in the Age of Vauban and Frederick the Great, 1660–1789* (London: Routledge and Kegan Paul, 1985).

11. Davide Maffi, *La cittadella in armi: Esercito, società e finanza nella Lombardia di Carlo II, 1660–1700* (Milan: Franco Angeli, 2010).

12. Providence, Hay Library, FT (1714?) France, 1–2.

13. Tonio Andrade, *The Gunpowder Age: China, Military Innovation, and the Rise of the West in World History* (Princeton, NJ: Princeton University Press, 2016), 219–30.

14. John P. LeDonne, *The Grand Strategy of the Russian Empire, 1650–1831* (Oxford: Oxford University Press, 2004), 26–27.

15. Brian Davies, *Warfare, State and Society on the Black Sea Steppe, 1500–1700* (Abingdon: Routledge, 2007), 205.

16. Charles Boxer and Carlos de Azevedo, *Fort Jesus and the Portuguese in Mombasa 1593–1729* (London: Hollis and Carter, 1960); James Kirkman, *Fort Jesus* (Oxford: Clarendon Press, 1974), 4–5.

17. William Gilbert, "'Ye Strength of Ye Place': Defence Works in the St. John's Narrows, 1638–1780," *Newfoundland and Labrador Studies* 25 (2010), 198–99.

18. Michael Hopkinson, "'French Connection': The Design and Roles of Urban Fortifications in Franche Comte and Quebec," *British Journal of Canadian Studies* 16, no. 2 (2003): 319–32; Ranjith Jayasena, "The Historical Archaeology of Katuwana, a Dutch East India Company Fort in Sri Lanka," *Post-Medieval Archaeology* 40 (2006): 111–28.

19. Engel Sluiter, "The Fortification of Acapulco, 1615–1616," *Hispanic American Historical Review* 29 (1949): 69–80.

20. Craig Keener, "An Ethnohistorical Analysis of Iroquois Assault Tactics Used against Fortified Settlements of the Northeast in the Seventeenth Century," *Ethnohistory* 46 (1999): 777–807.

21. Randall Lesaffer, "Siege Warfare in the Early Modern Age: A Study on the Customary Laws of War," in Amanda Perreau-Saussine and James Murphy, eds., *The Nature of Customary Law* (Cambridge: Cambridge University Press, 2007), 176–202.

22. NA. SP. 84/202, fol. 128.

23. John Wilson, ed., *From the Beginning: The Archaeology of the Maori* (Auckland: Penguin Books in association with the New Zealand Historic Places Trust, 1987).

5. THE EIGHTEENTH CENTURY

1. Diary of George Paterson, May 1770, BL. IO. Mss. Eur. E379/1, p. 184.

2. Wayne Lee, "Fortify, Fight, or Flee: Tuscarora and Cherokee Defensive Warfare and Military Culture Adaptation," *JMH* 68 (2004): 713–70.

3. Campbell Dalrymple to Barrington, January 20, 1762, NA. WO. 1/19, fol. 81.

4. Lee, *Fortify, Fight, or Flee*, 770.

5. Wadham College, Oxford, Swinton Diary, November 25, 1730.

6. Monson to Charles Townshend, Secretary at War, October 30, 1762, NA. WO. 1/319, p. 392.

7. Marcel Giraud, *A History of French Louisiana*, vol. I, *The Reign of Louis XIV, 1698–1715* (Baton Rouge: Louisiana State University Press, 1974), 33–34, 39–41, 45, 214, 218–21, 329, 353; Jay Higginbotham, *Old Mobile: Fort Louis de la Louisiane, 1702–1711* (Mobile: University of Alabama Press, 1977).

8. Anon. to Anon., August 20, 1758, BL. Eg. 3444, fol. 211; Colonel Richard Worge to Charles Townsend, Secretary at War, November 5, 1761, NA. WO. 1/319, p. 131.

9. Blankett to Lord Hawkesbury, March 1, 1791, BL. Add. 38226, fols. 114–16.

10. Thomas, Duke of Newcastle, Secretary of State for the Southern Department, to Charles, 2nd Viscount Townshend, Secretary of State for the Northern Department, June 27, 1729, NA. State Papers 43/78.

11. James Madison, *Papers*, ed. William T. Hutchinson and William M. E. Rachal (Chicago: University of Chicago Press, 1962), I:249–50.

12. David Weber, *The Spanish Frontier in North America* (New Haven, CT: Yale University Press, 1962).

13. Edward H. Spicer, *Cycles of Conquest: The Impact of Spain, Mexico, and the United States on the Indians of the Southwest, 1533–1960* (Tucson: University of Arizona Press, 1962).

14. Maurice, Field-Marshal Count de Saxe, *Rêveries* (London: J. Nourse, 1757), 84.

15. Dale Albert Gaeddert, "The Franco-Bavarian Alliance during the War of the Spanish Succession" (PhD diss., Ohio State University, 1969), 32–33.

16. Gaultier, French agent in London, to Torcy, French foreign minister, June 7, 1712, AE. CP. Ang. Sup. 4, fols. 150–51.

17. Horace St. Paul, campaign journal, June 8, 1758, Northumberland CRO. B2/3/25; Christopher Duffy, *The Fortress in the Age of Vauban and Frederick the Great, 1660–1789* (London: Routledge, 1985), 123–25.

18. Coote to Macartney, October 31, 1781, BL. Add. 22439, folios 63–67.

19. William Horsley, *A Treatise on Naval Affairs; or, A Comparison between the Commerce and Naval Power of England and France* (London: R. Wellington, 1744), 76.

20. Saxe, *Rêveries*, 77–78; Lieutenant General Henry Conway to Charles Townshend, September 20, 1762, NA. WO. 1/165, p. 182.

21. Beinecke, Osborn Shelves, pc. 224.

22. Thomas Orby Hunter to Henry Pelham, August 22, 1747, Beinecke, Osborn Shelves, Pelham Box.

23. Thomas Robert Keppel, *The Life of Augustus, Viscount Keppel, Admiral of the White, and First Lord of the Admiralty in 1782–3*, vol. I (London: H. Colburn, 1842), 321–22.

24. Horsbrugh diary, January 21, 1782, BL. Add. 50258, fol. 6.

25. Journal of siege of Dresden, papers of Horace St. Paul, Northumberland CRO. ZBU, B2/3/52, p. 51.

26. Francis to Jeremy Browne, October 26, 1762, BL. RP. 3284.

27. NA. WO. 1/319, p. 392.

28. Ken Alder, *Engineering the Revolution: Arms and Enlightenment in France, 1763–1815* (Princeton, NJ: Princeton University Press, 1997).

29. Jānis Langins, *Conserving the Enlightenment: French Military Engineering from Vauban to the Revolution* (Cambridge, MA: MIT Press, 2004).

30. Northumberland CRO, St. Paul, ZBU, B2/3/29.

31. For a contemporary account of the hard fighting, see BL. Add. 71172, fol. 13; see also Rohan Butler, *Choiseul* (Oxford: Oxford University Press, 1980), 689–95.

32. BL. Add. 32627, fols. 15–16.

33. James Hunter to Amherst, July 12, 1779, NA. WO. 34/1/6, fol. 89.

34. Holdernesse to Joseph Yorke, envoy in Berlin, May 3, 1758, NA. SP. 90/71.

35. Lincoln Diamant, *Chaining the Hudson: The Fight for the River in the American Revolution* (New York: Citadel, 1989); *Papers of George Washington*, Revolutionary War Series II (Charlottesville: University of Virginia Press, 1987), 81.

36. John Whitney Hall, ed., *The Cambridge History of Japan*, vol. IV, *Early Modern Japan* (Cambridge: Cambridge University Press, 1991), 475.

37. Alexander Querengässer, "Belagerungen im Grossen Nordischen Krieg," *Militär & Gesellschaft in der Frühen Neuzeit* 19 (2015): 101–24.

38. Koehler, memorandum, BB 36, fols. 99–160; Smith, BB 41, fol. 70; Monro, memorandum, BB 67.

39. Marie Bennigsen-Broxup, ed., *The North Caucasus Barrier: The Russian Advance towards the Muslim World* (London: Hurst, 1992).

40. Michael Khodarkovsky, *Russia's Steppe Frontier: The Making of a Colonial Empire, 1500–1800* (Bloomington: Indiana University Press, 2002).

41. Barry Lewis, "Village Defences of the Karnataka Maidan, AD 1600–1800," *South Asian Studies* 25 (2009), 91–111, at 106.

42. Barry Lewis, "British Assessments of Tipu Sultan's Hill Forts in Northern Mysore, South India, 1802," *International Journal of Historical Archaeology* 16 (2012): 164–98.

43. Watson to Robert, 4th Earl of Holdernesse, February 15, March 10, 1756, BL. Egerton Mss. 3488, fols. 140–41, 157–58.

44. Major John Corneille, *Journal of My Service in India*, Michael Edwardes, ed. (London: Folio Society, 1966), 39, 50, 63.

45. Cornwallis to the Court of Directors of the East India Company, April 20, December 26, 1791, NA. 30/11/155, fols. 19, 134–38.

46. BL. IO. Mss. Eur. Orme 197, pp. 95–100.

47. Cosby to ——, October 15, 1780, BL. IO. Mss. Eur. Orme 197, p. 148.

48. Skelly narrative, February 7, 1792, BL. Add. 9872, fols. 136–37.

49. Rudi Matthee, *Persian Crisis: Safavid Decline and the Fall of Isfahan* (London: Tauris, 2011), 217–41.

50. Robert W. Olson, *The Siege of Mosul and Ottoman-Persian Relations* (Bloomington: Indiana University Press, 1975); Michael Axworthy, "The Army of Nader Shah," *Iranian Studies* 40 (2007): 635–46.

51. John Waugh, *Carlisle in 1745: Authentic Account of the Occupation of Carlisle in 1745 by Prince Charles Edward Stuart*, George Gill Mounsey, ed. (London: Longman, 1846), 149.

52. Colonel Joseph Yorke to Lord Chancellor Hardwicke, December 24, 1745, in Philip Yorke, ed., *The Life and Correspondence of Philip Yorke, Lord Chancellor Hardwicke*, 3 vols. (Cambridge: Cambridge University Press, 1913), I:488.

53. Northumberland County Record Office, ZRI 27/4/50b; Windsor Castle, Royal Archives, Cumberland Papers (hereafter RA. CP.) 8/89, 109, 152, 161.

54. RA. CP. 8/161.

55. On the strategic importance of Stirling, see J. J. Sharp, "Stirling Castle," *British Heritage* 8 (1987): 62–68.

56. Robert Chambers, ed., *Jacobite Memoirs of the Rebellion of 1745* (Edinburgh: William and Robert Chambers, 1834), 98–99.

57. NA. SP. 43/6, fols. 244, 282.

58. HMC, *Eglinton MSS* (London: HMC, 1885), 444; Charles Sanford Terry, ed., *Albemarle Papers: Being the Correspondence of William Anne, Second Earl of Albemarle, Commander-in-Chief in Scotland, 1746–1747*, vol. I (Aberdeen: New Spalding Club, 1902), 289–90.

59. Conway to Duke of Devonshire, October 7, 1756, Derby, Library, Catton Collection, WH 3450.

60. Glenorchy to his daughter, April 15, 1746, Bedford, Bedfordshire CRO, Lucas Papers, 30/9/17/3.

61. Huntington Library, Montagu Papers, no. 4557.

62. Shelburne Diary, BL. Bowood Mss., vol. 104, fol. 9.

63. BL. Add. 61979A, fol. 40.

64. Allan Kuethe, *Cuba, 1753–1815: Crown, Military, and Society* (Knoxville: University of Tennessee Press, 1986).

65. Jamel Ostwald, *Vauban under Siege: Engineering Efficiency and Martial Vigor in the War of the Spanish Succession* (Leiden: Brill, 2007).

66. Frederick, Duke of York to Richard Grenville, May 24, 1786, BL. Add. 70958. On the situation at Portsmouth, see Philip Magrath, *Fort Cumberland, 1747–1850: Key to an Island's Defence* (Portsmouth: Portsmouth City Council, 1990), 12–13.

67. Douglas Marshall, "The British Military Engineers, 1741–1783: A Study of Organization, Social Origin, and Cartography" (PhD diss., University of Michigan, 1976), 167–68.

68. Cornwallis to Medows, January 4, 1791, NA. 30/11/173, fols. 43, 45.

69. Paul Harsin, *Les Rélations Extérieures de la Principauté de Liège* (Liège: H. Vaillant-Carmanne, 1927), 229–30.

70. Greene to General Thomas Sumter, March 30, 1781, Washington, Library of Congress, Sumter Papers.

71. William Cobbett, ed., *Cobbett's Parliamentary History of England*, vol. XX (London: T. C. Hansard, 1814), 791.

72. BL. Add. 21687, fol. 245.

73. NA. 30/11/74, fol. 101.

74. NA. 30/11/74, fol. 103.

75. O'Hara to Sir Evan Nepean, October —, 1787, Belfast, Public Record Office of Northern Ireland, T.2812/8/50.

76. James Whitman, *The Verdict of Battle: The Law of Victory and the Making of Modern War* (Cambridge, MA: Harvard University Press, 2012), 56–58.

77. Jean-Martin de La Colonie, *The Chronicles of an Old Campaigner: M. de la Colonie, 1692–1717*, Walter Horsley, trans. (London: John Murray, 1904), 184–85.

78. Alan David Francis, *First Peninsular War, 1702–1713* (London: Ernest Benn, 1975), 371–79.

6. THE NINETEENTH CENTURY

1. Don Horward, *Napoleon and Iberia: The Twin Sieges of Ciudad Rodrigo and Almeida, 1810* (Tallahassee, FL: Greenhill, 1994).

2. Bruce Collins, *Wellington and the Siege of San Sebastian, 1813* (Havertown: Pen and Sword, 2017).

3. Murray to Wellington, June 23, 1813, NA. WO. 1/259, p. 88.

4. Carl Nordling, "Capturing 'The Gibraltar of the North': How Swedish Sveaborg Was Taken by the Russians in 1808," *Journal of Slavic Military Studies* 17 (2004): 715–25.

5. Lowe to Colonel Bunbury, October 20, 1813, BL. Add. 37051, fols. 157, 162.

6. Roger Norman Buckley, ed., *The Napoleonic War Journal of Captain Thomas Henry Browne* (London: Army Records Society, 1987), 106–7.

7. James Shaw Kennedy, *Notes on the Battle of Waterloo* (London: J. Murray, 1865), 76.

8. Mark Lawrence, *Spain's First Carlist War, 1833–40* (Basingstoke: Palgrave, 2014), 152–56.

9. Patricia O'Brien, "*L'Embastillement de Paris*: The Fortification of Paris during the July Monarchy," *French Historical Studies* 9 (1975): 63–82.

10. Christopher Duffy, *Fire and Stone: The Science of Fortress Warfare, 1660–1860* (Newton Abbot: David and Charles, 1975).

11. James Glennie to Sidmouth, August 18, 1812, Exeter Devon CRO. 152/M/C1812/OF1A.

12. NA. WO. 1/141.

13. Larry Nelson, "'A Mysterious and Ambiguous Display of Tactics': The Second Siege of Fort Meigs, July 21–28, 1813," *Ohio History* 120 (2015): 5–28, quote on 27.

14. John C. A. Stagg et al., eds., *The Papers of James Madison*, vol. V (Charlottesville, VA: University of Virginia Press), 279, 311.

15. Joseph Whitehorne, *While Washington Burned: The Battle for Fort Erie, 1814* (Baltimore, MD: Nautical and Aviation Publishing, 1992).

16. Willard Robinson, *American Forts: Architectural Form and Function* (Urbana: University of Illinois Press, 1977); William Skelton, "Officers and Politicians: The Origins of Army Politics in the United States before the Civil Wars," *Armed Forces and Society* 6 (Fall 1979): 34–35; Emanuel Raymond Lewis, *Seacoast Fortifications of the United States: An Introductory History* (Annapolis, MD: Smithsonian Institution Press, 1979); Jamie Moore, *The Fortifications Board, 1816–1828, and the Definition of National Security* (Charleston, SC: Citadel, 1980); Russell Gilmore, *Guarding America's Front Door: Harbor Forts in the Defense of New York City* (Brooklyn, NY: Fort Hamilton Historical Society, 1983); Todd Shallat, "American Gibraltars: Army Engineers and the Quest for a Scientific Defense of the Nation, 1815–1860," *Army History* 66 (Winter 2008): 5–19.

17. Benjamin Hawkins, American government agent to the Creeks, to David Mitchell, July 7, Hawkins to John Floyd, September 30, Alexander Cornells, interpreter, to Hawkins, June 22, 1813, Auburn University Archives, Frank Owsley Donation, accession number 82-08.

18. Clarence Geier, "Confederate Fortification and Troop Deployment in a Mountain Landscape: Fort Johnson and Camp Shenandoah, April 1862," *Historical Archaeology* 37, no. 3 (2003): 31–45.

19. Ron Field, *American Civil War Fortifications III: The Mississippi and River Forts* (Oxford: Osprey, 2007), 45.

20. Gary Ecelbarger, *Slaughter at the Chapel: The Battle of Ezra Church, 1864* (Norman: University of Oklahoma Press, 2016).

21. Gary Gallagher, ed., *Fighting for the Confederacy: The Personal Recollections of General Edward Porter Alexander* (Chapel Hill: University of North Carolina Press, 1989), 435–36.

22. Edward Hagerman, "From Jomini to Dennis Hart Mahan: The Evolution of Trench Warfare and the American Civil War," *Civil War History* 13 (1967), 197–220; Richard J. Sommers, *Richmond Redeemed: The Siege at Petersburg* (New York: Doubleday, 1981); Earl J. Hess, *Field Armies and Fortifications in the Civil War: The Eastern Campaigns, 1861–1864* (Chapel Hill:

University of North Carolina Press, 2005); *Trench Warfare with Grant and Lee: Field Fortifications in the Overland Campaign* (Chapel Hill: University of North Carolina Press, 2007); and *In the Trenches at Petersburg: Field Fortifications and Confederate Defeat* (Chapel Hill: University of North Carolina Press, 2009).

23. Joseph Smaldone, *Warfare in the Sokoto Caliphate: Historical and Sociological Perspective* (Cambridge: Cambridge University Press, 1977), 26–37.

24. Peter Carey, ed., *The British in Java, 1811–1816: A Javanese Account* (Oxford: Published for the British Academy by Oxford University Press, 1992).

25. Inomjon Mamadaliev, "The Defence of Khujand in 1866 through the Eyes of Russian Officers," *Central Asian Survey* 33 (2014): 170–79.

26. Brian Robson, ed., "The Kandahar Letters of the Reverend Alfred Cane," *Journal of the Society for Army Historical Research* 69 (1991): 215.

27. Matthias Ogutu, "Forts and Fortification in Western Kenya (Marachi and Ugenya) in the 19th Century," *Transafrican Journal of History* 20 (1991): 77–97.

28. Barbara English, "Debate: The Kanpur Massacres in India in the Revolt of 1857," *Past and Present* 142 (1994): 169–89.

29. BL. Add. 41410, fol. 4.

30. Albert Nofi, "Profile—Defending London, 1858–1870," *Al Nofi's Combat Information Center*, no. 342 (April 2011), https://www.strategypage.com/cic/docs/cic342b.asp.

31. BL. Add. 5928, fols. 41–42.

32. BL. Add. 41410, fol. 2.

33. Gordon Bond, *The Grand Expedition: The British Invasion of Holland in 1809* (Athens: University of Georgia Press, 1979).

34. Robert Sutcliffe, *British Expeditionary Warfare and the Defeat of Napoleon, 1793–1815* (Woodbridge: Boydell and Brewer, 2016), 206–13.

35. Michael Partridge, *Military Planning for the Defense of the United Kingdom, 1814–1870* (New York: Greenwood, 1989); Ian Hogg, *Coast Defences of England and Wales, 1856–1956* (Newton Abbot: David and Charles, 1978).

36. Henri Ortholan, *Le Général Séré de Rivières: Le Vauban de la Revanche* (Paris: Bernard Giovenangeli, 2003).

37. Justin Solonick, *Engineering Victory: The Union Siege of Vicksburg* (Carbondale, IL: Southern Illinois University Press, 2015).

38. David Stevenson, "Fortifications and the European Military Balance before 1914," *Journal of Strategic Studies* 35 (2012): 829–59.

39. Nicholas Murray, "The Theory and Practice of Field Fortification from 1877 to 1914" (DPhil, University of Oxford, 2007).

40. Syed Tanvir Wasti, "The 1912–13 Balkan Wars and the Siege of Edirne," *Middle Eastern Studies* 40 (2004): 59–78.

41. Richard Hall, *The Balkan Wars, 1912–1913: Prelude to the First World War* (London: Routledge, 2000); Edward Erickson, *Defeat in Detail: The Ottoman Army in the Balkans, 1912–1913* (Westport, CT: Greenwood, 2003).

42. Mark Traugott, "Barricades as Repertoire: Continuities and Discontinuities in the History of French Contention," *Social Science History* 17 (1993): 309–23; Jill Harsin, *Barricades: The War of the Streets in Revolutionary Paris, 1830–1848* (Basingstoke: Palgrave, 2002); Dennis Bos, "Building Barricades: The Political Transfer of a Contentious Roadblock," *European Review of History* 12 (2005): 345–65.

43. Joanna Richardson, ed., *Paris under Siege: A Journal of the Events of 1870–1871* (London: Folio Society, 1982), 181, 191.

7. WORLD WARS

1. Richard DiNardo, "The Limits of Technology: The Invasion of Serbia, 1915," *JMH* 79 (2015): 990.

2. Nikolas Gardner, *The Siege of Kut-al-Amara: At War in Mesopotamia, 1915–1916* (Bloomington: Indiana University Press, 2015).

3. Graydon A. Tunstall, *Written in Blood: The Battles for Fortress Przemyśl in WWI* (Bloomington: Indiana University Press, 2016).

4. Alistair Horne, *The Price of Glory: Verdun 1916* (New York: St. Martin's, 1962).

5. Canberra, Australian War Memorial, 3DRL/6643; Nick Lloyd, *Hundred Days: The Campaign that Ended World War I* (New York: Basic Books, 2014).

6. *The Times*, October 28, 1933; Pablo Max Ynsfran, ed., *The Epic of the Chaco: Marshal Estigarribia's Memoir of the Chaco War* (Austin: University of Texas Press, 1950); Bruce Farcau, *The Chaco War: Bolivia and Paraguay, 1932–1935* (Westport, CT: Praeger, 1996).

7. NA. WO. 106/1576, pp. 1–7; NA. WO. 1580, pp. 2–7.

8. Agustín Guillamón, *Ready for Revolution: The CNT Defense Committees in Barcelona, 1933–38* (Oakland, CA: AK Press, 2014).

9. Enno Kraehe, "The Motives behind the Maginot Line," *Military Affairs* 8 (1944): 109–22; Joseph E. Kaufmann et al., *The Maginot Line: History and Guide* (Barnsley: Pen and Sword, 2011); Anthony Kemp, *The Maginot Line: Myth and Reality* (London: Frederick Warne, 1981).

10. Montgomery-Massingberd to Viscount Halifax, Secretary of State for War, August 17, 1935, LH. MM. 10/4/1.

11. Peter Harmsen, *Nanjing 1937: Battle for a Doomed City* (Havertown, PA: Casemate Publishers, 2015).

12. Edward Harris, *Bermuda Forts, 1612–1957* (Bermuda: Bermuda Maritime Museum Press, 1997), 250.

13. Samuel Van Valkenburg, "Geographical Aspects of the Defense of the Netherlands," *Economic Geography* 16, no. 2 (1940): 109–21. Published in April, a month before the conquest.

14. Andrea Santangelo, "Mareth 1943, La Battaglia Dimenticata," *Rivista di Studi Militari* 1 (2012): 173–88.

15. Andrew Holborn, *The D-Day Landing on Gold Beach* (London: Bloomsbury, 2015).

16. Steven Zaloga, *The Atlantic Wall III: The Sudwall* (Oxford: Osprey, 2015), 59.

17. Gordon Rottman, *Victory 1945: Western Allied Troops in Northwest Europe* (Oxford: Osprey, 2015), 30–31.

18. Harris, *Bermuda Forts*, 255–78.

19. Steven Zaloga, *Defence of the Third Reich, 1941–45* (Oxford: Osprey, 2012), 4–24.

20. Jak P. Mallmann Showell, *Hitler's U-Boat Bases* (Annapolis, MD: US Naval Institute Press, 2002).

21. Joseph E. Kaufmann and Hanna W. Kaufmann, *Fortress Europe: European Fortifications of World War II* (Cambridge, MA: Da Capo Press, 1999), and *Fortress Third Reich: German Fortifications and Defense Systems in World War II* (Cambridge, MA: Da Capo Press, 2003).

22. Louis Paul Devine, *The British Way of War in Northwest Europe, 1944–5: A Study of Two Infantry Divisions* (London: Bloomsbury, 2016).

23. Gordon Rottman, *German Field Fortifications, 1939–45* (Oxford: Osprey, 2004), and *US World War II and Korean War Field Fortifications, 1941–53* (Oxford: Osprey, 2005).

24. David Passmore and Stephan Harrison, "Landscapes of the Battle of the Bulge: WW2 Field Fortifications in the Ardennes Forests of Belgium," *Journal of Conflict Archaeology* 4 (2008): 87–107.

25. Mungo Melvin, *Sevastopol's Wars: Crimea from Potemkin to Putin* (Oxford: Osprey, 2017), 464–531, 553–66.

26. Samuel Mitcham, *Rommel's Greatest Victory: The Desert Fox and the Fall of Tobruk, Spring 1942* (Novato, CA: Presidio Press, 1998).

8. SINCE WORLD WAR II

1. Kwong Chi Man and Tsoi Yiu Lun, *Eastern Fortress: A Military History of Hong Kong, 1840–1970* (Hong Kong: Hong Kong University Press, 2014).

2. Harold Tanner, *Where Chiang Kai-shek Lost China: The Liao-Shen Campaign* (Bloomington: Indiana University Press, 2015), 191.

3. Ralph Sawyer, *Fire and Water: The Art of Incendiary and Aquatic Warfare in China* (Boulder, CO: Westview Press, 2004).

4. Geoffrey Demarest and Lester Grau, "Maginot Line or Fort Apache? Using Forts to Shape the Counterinsurgency Battlefield," *Military Review* 85, no. 6 (November–December 2005): 35–40.

5. Kevin Boylan, "No 'Technical Knockout': Giap's Artillery at Dien Bien Phu," *Journal of Military History* 78 (2014): 1349–83.

6. Peter Polack, *The Last Hot Battle of the Cold War: South Africa vs Cuba in the Angolan Civil War* (Philadelphia, PA: Casemate, 2013).

7. Thomas Eastler, "Military Uses of Underground Terrain," in Douglas Caldwell, Judy Ehlen, and Russell Harmon, eds., *Studies in Military Geography and Geology* (Dordrecht: Springer Netherlands, 2004), 21–37.

8. Quoting Aydin Dikerdem, a local Labour councillor, Wendell Steavenson, "The Nowhere Neighbourhood," *Prospect* 254 (May 2017): 43.

9. Edward Blakely and Mary Snyder, *Fortress America: Gated Communities in the United States* (Washington, DC: Brookings Institution, 1997), and "Separate Places: Crime and Security in Gated Communities," in Marcus Felson and Richard B. Peiser, eds., *Reducing Crime through Real Estate Development and Management* (Washington, DC: Urban Land Institute, 1998), 53–70.

10. Setha Low, "The Edge and the Center: Gated Communities and the Discourse of Urban Fear," *American Anthropologist* 103, no. 1 (2001): 45–58, at 56.

11. London, National Portrait Gallery, number 6998.

12. Barry Lewis, *Chitradurga in the Early 1800s: Archaeological Interpretations of Colonial Drawings* (Bangalore, ME: Indian Council of Historical Research, 2006), 36.

13. Barry Lewis, "Mayakonda: A Frontier Fort in Central Karnataka," unpublished draft.

14. Lester Grau and Ali Jalali, "The Campaign for the Caves: The Battles for Zhawar in the Soviet-Afghan War," *Journal of Slavic Military Studies* 14 (2001): 69–92.

15. NA. WO. 106/1576, pp. 1–7.

16. Mary Louise Roberts, *What Soldiers Do: Sex and the American GI in World War II France* (Chicago, IL: University of Chicago Press, 2013), 26.

17. Matthias Ogutu, "Forts and Fortifications in Western Kenya (Marachi and Ugenya) in the 19th Century," *Transafrican Journal of History* 20 (1991): 88.

9. CONCLUSIONS

1. Edinburgh, Scottish Record Office, GD. 170/1063/25.

2. Northumberland Record Office 1314/5.

3. William Cobbett, ed., *Cobbett's Parliamentary History of England*, vol. XX (London: T. C. Hansard, 1814), 982.

4. John McNeill, *Atlantic Empires of France and Spain: Louisbourg and Havana, 1700–1763* (Chapel Hill: University of North Carolina Press, 1985).

5. Thomas Barfield, *The Perilous Frontier: Nomadic Empires and China, 221 BC to AD 1757* (Oxford: Blackwell, 1989).

6. Petter Wulff, "Artillery, Light and Heavy: Sardinia-Piedmont and Sweden in the Nineteenth Century," *JMH* 80 (2016): 174–75.

7. Leonard Labaree et al., eds., *The Papers of Benjamin Franklin*, vol. XXII (New Haven, CT: Yale University Press, 1982), 359.

8. Julie Field, "Explaining Fortifications in Indo-Pacific Prehistory," *Archaeology of Oceania* 43 (2008), 1–10.

9. David Parrott, "The Utility of Fortifications in Early Modern Europe: Italian Princes and Their Citadels," *War in History* 7 (2000): 127–53.

SELECTED FURTHER READING

Chatelain, André. *Chateaux Forts, images de pierre des guerres médiévales*. Paris: Union Rempart, 1995 [1983].

Deloche, Jean. *Studies on Fortification in India*. Pondicherry: French Institute of Pondicherry, 2007.

Duffy, Christopher. *Fire and Stone: The Science of Fortress Warfare, 1660–1860*. London: Hippocrene Books, 1975.

———. *The Fortress in the Age of Vauban and Frederick the Great, 1660–1789*. London: Routledge, 1985.

Eaton, Richard, and Phillip Wagoner. *Power, Memory, Architecture: Contested Sites on India's Deccan Plateau, 1300–1600*. New Delhi: Oxford University Press, 2014.

Gravett, Christopher. *Medieval Siege Warfare*. Oxford: Osprey, 1990.

Rocchi, Enrico. *Le fonti storiche dell'architettura militare*. Rome: Officina Poligrafica Editrice, 1908.

Tracy, James, ed. *City Walls: The Urban Enceinte in Global Perspective*. Cambridge: Cambridge University Press, 2000.

Waldron, Arthur. *The Great Wall of China: From History to Myth*. Cambridge: Cambridge University Press, 1990.

Wiggins, Kenneth. *Siege Mines and Underground Warfare*. Princes Risborough: Shire Publications, 2003.

CREDITS

PHOTOS

1.1 Courtesy of the Ashmolean Museum's photographic collection.
3.1 Courtesy of MrNovel/iStock.
3.2 Courtesy of Ahazan.
4.1 Courtesy of Arenysam/iStock.
6.1 Courtesy of George Eastman House Collection.
8.1 Courtesy of Gammal Hammad, "Military Battles on the Egyptian Front," *Dār al-Shurūq* (Egypt).
8.2 Courtesy of Akabei/iStock.
9.1 Courtesy of Rex_Wholster/iStock.

MAPS

6.1 Courtesy of Gregory Fremont-Barnes, *The Encyclopedia of the French Revolutionary and Napoleonic Wars* (Santa Barbara, CA: ABC-CLIO, 2006), 992.
7.1 Courtesy of "*The Times* History of the War," *Times* (London, England, 1914–21), vols. 1–22 (pts. 1–273).

INDEX

ABOUT THE AUTHOR

Jeremy Black graduated from Cambridge University with a starred First and did graduate work at Oxford University before teaching at the University of Durham and then at the University of Exeter, where he is professor of history. He has held visiting chairs at the U.S. Military Academy at West Point, Texas Christian University, and Stillman College. He is a senior fellow of the Foreign Policy Research Institute. Black received the Samuel Eliot Morison Prize from the Society for Military History in 2008. His recent books include *Air Power: A Global History*, *War and Technology*, *Naval Power: A History of Warfare and the Sea from 1500 Onwards*, and *Rethinking World War Two: The Conflict and Its Legacy*.